medicine public & health

the power of collaboration

by Roz D. Lasker, M.D.
and the Committee on Medicine and Public Health

Foreword by
Mohammad N. Akhter, M.D., M.P.H., American Public Health Association
Nancy W. Dickey, M.D., American Medical Association

The New York Academy of Medicine
1216 Fifth Avenue
New York, NY 10029-5293

This project was supported by The Robert Wood Johnson Foundation.

Library of Congress Cataloging-in-Publication Data

Lasker, Roz Diane.
    Medicine & public health : the power of collaboration / by Roz D. Lasker
and the Committee on Medicine and Public Health
          178 p.   cm.
    Includes bibliographical references.
    ISBN 0-924143-05-3 (pbk. : alk. paper)—
    1. Public health—United States.   2. Medical care—United States.   3. Health planning—United States.   4. Medical cooperation—United States—Case studies.
I. New York Academy of Medicine. Committee on Medicine and Public Health.
II. Title. III. Title: Medicine and public health.
    [DNLM: 1. Delivery of Health Care—trends—United States.
2. Public Health—trends—United States.   3. Interinstitutional
Relations.   W 84 AA1 L25m 1997]
RA445.L37   1997
362.1'0973—DC21
DNLM/DLC
for Library of Congress   97-42385
                                               CIP

This monograph can be found on the World Wide Web:
http://www.nyam.org/pubhlth

Text design by Trejo Production
Cover design by Plumb Design

PROJECT STAFF

DAVID M. ABRAMSON, M.P.H., Senior Program Officer, Division of Public Health, The New York Academy of Medicine

KATHEL DUNN, M.S.L.S., Head of Public Services, Library, The New York Academy of Medicine

GRACE R. FREEDMAN, M.Phil., Executive Assistant to the Director and Program Officer, Division of Public Health, The New York Academy of Medicine

SUSAN R. LEWIS, M.P.A., Past Executive Assistant to the Director, Division of Public Health, The New York Academy of Medicine

MICHAEL J. PALICA, Administrative Assistant, Division of Public Health, The New York Academy of Medicine

DENIS J. PRAGER, Ph.D., Strategic Consulting Services

TO CHARLES C. HUGHES

Charles Hughes was a member of the Committee on Medicine and Public Health until his sudden death in August 1997. As an anthropologist, he broadened our understanding of the cultures of medicine and public health. As a peer, he pressed us to expand our thinking in many new ways. As a friend, he buoyed us with his tremendous enthusiasm and humor. Although Charles Hughes did not live to see the completion of this monograph, he embodied the spirit of our project, and his ideas and perspectives are reflected throughout the text. With great admiration and a deep sense of loss, we dedicate this book to his memory.

ACKNOWLEDGMENTS

This monograph, which is *about* medicine and public health collaboration, is also the *product* of such a collaboration. It could not have been accomplished without a collegial, multidisciplinary committee, whose members were willing to listen to different perspectives and to have their own ideas shaped by what they heard. Our work, in turn, depended on the willingness of a large number of health professionals to share their experiences with us, on the help of many individuals and associations in obtaining this information, and on the support of the project's staff and partners.

We are deeply indebted to the hundreds of health professionals who provided information from the field, either by participating in focus groups or meetings, or by submitting reports of their collaborative activities. Many of these individuals contributed a considerable amount of time to the project, clarifying their points of view and collaborative strategies in long, and often multiple, conversations. Their perspectives and experiences are the foundation of this work.

We also are grateful to the numerous organizations and agencies that facilitated the collection of information. In addition to our partners—the American Medical Association, the American Public Health Association, The New York Academy of Medicine, and The Robert Wood Johnson Foundation—these organizations include the Agency for Health Care Policy and Research, the American Association of Health Plans, the American College of Preventive Medicine, the American Hospital Association, the American Medical Group Association, the American Nurses Association, the American Osteopathic Association, the Association of Academic Health Centers, the Association of American Medical Colleges, the Association of Community Health Educators, the Association of Schools of Public Health, the Association of State and Territorial Directors of Nursing, the Association of State and Territorial Health Officials, the Association of Teachers of Preventive Medicine, the Centers for Disease Control and Prevention, the Health Resources and Services Administration, the Hospital Research and Educational Trust, the Institute for the Advancement of Social Work Research, the Medicine/Public Health Initiative Office at the University of Texas–Houston Health Science Center, the National Association of County and City Health Officials, the National Institutes of Health, the South Carolina Rural Health Association, and the Washington Business Group on Health. Energetic and dedicated individuals on the staffs of these organizations arranged meetings for us with key informants, publicized our project, distributed case study request forms, established Internet links to our World Wide Web site, and provided valuable references.

Collaborative undertakings are complicated, and this project was fortunate in having outstanding administrative, managerial, and analytic support. Special thanks to Denis Prager for facilitating good working relationships among the numerous and diverse individuals and organizations involved in the project. We also would like to thank those members of The New York Academy of Medicine staff who made important contributions to this project. David Abramson played a lead role in designing and implementing the strategy for collecting examples of medicine and public health collaboration, in managing the collaboration database, in interviewing case respondents, and in writing the case illustrations. He and Grace Freedman also contributed substantially to the analysis of case material. Together, Susan Lewis and Michael Palica formed an effective administrative and management team, coordinating the multiple, interrelated elements of the project and creating an environment that supported the free and vigorous exchange of ideas. Staff at the Academy Library—Kathel Dunn, Dixon Berry, Michael Minichino, and Jeffrey Alpi—provided us with valuable bibliographic support as well as an electronic communications network, which some of us were too "old fashioned" to use. They also developed and maintained the Internet case-collection tool.

In producing this monograph, we benefitted greatly from the skills of several individuals. The style and organization of the manuscript were enhanced by Molly McKaughan, who edited several iterations, and copyeditor Carol Chesler. Margaret Trejo designed the book with the reader in mind, and coordinated the complex activities involved in printing and distribution. Michael Freedman translated ideas into visual images, including some beautiful illustrations we were unable to use.

Two original members of the committee—Elizabeth Fee and Martin Wasserman—were unable to complete the project because of other obligations. Their insights, however, contributed to our discussions and are reflected in the body of the work. We also would like to acknowledge the skills of Vincent Breglio and Linda Rawls in organizing and conducting the focus groups.

We would like to express deep gratitude to the staffs of our organizational partners. Although some individuals are no longer with these organizations, during their tenure they provided us with invaluable encouragement and support. Special thanks to: James Allen, Patricia Byrns, Nancy Dickey, Arthur Elster, Robert Rinaldi, Roy Schwartz, Dana Swartzberg, and Reed Tuckson at the American Medical Association; Mohammad Akhter, Richard Levinson, Katherine McCarter, Rebecca Parkin, and Fernando Trevino at the American Public Health Association; and Jeremiah Barondess, Bradford Gray, and Patricia Volland at The New York Academy of Medicine.

Finally, we would like to thank The Robert Wood Johnson Foundation for making this project possible. Marilyn Aguirre-Molina and Nancy Kaufman had the foresight to recognize that the time was right to reevaluate the relationship between medicine and public health, and that a multidisciplinary team and multipronged approach would be needed to accomplish the task. Paul Tarini encouraged our efforts to assess current perceptions and collaborative activities. Together, these individuals catalyzed and nurtured the monograph project, demonstrating how a foundation can play a valuable role not only as a funder, but also as a partner.

The Committee on Medicine and Public Health

FOREWORD

The United States is currently undergoing significant changes in its health system. This restructuring, which is being guided by the rules of the marketplace, is forcing stakeholders in the health care arena to reexamine their present and future roles. Professionals and organizations in medicine and public health are under particular stress in this process, since the environment in which they operate is being altered to an unprecedented degree. For example, the solo practitioner, who traditionally has provided most of the medical care in the United States, is largely being replaced by corporate entities. Similarly, the governmental role in public health is being redefined. At the same time as major structural changes in the health system are occurring, both sectors are being challenged by increasingly severe fiscal constraints. These constraints are being applied to medicine by the managed care industry and to public health by governmental downsizing and privatization.

Although these forces pose a threat to medicine and public health, they also offer new opportunities. To respond constructively to current challenges, leaders from the American Medical Association and the American Public Health Association established the Medicine/Public Health Initiative in 1994. The Initiative provides a forum in which representatives from both sectors can explore their mutual interests in improving health and define collaborative mechanisms to achieve this goal. Thus far, it has revealed that the two sectors have many common interests and concerns.

As the Initiative evolved to include as members the leaders of 20 major professional, educational, and governmental organizations in medicine and public health, it developed an agenda of collaboration encompassing seven basic components: engage the community; change the education process; develop joint research activities; formulate a shared view of health and illness; work together in health care provision; craft health care assessment measures; and create national and local networks to transform Initiative ideas into action. These concepts were examined and elaborated upon in March 1996 when the Initiative held the first National Congress between medicine and public health. Almost 400 leaders from every state in the nation attended the Congress. It has been followed by several regional and state meetings, which addressed the issue of future collaboration around a series of programs and policies. These efforts have contributed to an assessment of the current status of the relationship between medicine and public health, and to the development of an infrastructure for the future enhancement of that relationship.

This monograph was prepared to support the Initiative, by providing professionals in medicine and public health with a practical framework for thinking about and implementing cross-sectoral collaboration. Toward that end, it reviews the historical relationship between the two health sectors and analyzes the current environment. As it does so, it identifies compelling reasons for the two sectors to work more closely together than they have in the recent past. Even more important, the monograph includes an analysis of over 400 cases of medicine and public health collaboration around the country, elucidating a set of collaborative strategies that have the potential to help many other health professionals and organizations deal with the challenges they face. These mutually beneficial strategies enable the two health sectors not only to promote the health of the individuals and populations they serve, but also to enhance their own effectiveness and economic stability.

Dr. Roz Lasker, the Committee on Medicine and Public Health, and the staff of the monograph project, are to be congratulated for producing a landmark analysis. They, and the numerous professionals and organizations who supported the effort, have furthered our understanding of the major issues facing medicine and public health and how these issues can be addressed effectively. Unless we take action on this information in a timely fashion, both health sectors face a future in which their contributions to the public good will be diminished. Should this occur, the health status of all residents of the United States will be affected adversely.

Accordingly, the American Medical Association and the American Public Health Association are making a major and long-term commitment to the Medicine/Public Health Initiative. Both also urge local medical societies, APHA affiliates, and members of the two associations to participate actively in the Initiative and to develop and implement effective models of collaboration at state, regional, and local levels. This monograph—and a multi-indexed compendium of the cases on which it is based—will be available through The New York Academy of Medicine web page (http://www.nyam.org/pubhlth). Our Initiative web page (http://www.sph.uth.tmc.edu/mph) will tell you how you can join Initiative efforts. We encourage you to get involved in these medicine and public health collaborations so that the 21st century will have a more positive outlook for health professionals and the health of the public.

Nancy W. Dickey, M.D.
President-Elect
American Medical Association

Mohammad N. Akhter, M.D., M.P.H.
Executive Director
American Public Health Association

CONTENTS

Figures

Case Illustrations

medicine & public health

the power of collaboration

Introduction

A reader opening this monograph might well ask "Why now? With the dramatic changes taking place in the American health system, which are demanding so much of my attention, why should I focus on the relationship between medicine and public health?" As this monograph will demonstrate, that relationship is important *precisely* because of the changes that are occurring. In the current environment, the medical and public health sectors are becoming increasingly dependent on one another—in achieving their missions, in addressing health problems, and in responding to economic and performance pressures. By engaging in various types of collaborative activities, some professionals and organizations in medicine and public health have identified powerful strategies for dealing with the problems they face. Although each of their collaborations is designed to deal with a particular situation, a set of common, and generally applicable, strategies emerge from analyzing their collaborations as a whole. The purpose of this monograph is to elucidate and present these collaborative strategies—which represent an unrecognized transformation in the American health system—to a broader audience. By doing so, we hope to give readers effective tools not only for improving health, but also for taking charge of, and shaping, their own professional futures.

THE CHARGE AND THE PROCESS

In 1996, The Robert Wood Johnson Foundation—joined by the American Public Health Association and the American Medical Association—charged The New York Academy of Medicine with examining why medicine and public health have functioned as separate and virtually independent components of the American health system, and how the current environment is influencing that relationship. Their interest in such a project was spurred by challenges that professionals and organizations in both sectors were facing, as well as by a new climate of collaboration fostered by the Medicine/Public Health Initiative.[138,139] To further the objectives of the Initiative, the partners sought a monograph that not only would articulate the desirability of medicine and public health collaboration in improving health, but also would assess whether a closer working relationship between the two health sectors is, in fact, achievable, and if so, how.

The Academy's first step in carrying out this charge was to convene a multidisciplinary committee (listed in the front of this monograph). Consistent with the diversity within medicine and public health, the committee reflects the broad range of perspectives within these sectors. We—the members of this committee—have backgrounds as physicians, nurses, administrators, economists, historians, and anthropologists. We represent the four domains of medicine and public health: practice, policy, education, and research. And we have experience working in both the public and private sectors, and at national, state, and local levels.

Soon after beginning our deliberations and literature review, we realized it would be important to obtain additional information from the field. Toward that end, we

- conducted a series of focus groups around the country with students and professionals in medicine and public health;

- held meetings with key informants, including nurses, professionals in preventive medicine, state health officials, and chief executives of integrated systems;

- solicited case examples of medicine and public health collaborations from a wide range of sources.

As a result of these activities, this monograph focuses not on what a collaborative relationship between medicine and public health might be or should be in an ideal world, but rather on what it can be today, and on how the experiences of those actively engaged in collaborative efforts can help other health professionals and institutions deal with the challenges they face in a very turbulent environment.

WHAT DO WE MEAN BY MEDICINE AND PUBLIC HEALTH?

As a first step, it is important to define what we mean by medicine and public health. Clearly, there are no universally accepted definitions for these terms—even by the people who work in both arenas. For the purpose of this study, we chose a broad construct that builds on the two vantage points that societies throughout the world have used to address health and disease. One is to provide "healers" to care for individuals who are sick. The other is to prevent disease from occurring by promoting healthful conditions for the community at large. In ancient Greece, these two approaches were epitomized by the daughters of Aesculapius, Panacea and Hygeia, goddesses of healing and of health. Today, in the American health system, the healers comprise the medical sector, while the promotion of healthful conditions in the community is spear-headed by public health.

The medical perspective focuses on the *individual* patient—diagnosing symptoms, treating and preventing diseases, providing comfort, relieving pain and suffering, and enhancing the capacity to function. Currently, the medical sector in the United States encompasses not only allopathic and osteopathic physicians, but also nurses, dentists, and a host of other personal health service professionals, such as physician assistants, social workers, psychologists, nutritionists, health educators, pharmacists, administrators, and managers. These professionals work in a wide range of settings, including medical practices, community clinics, hospitals, nursing homes, the delivery component of managed-care organizations and integrated health systems, and academic institutions.

The distinguishing feature of the public health perspective is that it focuses on *populations*—assessing and monitoring health problems, informing the public and professionals about health issues, developing and enforcing health-protecting laws and regulations, implementing and evaluating population-based strategies to promote health and prevent disease, and assuring the provision of essential health services. The broad range of professionals involved in public health includes nurses, sanitarians, physicians, epidemiologists, statisticians, health educators, environmental health specialists, industrial hygienists, food and drug inspectors, toxicologists, laboratory technicians, veterinarians, economists, social scientists, attorneys, nutritionists, dentists, social workers, administrators, and managers. They work not only in governmental agencies, but also in clinics, health centers, academic institutions, and community-based organizations.

THE STRUCTURE OF THE MONOGRAPH

This monograph is divided into three parts. The first part, *The Collaborative Imperative*, lays out a context for thinking about the relationship between medicine and public health. It begins with an analysis of the historical relationship between the two sectors, exploring their early connections and the factors that led to their progressive isolation. It then reviews previous attempts to bridge the gap between medicine and public health, describing not only the types of strategies that have been put forward, but also the reasons they failed to change the status quo. Finally, it reassesses the relationship between medicine and public health in the context of today's environment, identifying factors that are making the two health sectors increasingly dependent on one another, and new incentives that are making it advantageous for professionals and organizations in medicine and public health to work more closely together.

The second part of the monograph, *Models of Medicine and Public Health Collaboration*, is based on the 414 cases of medicine and public health collaboration that we collected. It documents and describes an important transformation in the American health system. In addition, it provides the reader with a practical framework for understanding and implementing collaborative strategies. This framework was developed from an empirical study of all of the cases collected. Aspects of this framework are illustrated with examples from the database.

One aspect of the framework focuses on ways that professionals and organizations in medicine and public health—and often other partners in the community as well—combine their resources and skills, and the benefits that can be achieved by doing so. We refer to these reinforcing combinations as "synergies." The six types of synergies observed in the cases cover a broad spectrum. They involve virtually every type of professional and organization in the two health sectors. They encompass all domains of medicine and public health: practice, policy, education, and research. And they occur at local, state, and national levels. Discussions of these synergies describe how partners in collaborative enterprises

- improve health care by coordinating services for individuals;

- improve access to care by establishing frameworks to provide care for the un- and underinsured;

- improve the quality and cost-effectiveness of care by applying a population perspective to medical practice;

- use clinical practice to identify and address community health problems;

- strengthen health promotion and health protection by mobilizing community campaigns;

- shape the future direction of the health system by collaborating around policy, training, and research.

The framework also addresses two additional aspects of collaboration: the structural foundations for combining partners' resources and skills, and partnership issues. The discussion of structural foundations describes how professionals engaging in collaborative endeavors can continue to work within their own organization while, at the same time, transcending the boundaries of that setting to link up with professionals and organizations in other sectors. The discussion of partnership issues describes strategies that enable professionals and organizations from different "cultures" to work together in a common enterprise.

The final part of the monograph, *Conclusions and Next Steps*, summarizes the benefits of cross-sectoral collaboration in today's environment. It then focuses on the paradigm that undergirds such interactions, examining whether—and, if so, how—collaboration affects the identity and roles of health professionals in the two sectors, and the way they think and work. It concludes with a discussion of issues that need to be addressed to promote productive medicine and public health interactions in the future, describing efforts currently underway to increase awareness and understanding of collaborative strategies, as well as to provide professionals and organizations engaged in these activities with technical and policy support. References cited throughout the monograph are enumerated in alphabetical order at the end of the text.

WHO SHOULD READ THIS MONOGRAPH?

This monograph will be of interest to a broad range of readers, including those who are currently engaged in, or are considering getting involved in, collaborative activities, and—the majority of the audience—those who are concerned about the direction of the health system and are seeking effective strategies for dealing with current challenges.

Clearly, professionals and students in medicine and public health are a key audience for this monograph. Since the spectrum of collaborative activity described is so broad, the findings are pertinent to virtually every type of professional and organization involved in medicine and public health, whether these function in the public or private sectors, or at national, state, or local levels. People in leadership roles in health organizations—such as medical practices, community-based clinics, hospitals, health systems, managed care organizations, health departments, academic institutions, professional associations, and voluntary health associations—may be in particularly good positions to act on the findings we report.

Many readers who are not health professionals will find the material relevant as well. Quite a few of the collaborations in this monograph involve partners beyond medicine and public health, and all have implications for the health and health care costs of individuals and/or communities. Consequently, the findings should be of interest to people involved in community groups—including boards of health, foundations, businesses, schools, and religious organizations—as well as to purchasers, insurers, health services researchers, and policymakers.

Part I

The Collaborative Imperative

An Initial Paradox

When the committee began considering the relationship between medicine and public health, we sought to get a better understanding of the status quo—how professionals in medicine and public health view each other, and the extent and nature of their current interactions. Toward that end we conducted a series of focus groups with professionals and students in the two health sectors. These focus groups included professionals in a broad range of specialties and disciplines who work in diverse settings in the public and private sectors. They were held in five locations around the country—Seattle, WA; New York, NY; Houston, TX; Boston, MA; and Columbia, SC—providing us with urban, rural, and regional perspectives.

The common themes that emerged from these sessions confronted us with an interesting paradox. On the one hand, most of the participants in the focus groups talked about the two health sectors as though they were closely related. It was common for medical professionals to describe public health as a sub-specialty of medicine, for example, and for public health professionals to refer to medicine as an arm of public health. Yet participants in both health sectors had quite a bit of difficulty articulating this relationship in practical terms. Most of them had little or no experience working with professionals or organizations in the other sector—in training or in practice. They did not feel that the other sector was particularly interested in their perspectives. They expressed considerable skepticism about each other's motivations. And very few could describe how the activities of the other sector were relevant to what they cared about or did.

These findings immediately raised several questions:

- What is the basis for the two health sectors' sense of connection?

- Why are they now functioning on separate tracks?

- Should anyone be concerned about the current relationship?

- Considering the dramatic changes that are occurring in the American health system, are there now compelling reasons for the medical and public health sectors to work more closely together?

The sections that follow attempt to answer these questions. We turn first to the historical relationship between medicine and public health, examining the scientific, political, and economic forces that first brought the two sectors together and that later contributed to their functional separation and cultural divergence. Over the years, leaders in medicine and public health have made a number of attempts to bridge that distance—in medical practice, in medical education, and in the orientation and allocation of health system resources. We review the strategies employed by these leaders and the reasons they failed to change the status quo.

Clearly, the way the medical and public health sectors evolved in this country reflects the response of health professionals and organizations to powerful external forces. In the current environment, however, these forces are changing substantially. We reassess the relationship between medicine and public health in the context of the crisis in health care costs, the market response to that crisis, the "reinvention" of government, and the emergence of challenging health problems. Our analysis reveals striking shifts in the American health system that are making the two health sectors increasingly dependent on one another. It also identifies new incentives and organizational structures that are making it advantageous and feasible for professionals and organizations in medicine and public health to work more closely together. While the discussion that follows is generally chronological, that is not always the case. To facilitate the reader's orientation, a timeline encompassing the key events in the relationship between medicine and public health that are discussed in the text is presented in Figure I-1.[30,107,153]

Figure I-I Medicine and Public Health Timeline (1847–1997)

Key Health System Issues: Professionalization .... Infrastructure Building .... Improving Access · Cost-Control · Market Forces .... Reinventing Government

Key Health Problems: Infectious Diseases — — — Chronic Diseases — — — Modern Challenges — — —

Key Health Strategies:
Quarantine —— Sanitary Reform —— Maternal & Child Health Programs —— Antibiotics —— Screen & Treat —— Managed Care — — —
Water Systems —— Pasteurization —— Personal Hygiene —— Hospital as Center of Care —— Categorical Health Programs —— Healthy Communities ——

Timeline / Era labels:

1850 — Civil War
1880
1910 — World War I
1920
1930 — Great Depression
1940 — World War II
1950
1960 — Great Society
1970
1980
1990

Events:

Founding of American Medical Association (AMA) (1847)

Metropolitan Board of Health–New York City (1866)
Massachusetts Board of Health (1869)
Founding of American Public Health Association (APHA) (1872)
Koch Discovery–Age of Bacteriology (1876)

Hygienic Lab (forerunner of National Institutes of Health) (1887)

Pure Food & Drug Act (1906)
Flexner Report on Medical Education (Carnegie Foundation) (1910)

Welch-Rose Report on Schools of Public Health (Rockefeller Foundation) (1915)

Maternity and Infancy Act (Sheppard-Towner) (1921)

Blue Cross Insurance (1929)

Social Security Act (Title V & Title VI) (1935)
Garfield/Kaiser Prepaid Group Practice (forerunner of Kaiser Permanente) (1938)

Center for Control of Malaria in War Areas (forerunner of Centers for Disease Control) (1940s)
Kark Community-Oriented Primary Care Clinic—South Africa (1940s)
Hospital Survey and Construction Act (Hill-Burton) (1946)

Salk Polio Vaccine (1952)

Surgeon General's Report on Smoking (1964)
Community Health Centers Program (1964)
Medicare and Medicaid Act (1965)
Health Professions Educational Assistance Act (1965)

Health Maintenance Organization (HMO) Act (1973)
LaLonde Report on Health of Canadians (1974)
Healthy People: Surgeon General's Report on Health Promotion and Disease Prevention (1979)

Medicare Payment Reform (1983, 1989)
Health of the Public Program (1986)
The Future of Public Health (Institute of Medicine) (1988)
U.S. Preventive Services Task Force: Guide to Clinical Preventive Services (1989)

HEDIS–Health Plan Employer Data and Information Set (1993)
Failure of Federal Health Reform (1993–94)
National Congress of the Medicine/Public Health Initiative (1996)

The Historical Relationship Between Medicine and Public Health

Historically, the relationship between medicine and public health in the United States can be characterized as having proceeded in three phases:

- an early supportive relationship prior to the early 20th century

- a period of professionalization and practice transformation spurred by the emergence of bacteriology

- an acceleration of functional separation in the post-World War II era

As the committee reviewed these phases, the perceptions of the focus group participants became easier to understand. Their tacit assumption of an interrelationship between medicine and public health is a vestige of a common framework the sectors once shared in addressing health and illness. Their inability to describe a cross-sectoral relationship in practical terms reflects the extent to which medicine and public health had become isolated—in training and in practice—by the time they embarked on their careers. While the factors accounting for this isolation are complex, the analysis that follows suggests that it has four underlying causes: (1) the progressive loss of any perceived need for the two sectors to work together; (2) the lack of adequate incentives or structural foundations to support cross-sectoral relationships; (3) recurring tensions deriving from overlapping interests; and (4) the development of striking cultural differences.

THE EARLY CONNECTION BETWEEN MEDICINE AND PUBLIC HEALTH

Although societies throughout the world have approached health problems from two distinct vantage points—public health and medicine—these perspectives have not been conceptualized independently. In Greek mythology, for example, the close relationship between healing and health was epitomized by two sisters: Panacea and Hygeia. In the fourth century B.C., Hippocrates espoused a framework that related medical and public health perspectives in practice. In approaching the individual patient, he urged physicians to pay attention to the environmental, social, and behavioral context in which illness occurs: the airs "peculiar to each particular region," the "properties of the waters" the inhabitants drink and use, and "the mode of life of the inhabitants, whether they are heavy drinkers, taking lunch, and inactive, or athletic, industrious, eating much and drinking little."[78]

In the United States, this type of comprehensive framework—encompassing prevention and treatment as well as a broad range of determinants of health—served as a common ground for leaders in medicine and public health from the mid-19th to the early 20th centuries. During this period, the nation's most pressing health problems were infectious diseases. Tuberculosis was "captain of the men of death." Influenza, pneumonia, streptococcal infections, and other airborne diseases struck the population with great force, mainly during the winter months. Infants died routinely as a result of acute communicable respiratory and diarrheal diseases. Measles and chickenpox were a "natural" part of childhood. It was not unusual for women giving birth to succumb to perinatal infections. Smallpox epidemics, with their considerable mortality, struck communities from time to time. Typhoid fever occurred on a small scale, spread within and between families, and occasionally erupted in outbreaks. Cholera epidemics created alarm and were a major cause of death in American ports.

With infectious diseases rampant, there was general agreement that an effective strategy required societal preventive action as well as medical care. Little could be done for patients once they were infected. Moreover, communicable diseases affected everyone—both the wealthy and the workforce—threatening not only people's health but also the economy. Although early public health workers lacked any knowledge of specific etiologic agents, they were able to relate infectious diseases to conditions associated with urbanization and industrialization. Citizen sanitary associations organized efforts to clean up squalid living conditions in the cities.[57] Health departments and boards of health were established to conduct and enforce sanitary measures, and to maintain birth and death records, which were needed to track disease. Together, these voluntary and governmental public health efforts were successful in addressing many of the important risk factors for transmission of communicable disease: overcrowding, poor nutrition, inadequate sewerage systems, uncollected garbage, and contaminated water and food.

At this time, with the public health movement focused on sanitary engineering, environmental hygiene, and quarantine—activities unrelated to the direct care of patients—the strategies of public health and medicine were distinct. Nonetheless, leaders in the two sectors overlapped considerably, and many physicians were actively involved in public health efforts. For example:

- John H. Griscom, a physician at the New York Dispensary and the New York Hospital, served as City Inspector of New York. In 1842, he conducted one of the first surveys of conditions in tenement housing and basement schools. He also advocated the construction of better homes and appealed for the study of occupational health, arguing that improved health and longer life expectancy among the productive population made a sound public health investment.

- Nathan Smith Davis, one of the founders of the American Medical Association (AMA) in 1847, was instrumental in proposing and getting approval for the construction of a sewerage system and a general hospital in Chicago. He also spearheaded the formation of a local medical society and a society for the care of the poor.

■ Stephen Smith, a surgeon in the Civil War, was a founding member of the American Public Health Association (APHA) in 1872. He was also a leading member of the New York Sanitary Association, the New York Citizens Association and the Special Council of Hygiene and Public Health, for which he directed a major sanitary survey of New York City, which led to the establishment of the Metropolitan Board of Health.

■ Henry Bowditch, one of the founders of APHA, served as president of the AMA in 1877. He helped establish the Massachusetts Board of Health in 1869, and served on the National Board of Health in 1879. A paper he wrote in 1874, "Preventive Medicine and the Physician of the Future," condemned the "error and stupidity which does not believe in the duty of studying the physical causes of disease and at least in endeavoring to crush out these originators of pestilence and death."[23]

The key reason that leaders in medicine and public health had such a close relationship during this period was that neither sector could address the infectious disease problem alone; each was in need of something that only the other could provide. Physicians supported public health measures because they could do relatively little on their own. Clinicians could comfort patients and inform them about their prognosis, but medical interventions were relatively ineffective in curing or preventing infectious diseases. Caring about public health was also a status symbol for physicians. It marked the "distinguished practitioner who was above the commercial competition of merely dealing in drugs, bleeding, and purging."[57]

A close relationship with the medical sector also was of benefit to public health. The influence of physicians with policymakers and the public was of substantial value in efforts to institute sanitary reforms and establish health boards. Equally important, clinicians' contact with patients was a useful resource in targeting public health interventions. This was highlighted in an 1852 report of The New York Academy of Medicine, which stated that no one is as "well qualified for the examination and correction of public sources of diseases, in the cellars, the garrets, the courts and cul-de-sacs, and the hollows" as medical practitioners, "whose business it is now to treat, in these very localities, the diseases produced by them."[129]

PROFESSIONALIZATION AND PRACTICE TRANSFORMATION

The emergence of bacteriology in the late 19th century profoundly affected both medicine and public health. On the one hand, the identification of bacteria as the causative agents of infectious diseases contributed to the professionalization of both health sectors. By providing the medical sector with a sound intellectual base and a scientific body of knowledge, bacteriology contributed to its transformation into an organized profession with control over the substance and evaluation of its work. The new science of bacteriology meant that medical practitioners could be held to new standards of knowledge. Licensing regulations and medical practice acts created statewide standards for the practice of medicine. A professional code of ethics established the obligation of physicians to exercise their knowledge and skills in the patient's best interest. In 1910, Abraham Flexner's report for the Carnegie Foundation for the Advancement of Teaching led to a single standard of science-based medical education, expediting the death of proprietary medical schools.[58,109]

Although the public health movement already had a strong scientific foundation in biostatistics and epidemiology, bacteriology also catalyzed the professionalization of public health. The bacteriological laboratory became the symbol of scientific public health. Its operation justified the need for full-time, educated public health personnel, rather than part-time voluntary reformers. In 1913, state legislatures began passing laws requiring public health officers to have specialized training.[56]

In 1915, a Rockefeller Foundation report led to the establishment of science-based schools of public health that could provide this training.[55] These schools were designed to be distinct from schools of medicine for several reasons. A diverse spectrum of personnel—including but going well beyond physicians—are involved in public health. Independent schools of public health were needed to bring together the broad range of expertise and intellectual disciplines integral to their work, to give them a common professional identification and outlook, and to disentangle public health from competing loyalty to medical practice. The early schools of public health were closely tied to medical schools, however. It was commonly believed that public health professionals needed exposure to and understanding of medicine to deal with the prevention and management of disease. There also was a desire to imbue medical schools with the spirit of public health.

The rise of bacteriology as a science did more than professionalize the two health sectors; it also transformed the nature of medical and public health practice. In the medical sector, bacteriology established the biomedical paradigm for elucidating biological causes of disease and for developing therapies—such as antitoxins, and later, antibiotics—that could be directed at patients. By doing so, it dramatically increased the effectiveness of medical diagnosis and treatment.

In public health, the new science led to targeted strategies for controlling specific routes of disease transmission, replacing nonspecific sanitation efforts, which had frequently involved politically contentious social reforms.[56] Some of these new public health initiatives were directed at the environment, for example, the detection and control of bacteria in water systems, the pasteurization of milk, and the eradication of mosquitos to control yellow fever. But other activities were directed at people, previously the sole purview of medicine. Bacteriological laboratories developed tests to diagnose infectious diseases. The prevention of disease through the use of vaccines became a powerful public health and medical strategy.

New Opportunities for Interaction

As the medical and public health sectors both began to target interventions at people, new opportunities arose for working together around health problems, which extended beyond the policy interactions that had led to health boards and sanitary reforms. In the area of communicable disease, complementary efforts of medical practitioners and public health professionals had the potential to assure that enough of the population was immunized to protect the health of the entire community. A close relationship between the two health sectors could provide medical practitioners caring for infected patients with valuable supports, such as laboratory testing, antitoxins, and vaccines. Effective avenues of cross-sectoral communication could link the diagnosis of infected individuals in private practices to the timely initiation of essential community-protection responses, such as isolation of the infected individual, disinfection of his or her home, and the identification and treatment of those who had been in contact with the patient.

The health benefits of working together were not limited to communicable diseases. In the early 20th century, the "New Public Health" increasingly focused its attention on health education, maternal and child health, and the detection of unrecognized but treatable impairments. Toward this end, well-baby clinics with home-visiting services were established that provided women with education about diet, child care, and living patterns. Public health nurses were posted in schools to test children for eye problems and other physical impairments that might interfere with learning. Public health campaigns were initiated urging everyone to get preventive health examinations.[160] In this context, a close working relationship between the medical and public health sectors had the capacity to assure that all women and children received appropriate health education; that all children diagnosed as having health problems were later treated by medical practitioners; and that all patients who were being urged to get preventive health examinations had a place to obtain them.

As the century reached its midpoint, and cardiovascular disease and cancer replaced communicable diseases as the major causes of death, further opportunities arose for the medical and public health sectors to combine their resources in addressing health problems. In part, chronic diseases emerged because people were no longer dying of infections in their early years. But these health problems also were a result of increasing economic opportunity, which allowed more people to avoid physical labor, eat fat-filled diets, smoke cigarettes, and consume alcohol. The medical sector tackled coronary artery disease, stroke, and cancer by attempting to elucidate the biological mechanisms of these diseases within the body and by developing effective procedures and drugs that could be used for diagnosis and treatment. The public health sector, on the other hand, worked to identify the environmental, social, and behavioral risk factors that caused such chronic diseases to emerge in susceptible individuals and to develop population-based interventions to reduce those risk factors.

One type of public health intervention centered on the promotion of screening, early diagnosis, and treatment. This approach was used for cancers for which there were effective screening tests (for example, breast and cervical cancer), and for asymptomatic but treatable diseases, such as hypertension and hypercholesterolemia, which increase the risk for stroke and coronary artery disease. Since most people in the country received personal health care services from medical practitioners in private practice, coordinated efforts by the medical and public health sectors had the potential to assure that all patients received appropriate clinical preventive services, and that all individuals identified as having abnormal results through population-based screening programs received follow-up medical services.

Another public health strategy for dealing with chronic diseases focused on modifying the behaviors that make susceptible people develop these problems in the first place. One aspect of this strategy involved counseling of high-risk individuals. Recognizing that lifestyle choices are not made in a vacuum, however, the strategy also entailed community-wide campaigns to promote conditions that would make it easier for people to follow medical advice. (For example, to address tobacco use—a key risk factor in the development of both cardiovascular disease and cancer—cigarette taxes, restrictions on tobacco advertising, and smoke-free zones have been instituted to create an environment in which people were more likely to stop smoking—or not to start.)[25] By combining their authority and influence, the two health sectors had the ability not only to promote the adoption of healthful social policies, but also to encourage the provision of behavioral counseling in a broad range of practice environments.

Early Barriers to Cross-Sectoral Collaboration

While opportunities for improving health by coordinating medical and public health activities expanded over the course of this century, few of these opportunities were realized in practice. One reason is that the heterogeneous and dispersed health system in this country has not provided a strong structural foundation to support cross-sectoral interactions. Until very recently, the loosely structured medical sector consisted of a vast number of autonomous professionals, most of whom were in solo or small group practices with no clear ties to defined populations. Its other main component, autonomous hospitals and medical centers, have had relationships with practitioners but no clear ties to public health. Although health departments originally were established to support community efforts aimed at the prevention of disease and the promotion of health, these agencies have varied substantially in their capacity to carry out this function. Moreover, they have had little or no jurisdiction over the medical sector.

Equally important, as public health activities increasingly focused on people—overlapping with what was considered to be the domain of the medical sector—thorny "turf" issues impeded the ability of the two health sectors to work cooperatively on health problems. To a large extent, tensions between the two sectors have been fueled by competition and concerns that public health—and government in general—was infringing on physician autonomy and interfering with the doctor-patient relationship. Problems of this sort were prominent in the early part of the century, when the medical sector had not yet solidified its stature in the public eye and when physicians were facing increasing competition from their own rapidly expanding numbers. For example, threatened by public health efforts that might provide free services to patients by whom they might otherwise be paid, some physicians actively resisted well-baby clinics, health centers, and mass immunization programs.[44,50] In the area of communicable disease control, the two sectors were at odds around compulsory reporting of tuberculosis and around the role of public health bacteriological laboratories in providing diagnostic testing for diphtheria and in producing diphtheria antitoxin.[50,57] While AMA and APHA have advocated the same policies in certain areas (for example, the short-lived National Board of Health in 1879, the Pure Food and Drug Act in 1906, and, more recently, the anti-tobacco campaign), they have tended to take opposite sides on issues involving patient care, such as the Sheppard-Towner Act of 1921, which provided federal funds for prenatal and child health clinics, and proposals for various forms of government-sponsored health insurance.[50,110]

Taken together, the lack of a structural foundation for coordinating overlapping activities and the tensions resulting from overlapping interests created significant barriers for medicine and public health collaboration. In 1924, William Henry Welch captured the situation well when he expressed his concern with "the lack of sufficient active participation of the general medical profession in public health activities, especially as developed in this country. The fault is on both sides. There has been encroachment upon the field of the private practitioner, and a lack of sympathy and cooperation with health officials and with health programs on the part of practitioners."[182]

FUNCTIONAL SEPARATION AND CULTURAL DIVERGENCE

These problems were serious, but they might have been overcome if further barriers to cross-sectoral collaboration had not emerged in the post-World War II era. During this period, rapid advances in scientific knowledge and the institution of new medical and public health programs made each health sector feel considerably more independent, dramatically reducing their perceived need to work together. As the American health system evolved, professionals and organizations had few, if any, incentives to interact with their counterparts in the other sector. With the proliferation of medical specialties, and the progressive categorization and fragmentation of public health, logistical impediments to collaboration became more of a problem. Finally, cultural differences and a growing imbalance in funding between the two health sectors compromised their capacity to trust, respect, and communicate with each other. As a result of these forces, the medical and public health sectors became increasingly isolated. Eventually, they functioned as separate, and virtually independent, parts of the larger health system.

The Impact of Science and Health Policies

A key factor in this separation was the success of the biomedical paradigm, which dramatically augmented the medical sector's ability to understand, diagnose, and treat disease. As an increasing array of pharmacological agents and diagnostic and therapeutic procedures became available in the post-World War II period, policies were adopted, which, through their funding streams and economic incentives, encouraged the medical sector to focus more and more exclusively on a "high-tech" curative approach.[57,68,105] Private health insurance—and, later, benefits through the Medicare program—primarily covered acute hospital care, laboratory tests, and procedures, providing generous reimbursement for these services through a fee-for-service payment system. The Hill-Burton Act of 1946 greatly increased the number of hospitals by providing states and localities with federal matching funds for hospital construction. Graduate medical education payments made through the Medicare program supported hospital-based training of large numbers of physicians, substantially increasing the proportion of procedurally oriented specialists. The country's impressive commitment to medical research, funded largely through the National Institutes of Health, centered on biological mechanisms and approaches to disease.

In this environment, careers in biomedical research and the provision of specialized, technologically sophisticated inpatient care were not only financially rewarding but also intellectually stimulating and prestigious. As a result, the medical sector expanded dramatically in the post-World War II period, and became increasingly specialized. In 1942, 15 specialty boards were in existence.[161] By 1992, the American Board of Medical Specialties recognized 24 primary boards and 70 subspecialties.[74] For nurses, as well as for physicians, training focused on preparing professionals to perform in specialized, acute care hospital environments.[162] From the point of view of the general public and policymakers, this investment paid off. The pace of biomedical advances accelerated, generating more knowledge about how to diagnose and treat disease, as well as more specialists and hospitals to deliver "state-of-the-art" care. Medical achievements were hailed as "miracles" that provided patients with relief from conditions that would otherwise cause disability and suffering and shorten life. As public expectations grew, policies to encourage the development of biomedical advances and the provision of specialty care became even stronger, establishing a self-sustaining positive feedback loop.

From the point of view of the relationship between medicine and public health, the most important consequence of these developments was that the medical sector became less dependent on and less interested in public health. In contrast to the situation in the 19th and early 20th centuries, medical professionals now had a powerful and growing therapeutic armamentarium at their disposal—one that seemed applicable not only to medical problems but also to the domain of public health. As antibiotics that could cure infectious diseases became available, the importance of prevention seemed to diminish. Moreover, taking a curative approach to chronic diseases seemed to circumvent the need to promote difficult lifestyle changes. Increasingly capable of making great strides on their own, medical practitioners and researchers no longer perceived much need to work with their colleagues in public health. They also lacked any economic incentives to do so. Public and private health insurance provided much higher reimbursement for diagnostic and therapeutic procedures than for clinical preventive services, such as immunization, screening tests, and counseling. Funding streams of the National Institutes of Health set clear priorities for biologically oriented research; very few grant programs encouraged the study of the behavioral, socioeconomic, and environmental factors that influence health. In this context, it was difficult to sustain much interest among medical professionals or schools of medicine in the public health perspective.

While there was significant expansion of the public health sector in the post-World War II period, it was much less extensive than that of the medical sector. Reflecting public demand for biomedical advances, funding was considerably less generous for population-based public health programs than for medical care; for health departments than for hospitals; for epidemiologic and social science investigation than for clinical studies and basic science research; and for the education and training of public health professionals than for those in medicine. In 1990, for example, 2.7 percent of the nation's health dollars went for public health.[34]

To some extent, the growing imbalance between the two health sectors is related to the fact that public health is a public good rather than an individual good. Medical care does well in a free-market economy like the United States because it is closely tied to individuals; the benefits of seeing a medical practitioner are realized directly by the individual receiving care. In public health, on the other hand, the benefits of community-wide strategies to prevent disease and promote health are received by everyone, including people who do not seek out these benefits and those who do not pay for them directly. Moreover, the benefits of public health—the absence of disease—are largely unrecognized. Because the universality and invisibility of these benefits reduce every person's individual interest in paying for public health, funding necessarily depends on taxpayer and other broad-based support.

Ironically, the impressive successes of public health have led to increasing difficulty garnering support for these activities among the general public and policymakers. Historically, the need for a strong public health presence has been closely tied to people's fear of contracting infectious diseases. But with the successful control of polio in the 1950s, and the availability of a formidable array of antibiotics and vaccines, the communicable disease problem seemed to have been conquered. It was more difficult for the public to appreciate the role of public health in dealing with chronic illnesses. Since cardiovascular disease is not contagious—and, until recently, cancer was not seen as related to infectious agents[108]—these problems were not perceived as a public health threat. Moreover, both the public and policymakers favored medical treatments and cures over prevention efforts. Changing the social and environmental conditions that cause susceptible individuals to come down with chronic diseases is difficult and, at times, politically contentious. Curative strategies, by contrast, do not typically require behavioral change or engender opposition from businesses, such as tobacco companies, anxious to protect their economic interests.[147]

Responding to changes in public perceptions—as well as to available funding streams—the public health sector became increasingly fragmented and disease-oriented, and it devoted a greater proportion of its resources to providing safety-net services for people left out of the mainstream medical system. Prior to World War II, public health funding primarily had supported the development of health agencies at federal, state, and local levels (with limited resources for the training of public health personnel).[57,105] With the control of communicable diseases, however, it became more difficult to obtain support for "generic" public health. Beginning in the 1960s, legislators created new government agencies, apart from health departments, to deal with problems such as environmental protection, occupational safety, water quality, air pollution control, community-based mental health, and substance abuse.[25] They also created a plethora of categorical public health programs, each of which addressed a specific disease or targeted services to a particular population, and each of which was supported by a defined interest group.[57] With federal funding for community and migrant health centers and the introduction of the Medicaid program, a large part of the expansion of the public health sector centered on providing medical care for the poor. Over the last three decades, state and local health departments have become major providers, directly and indirectly, of personal health services to indigent populations.[117,119] Recent estimates suggest that these activities account for two-thirds of state budgets for public health.[36,117]

The nature of public health expansion further contributed to the separation of the two health sectors. Through its categorical programs and safety-net services, the public health sector reinforced prevailing policies by accepting responsibility for certain activities that the medical sector had the expertise and training to perform but had little incentive or interest to do. In addressing categorical problems such as immunization, lead toxicity, sexually transmitted diseases, and tuberculosis, the public health sector provided not only population-based services—such as surveillance, public education campaigns, screening, linkage with medical services, contact-tracing, and environmental detoxification—but clinical services as well. In addressing the medical needs of the poor, the public health sector provided not only outreach and enabling services (which help people gain access to a medical practitioner), but also primary care. While other approaches may not have been feasible, taking on these responsibilities effectively relieved the mainstream medical sector of any obligation to provide certain types of clinical services or to provide medical care for certain types of patients. Moreover, by providing essential linkages between medical and public health services within the context of its own programs and clinics, the public health sector also created the impression that there was little need for the two health sectors to interact.

Even if medical professionals had wanted to develop a closer working relationship with the public health sector, it was becoming increasingly difficult to know "whom to call." The progressive fragmentation of public health activities among numerous categorical programs and government agencies made it hard for virtually anyone to define or relate to public health. With its increasing safety-net activities, many people developed a distorted and narrow view of public health, equating it either with publicly financed medicine or with medical care for the poor.

Separate and Independent Health Sectors

The divergence of the American health system during the post-World War II period led to the development of two distinct sectors—characterized more easily by their differences than by any common ground. The dominant, highly respected medical sector focused on individual patients, emphasizing technologically sophisticated diagnosis and treatment and biological mechanisms of disease. The considerably smaller, less well appreciated public health sector concentrated on populations, prevention, nonbiological determinants of health, and safety-net primary care. Medical investigation was based on biology, chemistry, and physics. Public health research was grounded in epidemiology and biostatistics, frequently making use of the social sciences as well. Medical practitioners were usually self-employed in the private sector, working autonomously in solo or small group practices. Virtually everyone in public health was employed by some type of organization, many by government agencies, which are closely linked to the political world. Payment in the medical sector tended to be on a fee-for-service or cost basis, which encouraged professionals to do everything possible for the patient at hand. Public health professionals typically worked from fixed budgets, juggling limited dollars to achieve the greatest benefit for the entire population.

Although these differences are striking, they need not have prevented constructive medicine and public health interactions in and of themselves. After all, the two sectors' professional perspectives and expertise were largely complementary, and professional relationships do not necessarily require that partners have the same views about financial matters and political strategies. For medicine and public health professionals, however, differences became stereotypical and, ultimately, a serious barrier because there was insufficient trust, understanding, and mutual respect to enable them to relate their activities and interests to each other or to accept differences in each other's points of view.[28] In part, this "cultural divide" stemmed from the striking imbalance between medicine and public health in terms of resources, income, value, and prestige, which created a virtual "class barrier" between the two sectors. It also was fueled by diminishing interactions. With little perceived need to work together—or meaningful incentives to do so—the two health sectors increasingly functioned as though they were separate and independent health systems, rather than reinforcing parts of a larger whole. By not working together—in training or in practice—they became more and more foreign to, and intolerant of, each other. As the cultural divide deepened, the capacity to trust, respect, and communicate with each other was weakened further, making collaborative relationships even more difficult than they had been before.

This environment, which shaped the training and practice experience of most health professionals working today, goes a long way toward explaining the results of our focus groups: the two sectors' lack of experience working together; their suspicions and skepticism about each others' motivations; their contention that the other sector is not particularly interested in their own perspectives; and their difficulty articulating what a meaningful collaborative relationship is or could be. It also helps to explain why so few cross-sectoral strategies—balancing prevention with treatment and addressing the full range of determinants of health—were implemented in the post-World War II period.

As medicine and public health became separate worlds, professionals in the two sectors lost the common framework they had shared in the 19th century, which had allowed them to appreciate the value and relevance of each other's perspectives. Without that mutually accepted framework, encompassing both prevention and treatment as well as the full range of determinants of health, it became very difficult for medical and public health professionals to understand each other's approaches to health problems or to see how the two sectors' unique skills and expertise could fit together in a coordinated strategy. As a result, approaches that were, in fact, complementary, were pursued independently by each sector, making them appear dichotomous and competitive.

In a health system increasingly dominated by the medical sector, it is not surprising that in the "contest" for resources, the biomedical approach usually "won." So, for example, preventive measures were difficult to sustain when drug treatment became available for tuberculosis. Strategies for addressing infant mortality focused far more on keeping low birthweight babies alive through neonatal intensive care units than on decreasing the incidence of low birthweight through the delivery of prenatal care or through community-wide strategies to reduce risk factors for low birthweight, such as smoking, drug abuse, and teenage pregnancy. For chronic diseases like noninsulin-dependent diabetes, far more attention was paid to developing pharmacologic interventions to control blood glucose levels than to addressing the social conditions and unhealthful lifestyles that triggered the development of diabetes in genetically susceptible individuals, for example, by increasing the availability of healthful food choices, by establishing incentives, opportunities, and safe environments for exercise, and by educating people at risk through individual counseling and media campaigns.

The point here is not to imply that either the medical or public health approach is better than the other—both clearly have important roles to play in any rational scheme to address these health problems. The real issue is that, in the diverging health system, the two sectors did not value each other's approaches or consider them together. Going off on separate tracks made it difficult to realize the full potential of the medical and public health perspectives or to allocate resources in the best interest of both individual and population health.

Previous Attempts to Bridge the Gap Between Medicine and Public Health

Although the separation of medicine and public health became the status quo for most health professionals, it was not universally accepted. Some observers raised concerns about the dissociation of prevention from treatment, especially the lack of attention to clinical and community-wide preventive strategies once drugs or procedures became available for treatment. Others focused on the changing nature of health problems in the country, noting that an overemphasis on biological mechanisms would divert attention from the behavioral, social, economic, and environmental conditions that make diseases emerge in susceptible individuals. Still others drew attention to the growing imbalance in resources between the two health sectors, and to the inability of medicine and public health, functioning separately, to meet the basic health needs of everyone in the country.

Over the years, two types of approaches have been put forward to bridge the gap between medicine and public health. One approach, spearheaded by some in the medical sector, has sought to change the nature of medical practice, with an aim toward making it more receptive to prevention and to nonbiological determinants of health. The second approach has focused on the growing imbalance between medicine and public health, proposing policies that would reorient health resources away from medical care and toward environmental, behavioral, and socioeconomic health determinants.

ATTEMPTS TO CHANGE THE NATURE OF MEDICAL PRACTICE

The desire for medicine to move beyond the biomedical paradigm harkens back to the broad view of health and illness that Hippocrates espoused in the fourth century B.C. Paradoxically, it also builds on words of the father of the biomedical paradigm, Abraham Flexner. In 1910, Flexner wrote that "the physician's function is fast becoming social and preventive, rather than individual and curative."[58] He urged practitioners "not to forget that directly or indirectly, disease has been found to depend largely on unpropitious environment."[109] These conditions—"a bad water supply, defective drainage, impure food, unfavorable occupational surroundings"—are matters for "social regulation," and doctors have the duty "to promote social conditions that conduce to physical well-being."[109]

In the post-World War II period, various attempts, involving both practice and academia, have been made to relate the care of the individual patient to the broader social and physical environments. Expressions of this theme include social medicine, community-oriented primary care, preventive medicine, and initiatives to broaden medical education and training.

Social Medicine

Although its origins date to the 19th century, social medicine[143] received particular attention in 1947 when Iago Galdston organized an Institute of Social Medicine in connection with the Centennial Celebration of The New York Academy of Medicine.[64] Recognizing the importance of the social sciences in the health of individuals and of groups, the Institute promoted social medicine as a framework that places "emphasis on man and endeavors to study him in relation to his environment: housing, drainage, water supplies, and the whole of the economic, nutritional, occupational, educational and psychological opportunity of the individual or community."[64] Members of the Institute of Social Medicine viewed public health as being narrowly focused on communicable diseases, sanitary law, and engineering. Consequently, they saw social medicine as more than a marriage of medicine and public health—it was a philosophy that could extend the perspective of public health as well as medicine.

Community-Oriented Primary Care

Primary care seeks to integrate the broad range of care that individuals need over time. Through the role of the generalist practitioner, it provides a mechanism for incorporating health promotion and clinical preventive services in medical practice, and for coordinating the care provided to patients by multiple specialists.[121,159,189]

Community-oriented primary care (COPC) goes even further in extending the perspective of medical practice—by linking epidemiology and a community perspective to primary care. In 1984, an Institute of Medicine (IOM) report defined COPC as "the provision of primary care services to a defined community, coupled with systematic efforts to identify and address the major health problems of that community through effective modifications in both the primary care services and other appropriate community health programs."[85] First implemented by Sidney Kark in the 1940s in South Africa, precursors of COPC in the United States included prepaid group practices, health maintenance organizations, and rural health associations centered around community hospitals. Other American examples of this model include some of the federally funded community and migrant health centers, such as the rural health center in Mound Bayou, MS, the Indian Health Service, and certain integrated health systems.

Preventive Medicine

The specialty of preventive medicine, which was recognized by the American Board of Medical Specialties in 1949, applies the broader medical perspective to postgraduate medical education. Preventive medicine focuses on elucidating and mitigating the causal factors of disease among individuals and populations.[51] While the majority of preventive medicine specialists deliver some clinical care, their training and expertise emphasize a population-based, quantitative approach to promoting health and preventing disease. Only a small proportion of the 600,000 physicians practicing in the United States today have received training in this field—as of 1991, 3,678 preventive medicine specialists had been board-certified nationally.[51] Yet, they could have an especially important role to play in bringing the two health sectors closer together. Coming out of residency programs that provide physicians with both formal public health training and M.P.H. degrees, preventive medicine specialists tend to have credibility in both sectors and an understanding of the perspectives, practices, and methodologic approaches of both medicine and public health. Consequently, they have the background and experience to serve as "boundary spanners"—professionals who can bridge the gap between more traditionally trained medical and public health professionals.

Initiatives to Broaden Medical Education and Training

In the post-World War II period, most medical schools have not trained their students to apply public health principles in clinical practice. Many students have been required to learn some of the principles of public health during their first two years of medical school, often through courses taught by faculty in departments of preventive, community, social, or environmental medicine. During their last two years in medical school and postgraduate training, however, students and residents seldom see faculty making use of those principles in clinical settings. In recent years, a number of educators have written eloquently about the need to extend the perspective of medical education and training.[21,37,79,187] In the United States, one of the most important initiatives along these lines has been the Health of the Public Program.[154] Launched in 1986 by The Pew Charitable Trusts and The Rockefeller Foundation, and later supported by The Robert Wood Johnson Foundation, it was designed to encourage academic centers to adopt a broad construct of health that emphasizes individuals' social and personal resources as well as physical capacity, and to integrate population and clinical perspectives into their education, research, and service programs.

The second type of strategy for bringing medicine and public health closer together has focused not on making medicine more receptive to public health, but on addressing the resource imbalance between two health sectors. Attributing current spending patterns to an erroneous interpretation of the effect of medicine in improving health, proponents of this approach have sought to reorient health resources away from medical care and toward environmental, behavioral, and socioeconomic determinants of health.

The scientific basis for this approach initially stemmed from studies by McKeown, which suggested that sanitary measures and nutrition, rather than medical care, had been responsible for the dramatic drop in mortality rates in the 19th century.[118] Later, the Black Report documented the persistence of socioeconomic differentials in health status in countries in which everyone has access to medical care through universal health insurance.[17] In a study of factors responsible for the ten leading causes of death in the United States in 1977 and 1990, the Centers for Disease Control and Prevention (CDC) concluded that less than 10 percent of premature deaths could have been avoided through improvements in medical care. The rest were dependent on personal risk behaviors, risk factors in the environment, and human biology.[173,175] In a complementary analysis of U.S. mortality data in 1990, McGinnis and Foege attributed half of all premature deaths to a small group of underlying causes (few of which appeared to be amenable to medical care): tobacco, diet and activity patterns, alcohol, microbial agents, toxic agents, firearms, sexual behavior, motor vehicles, and illicit use of drugs.[116] These studies suggested that strategies going beyond medical care would be needed to improve health status in the modern era.

Several attempts have been made to use these findings to shape health policy. In the 1970s, LaLonde, in Canada, and Dever, in the United States, suggested that a greater emphasis should be placed on nonmedical approaches to improving health, particularly those related to behavior and the physical and social environment.[47,101] Dever commented that "based on current procedures for reducing mortality and morbidity, little or no change in our present disease patterns will be accomplished unless we dramatically shift our health policy."[47] Seeing little change in resource allocation in 1994, Evans, Barer, and Marmor updated the analysis and literature review, emphasizing the need for policies that reflect the large extent to which health depends "on the structures of workplaces, families, schools, and communities, and on the policies of government agencies not traditionally associated with health (such as economic development, education, employment, income security, social services, and the environment)."[54]

These studies and policy recommendations were rebutted by the medical community. In 1977, McDermott suggested that the indices of health used in McKeown's studies—mortality statistics—were not a valid reflection of the medical sector's total impact on health because they did not account for the critically important supportive aspects of the encounter between physician and patient, such as reassurance, relief from pain and suffering, and improvements in capacity to function.[115] In 1995, a new analysis conducted by Bunker concluded that while the extraordinary increase in life expectancy early in the 20th century largely had been due to nonmedical factors, clinical preventive services and therapeutic interventions had substantially increased medicine's proportionate contribution to life expectancy and quality of life since 1950.[31]

IMPACT OF THESE ATTEMPTS

The initiatives described above—attempts to change the nature of medical practice and to reorient the allocation of health resources—were promoted with considerable enthusiasm and laid a strong foundation for change. Yet none received widespread support or could be said to have had much of a "mainstream effect" in bringing medicine and public health closer together. Despite these efforts, the medical sector—in education, practice, and research—continued to embrace a narrowly focused biomedical model. Moreover, the growth in spending for medical care continued to accelerate. In retrospect, the intransigence of the health system is not surprising. For most of the post-World War II period, neither health professionals, policymakers, nor the general public had any compelling reasons to change the status quo—or supportive incentives to do so.

In spite of the problems associated with the divergence of medicine and public health, the health of the general population did not seem to be suffering. Although disturbing gaps in health status were beginning to be identified among certain subgroups, measures of heath status for the public at large were showing substantial improvements. For example, longevity at birth, which had been only 47 years in 1900, had increased to 75 years in 1990. Infant mortality had decreased from more than 100 per 1,000 births to 9 per 1,000 births during the same period. Even without a close functional relationship between medicine and public health, substantial progress had been made in controlling the scourge of infectious disease that had plagued the country at the turn of the century, and in treating and addressing some of the risk factors for the chronic diseases that were now the leading causes of mortality. As a result, from 1950 to 1990, the age-adjusted death rate for diseases of the heart had declined from 307 per 100,000 to 152 per 100,000, and the age-adjusted death rate for cerebrovascular diseases had declined from 89 per 100,000 to 28 per 100,000.[176]

Medical professionals and institutions seemed to be thriving without any need for them to change their perspective or to work more closely with public health. Public expectations and economic incentives were congruent, encouraging the medical sector to develop new drugs and procedures to treat disease and to make up-to-date specialty care readily available to the public. As the medical sector was expanding, so was its economic and political power. Despite the claims of some researchers that improvements in longevity were largely unrelated to medical care, medical professionals were vividly aware of the importance of their activities to patients. Moreover, they knew that the value of these activities was growing as technological advances enhanced what medical practitioners could do.

Many professionals in the public health sector also considered themselves better positioned without a closer relationship to medicine. Clearly, they were concerned about the level of funding for public health, especially in the face of increasing pressure to provide safety-net services for the uninsured. In this context, they sought broader appreciation of the public health sector's efforts to prevent disease and promote health in the community, including better cooperation and support from the medical sector. At the same time, however, some public health professionals were wary of any proposal that would merge public health with medicine. The medical sector was considerably larger and more powerful than the public health sector. Consequently, attempts to have the medical sector adopt the perspective of public health risked the loss of all aspects of public health that did not directly overlap with the health of individuals or the practice of medicine. Moreover, some proposals focused entirely on physicians, ignoring the important role of other types of professionals in public health. John B. Grant of the Rockefeller Foundation—an advocate for the integration of preventive and curative health services—expressed the kind of view that fueled these concerns. He believed that if American medical schools became more oriented toward prevention, epidemiology, and the social sciences, schools of public health would no longer be needed.[56]

The Current Predicament

If the environment in which health professionals work had remained as it was in the late 1970s, it would be difficult to justify yet another attempt to bridge the gap between medicine and public health. The American health system, however, has undergone dramatic changes since that time. These changes have shattered any possibility of continuing the status quo, and they are making it not only desirable but also imperative for professionals in the two health sectors to re-evaluate their relationship. Today, in striking contrast to what had previously been the norm

- both sectors are concerned about the direction of the health system;

- both are under economic and performance pressure;

- neither can accomplish their mission alone.

DRIVING FORCES OF CHANGE

Several forces are driving the destabilization and growing interdependence of medicine and public health. The crisis in health care costs, the market response to that crisis, and the movement to reinvent government are radically altering the environment in which medical and public health professionals work. At the same time, the changing spectrum of health problems in this country is having a profound impact on the work that health professionals need to do.

Between 1960 and 1990, spending for health care grew at almost 6 percent per year (adjusted for inflation)—more than double the growth rate of the rest of the economy.[63] Health expenditures in the United States are now approaching $1 trillion per year (or $4,000 for every person in the country).[105] In part, the cost crisis is a consequence of the two health sectors' success in preventing and treating acute disease, which has led to an expanding older population and an increasing burden of chronic disease. It also reflects the increasing availability of expensive drugs and medical technology in an environment in which economic incentives—such as fee-for-service and cost-based payment—actively encourage their use.

By the late 1970s, skyrocketing costs of Medicare, Medicaid, and employer-sponsored health insurance, coupled with a troubled economy, forced government and business to confront the expenditure issue. Various strategies were implemented to reduce health cost inflation, including wage and price controls, prospective hospital payment, physician fee schedules, selective contracting, and prepaid health plans.[19] In the early 1990s, with U.S. health expenditures higher than any other country in the world, with U.S. health indicators lagging behind those of many other developed countries, with a growing number of workers uninsured, and with mounting fears among the middle class about the loss of health insurance, the federal government considered comprehensive proposals for overhauling the health system.[105] When government-driven efforts at health reform failed in 1994, market forces took over the health care system, and a movement to reinvent government swept America.[69,131]

Currently, the market solution to escalating health care costs is managed care. The term "managed care" describes strategies that health care organizations use to control the cost and quality of medical services. In some more experienced organizations, it is defined as a style of practice. While all managed care organizations insure plan members and furnish the care they receive, they carry out these functions in diverse ways. Managed care organizations can be for-profit or not-for-profit, local or part of a national chain, tightly managed staff models or looser organizations that contract with independent providers, group practices, or networks. The growth of managed care has been accelerating in recent years—in both the private market and government-funded health programs. In 1995, 54 million Americans were enrolled in health maintenance organizations and as many as 130 million were insured in one or another form of managed care (including preferred provider organizations and point-of-service plans).[18] Nationally, more than 25 percent of Medicaid recipients and 10 percent of Medicare beneficiaries are currently enrolled in managed care organizations.[145] The most rapid rate of growth has been in for-profit managed care organizations.

Managed care uses market leverage to achieve what Americans have not allowed government to do: reduce the excess capacity in the medical sector that was stimulated by post-World War II policies and curtail the inflation of health care costs.[11,141] For the most part, managed care organizations do this by imposing large price discounts or financial risk on providers. The latter reverses fee-for-service incentives for ever-greater consumption of medical care. As a result of market forces, hospitals have been downsizing, merging, and closing. Physicians have been moving to employed positions, and some (particularly specialists) have been experiencing reductions in their incomes. Power has been shifting from specialists to generalists, from physicians to nonphysician practitioners, and from medical professionals to managers, corporate executives, and investors. Recently, the country has begun to experience a backlash to managed care. As a result, policymakers are focusing increasing attention on consumer protection and quality issues.

At the same time as the market is playing a greater role in the health system, government's role is being redefined. The government reform movement that the country is currently experiencing reflects the voters' lack of faith in government programs. While government is a key instrument of community action, it is increasingly being perceived as bureaucratic, regulatory, and inefficient. In this context, taxpayers appear unwilling to pay more money for publicly funded health programs. Along with market forces, this tightening of public funds is threatening support for the health system's public goods: research, health professions education, population-based public health programs, and care for the substantial number of un- and underinsured.

Government reform is being implemented through five key mechanisms: devolution, downsizing, privatization, integration, and "results budgeting." Consistent with the trend in the private sector to move away from top-down hierarchical systems, devolution is moving authority and fiscal responsibility from the federal government to the states, and from the states to counties and cities. Downsizing is being spurred by tax reductions as well as by concerns about future tax increases. Its main consequences for the health system have been reductions in personnel and funding for public health programs, and, in some cases, termination of programs. Downsizing coupled with the need for greater flexibility (for example, to implement a program rapidly or to overcome "red tape") is leading many state and local health departments to privatize certain public health services. Fueled by frustrations in addressing persistent health problems, government agencies are attempting to integrate related programs, and legislatures are beginning to link the appropriation of funds to documentation that desired results are being achieved (a process known as "results budgeting").

Compounding the anxiety that is being engendered by market forces and the redefined role of government, today's health professionals also are facing an extremely challenging and disconcerting set of health problems. They are witnessing the reemergence of diseases that many thought were "conquered," such as measles and tuberculosis. Drug resistance is becoming an increasingly common and worrisome phenomenon. New diseases are emerging, such as HIV/AIDS, that resist easy approaches to prevention or cure. "Old" diseases, such as cervical cancer and peptic ulcer, are being found to have new and unexpected causes. Chronic diseases are persistent, and, some, like noninsulin-dependent diabetes, seem to defy translating what is known about prevention and treatment into routine public health and medical practice. Problems with prominent social components, such as violence, substance abuse, and teenage pregnancy, which do not fit easily into the disease model, are being classified as health problems. And striking differences in health status—according to race, ethnicity, and socioeconomic status—are becoming a disturbing "norm" in America's increasingly diverse society.

GROWING
INTER-
DEPENDENCE
OF MEDICINE
AND PUBLIC
HEALTH

In this "brave new world," professionals and organizations in medicine and public health are under intense pressure. All are facing challenges to their stature and authority, all are concerned about their economic viability, and all are having difficulty carrying out their professional roles. At the same time, certain aspects of the current environment are increasing the relevance of each sector's perspectives, resources, and skills to the other sector. Striking shifts in the health system are making the medical and public health sectors increasingly dependent on one another. New incentives are making it advantageous for professionals and organizations in the two sectors to work more closely together. And new organizational structures are making cross-sectoral interactions easier and more efficient to carry out. In this environment, continuing on separate tracks is not in the best interest of either medicine or public health. Today, professionals and institutions in the two sectors need each other and can help each other—not only in addressing their patients' and populations' health problems, but also in promoting their own professional and economic health.

Below, we discuss six factors that are contributing to these changes:

- shifts in patient populations

- shifts in clinical services

- shifts in perspectives

- shifts in financing streams

- economic and performance pressures

- consolidation and partnerships

Shifts in Patient Populations

As states are moving to managed care contracts and "medical home" initiatives to control costs in their Medicaid programs, increasing numbers of patients who previously had received care through public hospitals and public health clinics are being shifted to "mainstream" medical settings.[141] As a result, hospitals and physician groups that previously had little experience with Medicaid patients are now becoming involved in their care. As a group, Medicaid recipients differ in important ways from patients traditionally seen in the private sector. They tend to be poorer and less well educated. They also are more likely to have multiple risk factors for disease and to suffer from serious mental and physical health problems, such as cardiovascular disease, sexually transmitted diseases (STDs), lead toxicity, multidrug-resistant tuberculosis (MDR-TB), substance abuse, and HIV/AIDS.[32]

Because of these differences, it is more difficult to deliver medical care successfully to Medicaid recipients than to the healthier, more affluent enrollees traditionally covered by managed care organizations. Rather than simply waiting for patients to come into the office, effective care for many Medicaid recipients depends on the ability to overcome physical, cultural, and social barriers to care, to get into the home environment and provide follow-up services, and to link patients with other relevant services and programs in the community.[45]

In governmental and community-based public health clinics, medical care for Medicaid recipients traditionally has been linked to special "wraparound" services designed to meet these needs. Some of these services, such as transportation, translation, and child care, help patients gain access to and communicate with their practitioner. Others, such as home visits, reinforce and extend what takes place during an office or clinic visit. Home visits often are invaluable in providing follow-up care—for high-risk mothers, for instance—and in helping patients and their families deal with complex medical regimens, such as those used to manage asthma, diabetes, or HIV/AIDs. They also are of benefit in promoting compliance with treatment programs. For example, visits to a patient's home can reinforce the need for treatment in asymptomatic conditions, such as hypertension, and they can be used to verify that medications actually are taken by patients with problems like MDR-TB.

In addition to providing wraparound services, public health clinics also frequently have provided their medical practitioners with ways to link patient care to population-based public health services and to social support services in the community. Easy access to public health services is important in dealing with certain health problems that are prevalent in the Medicaid population, such as lead poisoning. To prevent the recurrence of lead toxicity in a child with that condition—and to protect other children from being exposed to lead from the same source—appropriate follow-up is needed to identify the source of the contamination, to educate the child's family, and to remove the lead hazard from the child's school or home. The availability of effective links to social support services also is valuable to clinicians caring for Medicaid recipients. These services can help assure that patients retain their health insurance coverage, obtain access to available nutritional support, and are referred to needed ancillary services, such as substance-abuse treatment programs.

With the shift to Medicaid managed care, many of these same wraparound, public health, and social services are now needed in mainstream medical settings. Without this support, it is virtually impossible for medical practitioners to provide effective medical care to many Medicaid recipients. But few managed care organizations, and even fewer medical practices, have the experience, expertise, or structures to provide such services themselves. Moreover, no states include in their contracts with managed care organizations all of the care and services they have been covering under their Medicaid programs.[32] To assure the provision of effective care to Medicaid recipients in mainstream medical environments, new relationships need to be established between professionals and organizations in medicine and public health.

Shifts in Clinical Services

The new health care environment is characterized not only by a shift of Medicaid recipients from public health settings to the mainstream medical sector but by a shift of clinical services as well. This shift in services goes beyond the medical care required by Medicaid patients themselves. It also encompasses clinical services that public health professionals previously had provided to some privately insured patients and Medicare beneficiaries: preventive services that the medical sector had few incentives to provide, and certain diagnostic and treatment services that are critical to protecting the entire community's health.

Two important changes in the health system are driving this shift in services. One impetus is the expanded coverage for clinical preventive services—such as immunizations, mammograms, Pap tests, and counseling—in private and publicly sponsored health insurance programs. Until recently, clinical preventive services were not commonly included in private health insurance, and were not part of the benefits package in the Medicare program. Consequently, most people either paid their regular medical practitioner for these services "out-of-pocket," obtained them in public health settings (such as clinics, health fairs, or other public health-sponsored events), or did not receive them at all.

In the current environment, however, public and private purchasers are increasingly requiring the inclusion of clinical preventive services by the plans with which they contract. These plans, in turn, are either reimbursing medical practitioners for the delivery of these services or including them as part of the capitation payments made to primary care practitioners. Through report cards such as the Health Plan Employer Data and Information Set (HEDIS), developed by the National Committee for Quality Assurance (NCQA), managed care organizations are reporting to purchasers the rate at which certain clinical preventive services are actually being delivered.[126] In part, expanded coverage for clinical preventive services reflects the increasing emphasis on primary care in the health system, the development of evidence-based guidelines for these services by the U.S. Preventive Services Task Force,[180] and the growing interest in wellness on the part of the public. It also has been fueled by the savings that can be achieved through the delivery of certain preventive services, such as childhood immunization, prenatal care, intensive ophthalmic screening in patients with insulin-dependent diabetes, and influenza immunization in the elderly.[166]

The other driving force behind the shift in clinical services is that managed care organizations are giving their enrollees fewer options to go "out-of-network" for care. Under unrestricted indemnity insurance, which is rapidly becoming extinct, all qualified providers—including public health clinics—were eligible to receive payment for covered services. Consequently, individuals who had such insurance could selectively obtain certain services in public health settings. Often they chose this route for concerns or problems that they did not want their regular practitioner (or parent or spouse) to know about, such as family planning, STDs, and HIV/AIDS. Under most forms of managed care, however, clinical services related to these problems are usually part of "in-network" benefits. If a public health clinic is not part of a managed care organization network, services provided in that setting are either partially covered by the managed care organization or not covered at all. Equally important, if certain services are covered under public managed care contracts, taxpayers are less likely to be willing to subsidize such services for managed care enrollees in publicly funded clinics as well. In some areas, and for some services, the impact of these forces is substantial. In San Francisco, for example, two-thirds of all STD cases are now diagnosed and treated in managed care settings rather than in traditional STD clinics.[89]

These shifts in services have the potential to improve clinical practice by integrating prevention and health maintenance more fully with medical diagnosis and treatment. At the same time, however, they are disrupting critical linkages between clinical and population-based services that had been established through categorical public health programs. Even more important, they are making the medical sector a key player in public health strategies that are critical to the entire community's health.

As the medical sector is becoming a *de facto* arm of prevention, the two health sectors are becoming considerably more dependent on each other than they have been for much of the post-World War II period. In the area of immunization, for example, the public health sector needs to be sure that immunizations included as medical benefits are, in fact, delivered. Otherwise, not enough of the population will be immunized to protect the community at large. The medical sector, on the other hand, is increasingly under pressure to document that target immunization rates have been achieved—not only for the sake of public health, but also for report cards, such as HEDIS.

Numerous studies have shown that it is not possible to achieve either of these goals simply by making immunizations available. In managed care organizations, for example, rates were found to be low even among children with multiple encounters per year, and even when immunization was not associated with any copayment.[80] In 1989–91, a failure in preschool immunization resulted in over 55,000 cases of measles in the United States with 130 measles-associated deaths.[14] To achieve adequate childhood immunization levels in today's environment, the medical sector's increasing attention to this problem needs to be reinforced with strategies that can help clinicians identify and influence parents who are not seeking out indicated immunizations, and account for children in their practices who are getting their immunizations elsewhere. Managed care organizations and structured practices can offer clinicians valuable supports in this regard, including patient education and outreach; reminders; tracking and feedback of results; and various incentives and rewards.[169,170] These can be reinforced substantially by community-wide public health strategies. Public education and media campaigns, for example, can help "funnel" patients in need of immunizations to their practitioners' offices; wraparound services can help address logistical barriers that some patients face in accessing care; and community-wide immunization registries can keep track of the immunization status of individual patients, regardless of where they obtain their care or whether they are stable members of a practice or managed care organization population.

The shift in services is making the two health sectors interdependent not only around immunization, but in other areas as well. As health problems such as lead poisoning, MDR-TB, and STDs increasingly are being diagnosed and treated outside of categorical public health programs, new linkages are needed between mainstream medical practice and public health agencies to assure that an adequate community protection response occurs. The discussion around shifts in the Medicaid population highlighted the importance of linking the diagnosis and treatment of children with lead toxicity to environmental lead-abatement interventions. Without such linkages, lead toxicity is likely to recur in affected children, as well as in other children in the same environment who also are at risk of developing the problem. Effective linkages also are needed in the area of communicable diseases, such as STDs, TB, and HIV/AIDS. For example, to limit the spread and long-term sequelae of these diseases, the diagnosis and treatment of an individual patient needs to be linked to public health efforts to identify and test those with whom the patient has been in contact. To assure compliance and prevent the development of drug resistance, mainstream medical practices need ready access to wrap-around services, such as home visits and transportation, that can help patients manage complex medical regimens, and to programs providing directly observed therapy.

Shifts in Perspectives

Another important aspect of the new environment is that certain perspectives and tools of public health are becoming considerably more relevant to the medical sector. To a large extent, this is happening because of the financial risk associated with managed care. All managed care organizations, regardless of type, contract with purchasers to provide a predetermined set of benefits to a defined population of enrollees for a fixed annual price. The risk for delivering medical care within this budget can be assumed by a managed care organization or integrated system that employs or contracts with medical professionals. Alternatively, it can be borne by practitioners themselves through capitated physician networks and large group practices.[142] In either case, as medical organizations and physicians take on financial risk, they are under increasing pressure to anticipate health service demands accurately and to practice cost-effectively. In effect, their economic viability is becoming dependent on population-based data, epidemiologic analyses, and public health strategies.

Managing financial risk successfully requires up-to-date information from the scientific literature about what works, what doesn't, for whom, and at what cost. It also requires a solid understanding of one's own medical organization: the health needs of the patient population in a medical practice, integrated system, or managed care organization; the way medical care is provided to that population; and the outcomes of that care. Data about the health status and health risks of the patient population are relevant to this need, as are epidemiologic analyses that assess the effectiveness and costs of the organization's medical practices. In addition to organizational-level data, information about the community at large—the pool from which the enrolled or practice population is drawn—is often critical as well. This is particularly true for managed care organizations, integrated systems, and group practices that are considering taking on financial risk for a new population, or that seek to expand their presence in a geographic area. In the latter case, the health of the entire community becomes relevant, since the health and behavior of those not enrolled in the organization can affect the medical needs (and costs) of its members. Moreover, anyone not enrolled today has a good chance of becoming enrolled tomorrow.[1]

Clearly, these changes are making the public health perspective more pertinent to the medical sector. Indeed, a growing number of medical professionals are seeking training in biostatistics, clinical epidemiology, and cost-effectiveness analysis.[174] At the same time, the move to managed care and the bearing of financial risk is making the medical sector more dependent on public health, and vice versa. Increasingly, professionals in medicine and public health have a common need for population-based data about health and functional status, the prevalence and underlying causes of disease and disability, and the utilization, costs, and effectiveness of health services.[75] Yet, in the current environment, neither sector is able to amass this information alone. As a greater proportion of the population is moving into managed care, public health agencies are losing certain sources of information (for example, fee-for-service claims data, and information they had collected about clients in their own programs), making it more difficult to compile community-wide health statistics. The medical sector also is experiencing information problems. The instability of some enrolled populations (especially those in the Medicaid program) is creating a need among managed care organizations and group practices for information frameworks, such as immunization registries, that go beyond the data that they can collect themselves.

As the medical sector takes on financial risk, it also is becoming economically dependent on the public health sector, particularly on the capacity of public health agencies to prevent unnecessary disease from occurring in the community. Under capitation—in striking contrast to fee-for-service or cost-based payment—treating medical problems consumes the medical sector's resources instead of increasing its revenues. Consequently, in today's environment, managed care organizations and capitated medical practices bear the costs of treating patients who come down with diseases that occur when efforts to protect the community's food, water, housing, and environment fail.[134] These costs can be substantial. The 1993 cryptosporidium outbreak in Milwaukee, for example, a result of a failure to protect the water supply, affected 370,000 people at a cost of $15.5 million.[105] To avoid such expenses, the medical sector has an incentive to pay more attention than it has in the past to the effectiveness and funding of agencies carrying responsibility for community health protection. It also has an incentive to work more closely with the public health sector in a variety of other prevention activities, such as immunization, bicycle helmet use, and initiatives to discourage drunk driving.

Shifts in Financing Streams

With the move to Medicaid managed care, managed care organizations are not only taking over Medicaid patients, they also are taking over these patients' Medicaid revenue. This shift in financing streams is making it extremely difficult for public health "safety-net" providers to subsidize care for the uninsured. Equally important, it may be compromising the capacity of some public health agencies to provide population-based services that are essential to protecting the community's health.

A particularly disturbing aspect of the current environment is that a large number of people in the United States have no health insurance or inadequate coverage. Estimates suggest that 39 to 42 million people are uninsured at any one time, and as many as 60 million people are uninsured at some time during the calendar year.[141] People without health insurance have less access to medical care, and are twice as likely to be hospitalized for avoidable conditions.[141]

For most of the post-World War II period, medical care for the un- and underinsured has been provided primarily by a safety net of public health agencies, not-for-profit public health clinics, public hospitals, and academic health centers. To a large extent, these safety-net providers have funded their services with tax dollars and cross-subsidies from Medicaid reimbursement.[89] Mainstream hospitals and medical practitioners also have played a role, subsidizing the care they have provided to the uninsured by raising the fees they charged to paying patients. In the current context of discount pricing and financial risk, private hospitals and medical practices are less able to cross-subsidize care for the indigent. Moreover, as safety-net providers are losing both their Medicaid patients and Medicaid revenue, they are finding it increasingly difficult to finance the care of a rising proportion of uninsured patients.[45] The economic impact of these changes is being felt by both health sectors. Obviously, it is threatening the survival of many safety-net providers. But it is also a problem for the mainstream medical sector. When uninsured people lack access to timely medical care, high emergency room costs are borne not only by public hospitals but also by private hospitals and integrated systems. If public health clinics and public hospitals do not remain viable, the financial burden on these private institutions is likely to increase.

The shift in the Medicaid financing stream also may be having a less anticipated effect—it may be undermining the capacity of governmental public health agencies to deliver population-based services, such as monitoring of health status, disease investigation, and protection against outbreaks of disease. Recent estimates suggest that approximately 1 percent of the nation's health expenditures are devoted to these types of activities.[36,117] The reemergence of "conquered" health problems like tuberculosis, as well as recent outbreaks of preventable childhood diseases and of food-borne and water-borne diseases, have raised concerns that this level of funding is not adequate to protect the public's health. Indeed, the 1988 IOM report, *The Future of Public Health*, described the American public health system as in "disarray" and a "threat to the health of the public."[86] Since the publication of that report, a number of public health agencies have been reevaluating their role, and many are attempting to strengthen their capacity to provide essential population-based services, in some cases by moving away from direct patient care.

The delivery of personal health care services can either support or detract from population-based public health activities. With limited funds for population-based services, some health departments have used home health visits to underwrite community-wide prevention functions. For others, fulfilling the safety-net role has claimed staffing and funding that otherwise might have supported essential population-based activities.[68] Regardless of the approach used, the loss of Medicaid revenue is likely to have a detrimental effect on the capacity of these health departments to fulfill their community-wide responsibilities. It either will result in a loss of funds that previously were used to subsidize essential population-based services, or it may redirect limited health department resources away from population-based activities to more "urgent" safety-net medical care.

Various aspects of the current environment are influencing the ability of health departments to obtain public funds for generic population-based services. As described earlier, funding for such activities has been very difficult to achieve in the post-World War II period. On one level, it is even more difficult in the current environment. With the new focus of managed care on patient populations and on clinical prevention, some people have the misperception that managed care organizations are taking over responsibility for the entire population and for community-wide prevention activities. In this context, public health agencies are under increasing pressure to justify the need for what they do. On the other hand, the assumption of financial risk is making the capacity of public health agencies to prevent or quickly address community health problems a real economic concern to the medical sector. Consequently, managed care organizations and capitated practices could become a vocal constituency for adequate health department funding and staffing.

Economic and Performance Pressures

The striking shifts in the American health system—in patients, services, perspectives, and financing streams—are revealing various ways that the medical and public health sectors are becoming dependent on each other and can reinforce each other in today's challenging environment. The strongest impetus for actually *establishing* cross-sectoral relationships, however, may come from the health system's growing emphasis on cost containment and on documenting results. As economic and performance pressures intensify, success is much more likely if professionals and institutions in the two health sectors work together than if they continue to work alone.

As health expenditures in this country approach $1 trillion per year, pressures to contain costs are mounting. Purchasers of medical and public health services—government, employers, and consumers—are resisting increases in health insurance premiums, in taxes, and in out-of-pocket expenses. Moreover, they want every dollar that they spend to count—to go toward results they care about. These expectations are having a profound impact on the environment in which the two health sectors work. Through market forces and government reform, professionals and organizations in medicine and public health are expected to carry out their roles with fewer personnel and for less money. Through report cards, which sometimes are used for accreditation and performance-based contracting, they are expected to show that meaningful results are being achieved for that money. Increasingly, the types of results that they are being asked to document are not institutional process measures, but rather indicators of health outcomes and quality, such as access to care, satisfaction with care, delivery of essential health services, reductions in morbidity and mortality, reductions in risk factors, and improvements in health status and functional status.

In the medical sector, a variety of datasets are being used to assess the quality and results of clinical care for defined patient populations. These datasets include HEDIS (the National Committee on Quality Assurance report card referred to earlier), New York's Quality Assurance Reporting Requirements (QARR), and sets of performance indicators developed by the Joint Commission on Accreditation and Healthcare Organizations (JCAHO) and the Foundation for Accountability.[60,92,93,126] JCAHO also requires community health status measures from hospitals.[92,93] In the public health sector, where health assessment focuses on the community at large, performance measurement has centered around *Healthy People* objectives. Beginning in 1980 with *Promoting Health/Preventing Disease: Objectives for the Nation*, these measures have been updated every ten years (the latest version is *Healthy People 2000*), and are reported nationally on a regular basis.[177-179] Faced with limited resources and a range of difficult health problems, state and local governments are prioritizing health objectives to address in their own communities. While these "health priorities," usually are selected from the measures included in *Healthy People*, they sometimes go beyond them.

Economic and performance pressures are providing compelling reasons for professionals and organizations in medicine and public health to work more closely together. In this type of environment, both sectors are looking for ways to achieve economies of scale, to provide services more efficiently, to reduce duplication of effort, and to increase productivity. When neither sector has the time or resources to do everything itself, collaborative relationships begin to make sense, particularly if each sector focuses on areas in which it has special expertise or which would be inefficient for the other sector to perform. In the medical sector, the shift from fee-for-service and cost-based payment to capitation and financial risk is reinforcing this incentive to partner. Under the old payment structure, medical practitioners and institutions were rewarded financially for doing more themselves. In the current environment, by contrast, they have an economic incentive to focus on what they do best and to work with others whose skills and resources complement their own.

Another compelling reason to collaborate is that the health outcomes that are being measured—whether they relate to improvements in health status for the community at large or to the delivery and quality of clinical services for defined patient populations—often depend on factors beyond any one sector's direct control. In today's environment, the medical sector's performance in HEDIS and JCAHO measures frequently is dependent on public health strategies. Similarly, the public health sector's capacity to achieve health priorities and *Healthy People 2000* objectives often is dependent on the involvement of a broad range of partners in the community, including the medical sector. Considering economic and performance pressures together, the two health sectors are likely to experience particularly strong incentives for working together around health outcomes that are being monitored in both sectors (for example, by HEDIS or JCAHO and by *Healthy People* or locally set health priorities) and in areas where collaborative relationships allow each sector to achieve its goals more efficiently as well as more effectively.

While the move to managed care has made performance measurement in the medical sector possible (by establishing clear denominator populations of sufficient size to be measured reliably), medical professionals, on their own, face serious challenges in meeting performance goals. For one thing, performance measurement dramatically changes the expectations of practice. Previously, a clinician's responsibility was to do everything possible for patients who took the initiative to visit the office. But achieving specific health outcomes means paying attention to patients who do not actively seek out care, and to factors, such as compliance and health-seeking behaviors, that depend on more than what medical practitioners can do in their offices. Linking some of the public health strategies described in this chapter to medical practice could be useful in addressing these challenges. Wraparound and outreach services, for example, can help patients overcome logistical barriers to accessing care and help them manage and comply with treatment regimens. Community-wide screening programs and public education campaigns can help funnel patients in need of care to their practitioner's offices. Community-wide information systems, such as immunization registries, can keep track of whether individuals have received particular clinical services, regardless of where these services are provided.

While the public health sector always has had a clear geopolitical population for measuring performance, making headway on the types of health problems that the public and policymakers care about requires considerably more than what public health professionals and agencies can do on their own. On the one hand, today's most pressing health problems have multiple, intertwined medical, social, and economic causes.[89] Equally important, the shifts in patient populations, clinical services, and financing streams that characterize the current environment are making it essential for the public health sector to work with and through the mainstream medical sector in achieving many of its *Healthy People 2000* goals. A number of medicine and public health linkages described earlier in this chapter could be useful in this regard. For example, public health goals that depend on the delivery of covered clinical services, such as up-to-date childhood immunizations, can be furthered by the institution of organizational supports—reminder systems, practitioner feedback, incentives and rewards—by managed care organizations and medical practices. Goals that depend on "screen and treat" strategies, such as the control of hypertension, are easier to achieve if mechanisms are in place to assure that individuals with abnormal results actually see a medical practitioner for follow-up diagnostic testing and treatment. The large number of health promotion goals that depend on influencing behavior are more likely to be achieved if medical practices and managed care organizations put in place incentive systems and organizational supports that promote the delivery of counseling to their patient populations—in such areas as smoking cessation, diet, physical activity, seat-belt use, and alcohol abuse—and if a broad range of groups within the community, including the medical sector, become involved in community-wide efforts to make the social environment more conducive to following counseling advice.

Consolidation and Partnerships

Even with compelling reasons for medicine and public health to develop a closer working relationship—and real incentives for doing so—it is difficult to put collaboration into practice without organizational structures that can bring together the perspectives, resources, and skills of diverse health professionals and organizations. As noted earlier, the loose structure of the American health system, and its increasing fragmentation, has served as one barrier to the coordination of medical and public health services. Moreover, little public support accrued to various attempts to rationalize the organization of the health system through the comprehensive health planning proposals in the 1960s and 1970s.[3,84,105] While some of the changes that are occurring in the health system are disrupting linkages of medical and public health services that had been established in the context of public health clinics and categorical programs, new organizational structures are beginning to emerge that may be better suited for supporting cross-sectoral interactions.

In some cases, partnerships between the two health sectors are occurring in response to mandates. Kentucky's 1115 waiver, for example, calls for the formation of cross-sectoral partnerships in Medicaid managed care. These partnerships are required to undertake community needs assessments and wellness-promotion programs, and to develop health education materials on topics such as nutrition, well-child care, childhood screening, injury prevention, and smoking cessation.[45] In Minnesota, managed care organizations are required to produce action and collaboration plans that demonstrate how they intend to work with local public health agencies to improve community health.[1]

Other relationships and organizational structures are being driven by market forces and the redefined role of government. As managed care becomes more widespread and as government funding declines, professionals and institutions in both sectors are perceiving the need to become part of larger systems in order to enhance their negotiating leverage, to achieve economies of scale, to manage risk more successfully, to maintain or expand their patient base, to enhance opportunities and venues for research, and to provide meaningful training experiences for students and residents. This trend toward consolidation has been associated with a plethora of mergers and joint ventures among and between hospitals, academic institutions, and medical practices.

It also is producing a remarkable transition in the practice organization of patient-care physicians. Between 1983 and 1994, the proportion of patient-care physicians practicing as employees increased from 24 to 42 percent, while the proportion in solo practices fell from 41 to 29 percent.[100] While much of the change is being driven by competitive pressure, it also is a response to the growing complexity of medical management and care. In the past, physicians "had everything they needed between their ears and in their black bags."[18] Now, in order to do their jobs, they need an organizational structure that provides them not only with access to human resources—such as specialists, support staff, home care, and nursing home care—but also with information and computer systems that can help them keep up-to-date with the latest advances and apply that knowledge in their practices.

On the one hand, the forces that are driving consolidation are establishing an incentive for professionals and institutions within each health sector—and sometimes across health sectors—to come together. At the same time, the organizational structures that are emerging have the potential to facilitate new relationships between medicine and public health, and to reduce the costs of collaboration. At the least, the dramatic shift of physicians from solo practices to larger group practices and networks is reducing the number of independent medical practitioners with whom a public health agency needs to interact.[145] At best, highly integrated systems have the infrastructure to support the coordination of services among a broad range of organizations and personnel.

A New Dilemma

Reviewing the historical relationship between medicine and public health in the United States, it is clear that two sectors have worked together around health problems in the past, and have continued to have ample opportunities to do so. For much of this century they have taken little advantage of these opportunities, however, because critical conditions for collaboration have not been met. Without a compelling need to work together, and without supportive incentives and organizational structures, the medical and public health sectors evolved along separate, and virtually independent, tracks. By not working together, their cultural differences became increasingly pronounced, making the possibility of future interactions less and less likely.

In the current environment, some of these conditions have changed dramatically. Today, professionals and organizations in medicine and public health clearly need each other—to achieve their missions, and to respond to the economic and performance pressures that they face. Moreover, with the emergence of new incentives and organizational structures, it should be more feasible for them to establish cross-sectoral relationships than it has been in the past. The changes in the health system have not influenced the cultural divergence between medicine and public health, however. Consequently, we now face a new dilemma. Will professionals and organizations in sectors that have become very foreign to each other be able to identify their mutual interests? Will they be able to overcome enough of their suspicions and skepticism to initiate a working relationship? Having had so little interaction over the last 50 years, will they be able to identify potential partners? Will they have a clear idea of how partners can combine their resources and skills in a collaborative endeavor?

The focus groups that we conducted around the country suggest that many health professionals in both sectors would not know where to begin. Overwhelmed by the changes that are occurring, and with little experience working with the other health sector, they do not look to collaboration as an obvious strategy for dealing with current challenges. In spite of these barriers, however, a substantial foundation for collaboration has been laid. Greater attention is being paid to primary care and to its relationship with public health.[159] Through the Health of the Public and other programs, some academic medical centers are increasing their focus on population-based medicine.[73,150,154] The public health sector is reexamining its role, emphasizing the need for broad-based community partnerships.[6,86,89,90] Numerous activities are underway examining the relationship between managed care and public health.[35,137,149,184] New community alliances are being established through Community Care Networks and the Healthy Cities and Healthy Communities movements.[4,39–41,59,76] And in many parts of the country, the medical and public health sectors have found it essential to work together to address emerging health threats such as the measles outbreak, MDR-TB, and HIV/AIDS.

In this context, it is not surprising that we collected 414 examples of medicine and public health collaboration. These cases suggest that for many health professionals around the country, current circumstances are providing compelling reasons to work more closely with the other health sector, and that it is possible to overcome the "cultural divide." In the next part of this monograph, we turn our attention to these collaborations, examining *what* the two health sectors can accomplish by working together and *how* collaborative work gets done.

Part II

Models of Medicine and Public Health Collaboration

The Case Study

As soon as several of the inhabitants of the United States have taken up an opinion or a feeling that they wish to promote in the world, they look out for mutual assistance, and as soon as they have found each other out, they combine. From that moment, they are no longer isolated men, but a power seen from afar whose actions serve for an example and whose language is listened to.

— Alexis de Tocqueville, 1848[171]

Gentlemen, the world has found that there are tasks which one man cannot do alone; the day of isolated individual labor is forever gone. There are also tasks in our world of medicine which no man can accomplish alone . . . Cooperation! What a word! Each working with all, and all working with each. Can anyone doubt that we shall win our battle against low standards, indifferent laws and deadly disease if all work as one.

— Edward C. Register, 1915[110]

None of us is as smart as all of us . . . We all know that cooperation and collaboration grow more important every day. A shrinking world in which technological and political complexity increase at an accelerating rate offers fewer and fewer arenas in which individual action suffices.

— Warren Bennis, 1996[10]

Collaboration is damn tough.

— Focus Group Participant, 1997

The power of combining resources to achieve a shared objective has been appreciated for a long time. As the quotations above illustrate, collaboration has been discussed in general terms, medical terms, business terms—and even in what would now be considered sexist terms—over the course of the last 150 years. At an abstract level, few would oppose the application of this concept to medicine and public health. In the focus groups we conducted around the country, students and practitioners in both health sectors were open to the idea of collaboration. Moreover, the current environment provides compelling reasons for professionals and organizations in medicine and public health to give serious consideration to establishing closer working relationships. Yet, a concrete, practical framework for moving forward with cross-sectoral collaboration seems to be lacking. Very few professionals in the focus groups have had experience working with the other sector. Consequently, they had difficulty describing exactly what cross-sectoral collaboration means or how it could be beneficial to them or to the people they serve. Since working with other people and organizations is not easy, it is unrealistic to encourage the two health sectors to establish a closer relationship without a clear understanding of whether cross-sectoral collaborations can work—and, if so, how they work—in the real world.

To develop such an understanding, we solicited examples of medicine and public health collaboration from a wide range of sources. Beginning in August 1996, cases were requested by mail and through electronic postings to members of major medicine and public health associations, to officials in government health agencies, and to participants in potentially relevant foundation-sponsored initiatives. Using a self-administered written or Internet questionnaire, respondents were asked to provide some basic demographic information about themselves and to answer five open-ended questions: What made the collaboration happen? Who was involved? What was the collaboration trying to achieve? What actually happened? What do you think were the critical elements that determined the project's success or failure?

The response to the solicitation was far greater than any of us expected. Ultimately, over 500 cases were identified, of which 414 involved professionals and/or organizations in both medicine and public health. These collaborations, which also frequently involved other community partners as well, were entered in the database. Over 150 hours of telephone interviews were conducted with a subset of respondents to clarify and extend the information provided in their case reports.

The database of medicine and public health collaborations provides a rich and valuable resource for analysis. The cases are well-dispersed geographically, encompassing not only diverse regions of the country but also urban and rural communities (Figure II-1). They were submitted by a broad array of professionals working in virtually every type of venue relevant to medicine and public health. They encompass all of the domains of medicine and public health: practice, policy, education and training, and research. In addition, they reflect activities at local, state, and federal levels. Because of this diversity, the database is likely to include most of the common types of medicine and public health interactions occurring in this country. Nonetheless, because the cases in the database are not a random sample, we cannot generalize from the frequencies observed.

A "grounded theory" approach was used to analyze this case material.[67,192] Starting with an open mind—without any preconceptions about what medicine and public health collaboration is or should be—we searched for commonalities and concepts that would elucidate the nature of these collaborative activities. In particular, we sought to answer three questions:

Figure II-1 Geographic Distribution of Cases (N = 414)

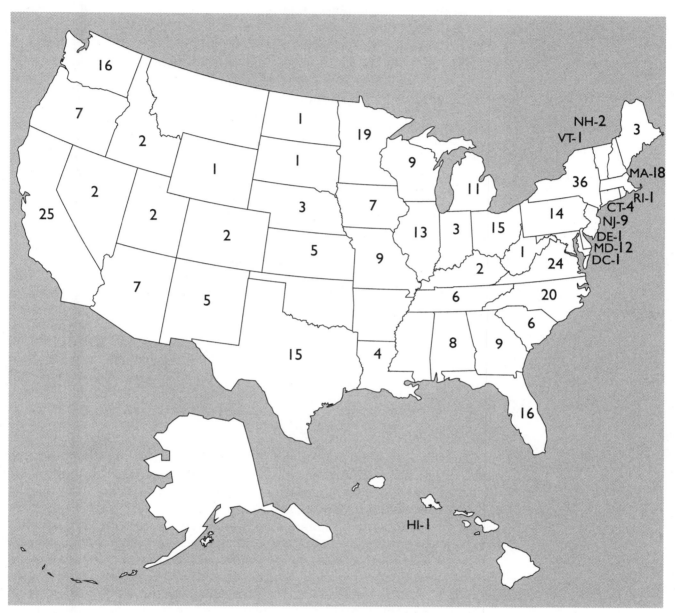

Note: *Most collaborations are at community-level within the state. The database also includes 28 national, 2 multi-state, and 5 international medicine and public health collaborations.*

- How do professionals and organizations in medicine and public health combine their resources and skills?

- What is the structural foundation for interactions among the two health sectors?

- Considering the "cultural divide" that characterizes medicine and public health, how are relationships between the two health sectors established? What makes people and organizations willing to engage in collaborative enterprises, and what makes these partnerships work?

The sections that follow summarize the results of our findings. First, we describe six powerful ways that the medical and public health sectors can combine their resources and skills. The case database shows partners from the two health sectors—and often other sectors of the community as well—contributing the following array of assets to collaborative endeavors:

- technical, scientific, and pedagogic expertise

- methodologic tools

- individual-level services and population-based strategies

- administration and management skills

- legal and regulatory authority

- convening power

- influence with peers, policymakers, and the public

- data and information systems

- buildings and space

- financial support

These assets are valuable in and of themselves. But by combining them in certain ways, the individual partners in a collaboration are able to transcend their own limitations and achieve additional benefits that are important to their patients, their populations, and themselves.

We refer to reinforcing combinations of resources and skills as "synergies." In sections describing six distinct types of synergies, we discuss the particular building blocks involved, the value to different partners of combining them, and the models that people use to put the combination into action (Figure II-2). Each model is "brought to life" with an illustrative example of a case from the database. Taken as a whole, the synergies clearly document the relevance of each health sector's activities to the other. Moreover, they show that the medical and public health sectors can reinforce each other in virtually everything they do: efforts related to individuals (Synergies I and II), to populations (Synergies V and VI), and to combinations of the two (Synergies III and IV). In all of these interactions, both sectors benefit. Although the various synergies are described separately in the text, it should be pointed out that they are not

Figure II-2 Models of Medicine and Public Health Collaboration

Synergy	**Models**
I Improving health care by coordinating services for individuals	A. Bring new personnel and services to existing practice sites B. Establish "one-stop" centers C. Coordinate services provided at different sites
II Improving access to care by establishing frameworks to provide care for the uninsured	A. Establish free clinics B. Establish referral networks C. Enhance clinical staffing at public health facilities D. Shift indigent patients to mainstream medical settings
III Improving the quality and cost-effectiveness of care by applying a population perspective to medical practice	A. Use population-based information to enhance clinical decision-making B. Use population-based strategies to "funnel" patients to medical care C. Use population-based analytic tools to enhance practice management
IV Using clinical practice to identify and address community health problems	A. Use clinical encounters to build community-wide databases B. Use clinical opportunities to identify and address underlying causes of health problems C. Collaborate to achieve clinically oriented community health objectives
V Strengthening health promotion and health protection by mobilizing community campaigns	A. Conduct community health assessments B. Mount health education campaigns C. Advocate health-related laws and regulations D. Engage in community-wide campaigns to achieve health promotion objectives E. Launch "Healthy Communities" initiatives
VI Shaping the future direction of the health system by collaborating around policy, training, and research	A. Influence health system policy B. Engage in cross-sectoral education and training C. Conduct cross-sectoral research

mutually exclusive in practice. Cases in the database can, and often do, involve more than one synergy.

We turn next to the structural foundations for combining the two health sectors' resources and skills. While some medicine and public health collaborations take place within the confines of a single organization, the vast majority of cases in the database bring together health professionals from diverse disciplines who work in or represent an array of organizations, including:

- medical practices and community-based clinics

- laboratories and pharmacies

- hospitals and health systems

- managed care organizations

- health departments and other government agencies

- academic institutions

- professional associations

- voluntary health organizations

- community groups, such as businesses, labor organizations, schools, and religious organizations

- the media

- foundations

In each of these collaborations, professionals continue to work within their own organization while, at the same time, transcending the boundaries of that organization to link up with professionals and organizations in other sectors. Much has been written about inter-organizational arrangements within a particular sector (business or medical care, for example), and some investigators have begun to examine arrangements between health departments and managed care organizations.[2,75,95] Prior research, however, has not focused on cross-sectoral arrangements involving the range of partners seen in the database cases. In the section on structural foundations, we discuss the attributes of five types of arrangements used in the cases:

- coalitions

- contractual agreements

- administration/management systems

- advisory bodies

- intra-organizational platforms

Finally, we turn to partnership issues, which are a key determinant of success in the cases in the database. For collaborations to proceed smoothly, working relationships need to be established that allow a broad range of professionals and organizations to work together in a common endeavor. This is not an easy task in an environment in which all of the potential partners are under siege, few have any history of working together, and many are separated by suspicions, preconceptions, and deep cultural differences. Examining cases in the database that succeeded as well as those that did not, we discuss eight strategies that collaborations use to make the enterprise a high priority for all participants and to build and sustain confidence and trust:

- build on self-interests as well as health interests
- involve a "boundary spanner" in the project
- seek out influential backing and endorsements
- don't expect other partners to be like you
- be realistic
- pay attention to the process
- ensure adequate infrastructure support
- be "up-front" about competition and control issues

Synergy I

Improving Health Care by Coordinating Services for Individuals

Our findings suggest that one of the most powerful ways that professionals and institutions in medicine and public health can interact is by coordinating the broad array of services they provide for individuals. Over 100 of the cases in the database illustrate how collaboration can enhance the success of medical care and address determinants of health that go beyond medical care. They achieve these objectives by combining

- *clinical services*, encompassing diagnosis, prevention, treatment, and rehabilitation

with one or more of the following:

- *wraparound services* that overcome logistical, cultural, and social barriers to care
- *counseling and educational services* directed at personal risk behaviors, the management of particular health problems, and the use of health services
- *outreach services*, such as home visits, that assure the delivery of needed care and that promote compliance with complex treatment programs
- *case management services* that identify health-related needs of individuals, link individuals with health professionals and programs in the community, and coordinate care
- *social services* that address socioeconomic determinants of health

THE VALUE OF COORDINATING SERVICES FOR INDIVIDUALS

The highly specialized and categorical nature of the American health system has contributed to important advances in medicine and public health. But specialization also has fragmented the care that individuals receive, creating problems for patients, practitioners, and health care organizations.[84] Spurred, in part, by the primary care movement, each of the health sectors has made attempts to promote more integrated, comprehensive, and longitudinal care for selected populations, often by establishing interdisciplinary teams that connect medical care to various types of wraparound, outreach, or social services.[52] People targeted for this approach have included indigent patients receiving care in public health clinics and certain elderly and chronically ill patients treated in mainstream medical practices. In today's environment—characterized by intense economic and performance pressures, as well as by shifts of Medicaid patients from public health settings to the mainstream medical sector—the coordination of individual-level services both within and across health sectors is becoming increasingly important.

The cases in the database demonstrate how linkages of services directed toward individuals can address many of the frustrations that clinicians and patients experience with medical care, and improve the outcomes of that care. By doing so, they support and expand upon reports in the literature.[99,112,114,130] Transportation and child care services, for example, can make it possible for patients to keep appointments, assuring the delivery of needed care and decreasing "no-show" rates in medical practices. Translation and specially designed educational materials can help practitioners and patients from different cultural, educational, and socioeconomic backgrounds communicate more clearly with each other. Outreach services can promote effective health and treatment-seeking behaviors among patients, leading to more appropriate use of emergency rooms, for instance, and can enhance patient involvement in, and compliance with, preventive care and treatment programs. Case management services can help patients navigate their way through an increasingly complex health system, assuring that they have access to needed health professionals and programs while, at the same time, diminishing the risk of conflicting care or missed care when they are seen by multiple practitioners.

Connections between clinical and social services—for which, in some cases, public health professionals act as the bridge—appear to be useful not only in enhancing medical care but also in addressing important determinants of health that go beyond medical care. From a clinical perspective, social services can help patients retain their health insurance coverage, and obtain essential medications, supplies, and tests that they cannot afford on their own. Equally important, these services can provide patients with social and economic supports that are essential to their health, such as food, housing, education, supplemental income, parenting skills, job training, or protection from domestic violence.

Taken together, the coordination of clinical, wraparound, outreach, and social services appears to be valuable in efforts to achieve clinical performance goals (as measured by HEDIS, for example).[126] By addressing barriers that some patients face in obtaining care, and by identifying and influencing individuals who do not actively seek out needed medical services, this strategy can contribute to achieving clinical health objectives, such as immunization targets, for patients enrolled in a medical practice or managed care organization. Support services also can improve patient satisfaction with care, both by making the health system more seamless and responsive to individual needs and by reducing the dangers and inconvenience of fragmentation.

From an economic perspective, coordination of individual-level services is a pivotal component of the current trend to provide quality medical care more efficiently and to build more integrated health delivery systems. As a number of cases in the database demonstrate, linking support services to medical care can enhance the productivity of health professionals, reduce the underutilization of needed health services and programs, and curtail duplication of effort. Economies of scale can be achieved by centralizing these support services across multiple practices and health programs.

PARTNERS INVOLVED IN THESE COL-LABORATIONS

Consistent with the diversity of services involved, cross-sectoral collaborations coordinating health services for individuals bring together a broad range of health professionals, including physicians, nurses, social workers, nutritionists, health educators, therapists, pharmacists, administrators/managers, and other allied health professionals. They also involve various types of health organizations—such as medical practices, clinics, public health and social service agencies, community-based organizations, hospitals, managed care organizations, and academic institutions—that play important roles in "housing" and coordinating the activities of different types of professionals. The involvement of academia in these cases is frequently associated with efforts to expand the patient base for academic referrals, to provide meaningful training opportunities for students and residents, or to provide research opportunities for faculty who conduct scientific evaluations of the effectiveness of service coordination. Because social services are significant in many of these collaborations, partners often extend beyond the traditional health sectors.

It is important to point out that, depending on the case, wraparound, counseling, outreach, and case-management services can be provided by professionals with a variety of backgrounds. Moreover, organizations in either sector can hire or contract with outside professionals to provide a particular support service. Ultimately, decisions depend on local factors: who in the area has special expertise in providing the service; which organization or agency can provide the service most efficiently; what sources of funding are available; and whether there is a perceived value in having a professional on the team with perspectives and contacts in another sector.

In some of the cases we have collected, roles change during the course of a collaboration, usually because professionals providing a service become employed by an organization in the other sector. While changing roles is often stressful, doing so within the context of a collaborative process offers certain advantages: essential support services are less likely to be "lost in the shuffle"; expert knowledge is more likely to be maintained; disruption of services to clientele can be minimized; and institutional ties can be created that help assure employment of qualified professionals as they move from one health sector to the other.

The cases in the database connect services for individuals in three distinct ways:

- by bringing the other sector's personnel and services to existing medical or public health practice sites

- by creating "one-stop" centers that locate a broad range of services in one place

- by coordinating services provided at different locations in the community through an integrated systems model

Synergy I-A

Bring the Other Sector's Personnel and Services to Existing Medical or Public Health Practice Sites

Reflecting the current shift of Medicaid patients to the mainstream medical sector, a number of collaborations in the database place governmental public health professionals—paid through health department funding streams—in private medical practices. These sites are usually pediatric or obstetrics and gynecology practices, which receive support staff and services as part of state and local efforts to establish "medical homes" for Medicaid recipients. In some cases, nurses from public health agencies reinforce physicians' office visits by providing home follow-up and case management services for pregnant women, new mothers, and children who receive care through these practices. In others, the practices provide free space for the local WIC program (Special Supplemental Food Program for Women, Infants, and Children), increasing WIC participation among the practice's eligible patients.

Specialty practices and academic institutions are involved in these types of collaborations as well. In one example, a health department nurse works with a private infectious disease specialist, assuring that patients with HIV/AIDS have access to primary care, medications, and needed social services. In another, researchers in a local academic institution conduct a randomized trial to assess the impact on health outcomes for Medicaid mothers and their infants of linking home and office-based services.

The database also contains cases in which hospitals and integrated systems bring in outside personnel to provide individual-level support services for their patients. Unlike the collaborations involving medical practices, these activities usually are not financed by health departments unless they receive a direct benefit, as in a case in which a hospital houses the home visiting staff of a local health department in exchange for home visits for its patients. More commonly, the medical institution hires or contracts with professionals that have expertise and experience in providing the desired service. In attempts to decrease recurrent emergency room use, for instance, hospitals use support services to link certain types of patients (such as asthmatics or victims of domestic violence) with follow-up primary care, home visits, and community-based programs. To improve pregnancy outcomes, integrated systems hire staff to connect pregnant women to the WIC program. Some cases have documented improvements in health outcomes through these types of collaborative activities.

Although rarer, the database also includes collaborations that connect individual-level services by bringing mainstream medical personnel to public health clinics. This occurs when a health department contracts with physicians or medical organizations to provide clinical services in health department settings. As part of the contract, the medical professionals working in the public health clinic have access to health department nurses and community health educators who provide patients with a range of wraparound and outreach services, such as education and counseling, home visits, and case management. One case describes an interesting advantage of using health department staff to provide these support services: the new medical professionals in the clinic also obtain access to public health data and population-based services.

Case Illustration: Synergy I-A

SOUTH CAROLINA "PARTNERSHIPS FOR CHILDREN" (SC)

In 1993, South Carolina's Marie Meglen, C.N.M., Director of the Bureau of Maternal and Child Health, invited a select number of pediatricians from around the state to join with their local health departments in an experimental partnership. The state health department was concerned about the dwindling number of children in the Medicaid program who had access to a family doctor or pediatrician. Over half the babies born in the state were Medicaid-eligible, but fewer than half saw a primary care provider. The state knew all too well how fragmented and sporadic the newborn care was—Early Periodic Screening, Detection, and Treatment (EPSDT) was provided in health department clinics, acute care often was provided by emergency rooms, and many babies were either under-immunized or double-immunized because of poorly coordinated care. Also, most one-year-olds in the Medicaid program had been seen for only two primary care visits in their first year of life, despite the American Academy of Pediatrics' guideline of five primary care visits.

Meglen believed that by adding public health services to the medical services provided by private doctors, "We could assure medical homes for every child in the state. A doctor could see twice or maybe three times as many children if he or she didn't have to do all of it—public health could help." Being on the cusp of a crisis—the potential changes foreseen with Medicaid managed care—was fortuitous. "It seemed like a good time to capitalize on everyone's anxiety," said Meglen, "and in turn get something good for children."

The five pediatricians invited to the state capital were chosen carefully. All served a large Medicaid population in their community, and all had good relationships with their respective local health officers. Meglen proposed launching pilot projects in which public health nurses would be assigned to the private pediatricians' offices to assist the doctors with Medicaid children from infancy to two years of age. The state would fund these partnerships as Child Health Initiatives; specific strategies were left to the discretion of each partnership.

In rural Lancaster, pediatrician Dexter Cook, M.D.; the local health officer, Sandra Catoe, M.D.; and the public health nursing director, Miriam Cauthen, R.N., designed a model in which public health nurses are outfitted with beepers to alert them to every Medicaid birth in the county. "We took the best nurses we had and put them in the partnership," said Catoe. At the partnership's inception, Cook was the sole participating pediatrician in the county (the program has since expanded to other physicians). In his partnership, the nurses visit the new mothers at the hospital nursery, inform them of the voluntary program, and recruit their babies to Cook's practice. The nurse becomes each family's primary medical liaison, arranging for office visits with Cook, conducting a number of clinical preventive services (such as vaccinations) either at the baby's home or in Cook's office, and assisting the mothers in keeping their appointments and finding other necessary health and social services. Part of the bargain is that the nurses also "take call" for the Medicaid families in Cook's practice up to ten o'clock each night, seven days a week, and follow his patient protocols. The nurses note their findings in the office chart, and consult with Cook about family concerns that impinge on the children's care. Each nurse maintains an average caseload of 60 Medicaid babies. "These public health nurses are the eyes of the physician," said Jan Cauthen, R.N., a state nursing coordinator. "They can make a home visit, see the family's environment, and tell the physicians about factors that might influence the baby's health. Also, many people are intimidated by physicians. They're more willing to talk to the nurses."

The state's five pilot partnerships were so successful that the South Carolina Medical Association (SCMA) was awarded a Robert Wood Johnson Foundation (RWJF) "Reach Out" grant to expand the public-private partnerships statewide in collaboration with the state health department. Cook was designated the project's medical director, SCMA's research foundation became the administrative and fiscal agent, and the state health department assigned Jan Cauthen to oversee the partnership operations in the local health offices. In addition, the state health department bundled together many of the assessment and support services into the category of "family support services" under its Medicaid contract. This way, the public health units could fund their collaborations with the pediatricians by billing Medicaid for the family support services provided through the partnerships. The health department defined this category to include services provided by indigenous community outreach workers, public health nutritionists, social workers, and health educators, in addition to the nurses.

Since there was no fixed model for a partnership, the specific arrangements varied by practice. In some offices, for example, the physician arranged for a public health pediatric nurse practitioner to provide both sick care and well care in the office, whereas in other practices the pediatrician referred high-risk Medicaid families to the health department for family support services. Throughout the state, though, the principle was consistent: by working with individual medical practitioners, local public health agencies could support the primary care needs of the babies covered by Medicaid.

Meanwhile, Cook brought another pediatrician into his practice, which has grown from 1,500 to 6,000 patients in five years, and used the RWJF grant money to promote the partnership program to his colleagues and their local health officers around the state. "In some places, you could throw a rock from the pediatrician's office to the local health department," recalled Cook, "yet they had no communication. The private pediatricians were wary—they didn't know what the public health sector was doing. They thought that public health was trying to take control. It helped a great deal that it wasn't someone from the state health department pitching this but a private physician, someone with experience who knew what it was like to have a waiting room full of patients."

Cook described the benefits he derived from the partnership as a model. He noted that his "show" rate for appointments has increased from 50 percent to over 90 percent, that it is easier now to catch serious problems at an early stage given the public health nurse's home visits and attention to the family, and that the partnership has increased the capacity of his practice. "It's a great deal for the physicians," said Cook. "The pediatrician gets the public health nurse teaching the patient parenting skills, doing follow-up, and making emergency calls." In Cook's practice, immunization of two-year-olds increased from 62 percent to 95 percent over three years.

"This has done a great deal to change perspectives," noted Cook of the partnerships, which have expanded to 54 practices around the state, "and it has gone a long way to linking these parallel delivery systems."

Synergy I-B   Establish "One-Stop" Centers

Another way to connect clinical, wraparound, outreach, and social services is to bring the professionals and programs engaged in these different types of activities together at one site. Some of the one-stop centers described in the database are organized around the primary care and social needs of the general population. Others focus on selected groups, bringing together diverse services that can benefit homeless persons, for instance, or patients with HIV/AIDS or tuberculosis.

The people involved in cases that take this approach cite the broad range of services and programs that can be co-located at one-stop centers—considerably more comprehensive and diverse than what most medical practices, clinics, or hospitals can support. All of the one-stop centers in the database offer primary, specialized, or urgent medical care, often through community health center clinics. In some cases, students, residents, and faculty affiliated with academic institutions contribute to providing these clinical services. The centers also house a spectrum of public and voluntary agencies, which offer such services as benefits counseling, nutrition support, family planning, parenting skills, child care, youth programs, education, library services, and sports opportunities.

One objective of bringing so many services together in one place is to make them more convenient to consumers. Comprehensive centers can reduce the travel time and expense involved in accessing multiple services. Moreover, centers that include children's programs offer parents more freedom to attend to their own needs.

Another advantage of co-location is that it provides an opportunity to actively coordinate the services and programs of the different partners in the center. Some of the cases do this by centralizing certain support services that benefit all of the participating partners, for example, through offices that help consumers understand and use the services in the center or that provide common transportation and translation services. Other centers integrate the activities of partners by promoting referrals of individuals across the different programs in the center through mechanisms such as common face sheets, or by arranging meetings to identify opportunities to share staff or to reduce duplication of services. In some cases, these types of strategies have led to documented efficiencies and improved utilization of program services.

Case Illustration: Synergy I-B

SOUTH MADISON HEALTH AND FAMILY CENTER (WI)

Madison, Wisconsin, is a bucolic university town. The environment is clean, hills and lakes dot the landscape, employment is high, and the crime rate is low. Despite this allure, though, Madison does have pockets of poverty, with segregated minority communities suffering from the same social ills as those in other urban areas. According to a 1990 community health assessment, there are higher incidences of infectious diseases, untreated diabetes, hypertension, and pediatric asthma in South Madison than elsewhere in the city. Access to health and social services was listed as the top priority by community residents. Although the city is "resource rich," according to health department planner Gay Gross, the resources are not always accessible to those without cars. It can take up to two hours by public transportation from South Madison to reach a health or social service agency.

As a result of the community health assessment, the city renovated an old bowling alley to house a "one-stop" center, the South Madison Health and Family Center. In addition to inviting the city-supported community health clinic to join the center, the Madison Health

Department recruited five other agencies as well: Planned Parenthood, Head Start, the public library, Family Enhancement (a parenting and family resource center), and the Dane County Health Department. The city health department agreed to organize and staff a coordination office for the Center and its partners, and helped to craft partnership agreements between the partner agencies and the newly created Center.

In Madison, one of the largest health care providers in town is the University of Wisconsin's academic health center—it runs a hospital and a series of ambulatory clinics, has a highly regarded medical school, and, until recently, also operated its own health maintenance organization (HMO). According to the vice president of the university's hospital and clinics, Mark Hamilton, F.A.C.H.E., while the university has considerable research and clinical resources, it needed to find more community-based training sites for its medical and nursing students, to demonstrate a greater commitment to community service, and to obtain more primary care access points for its affiliated HMO.

The medical school, nursing school, and faculty practice plan agreed to donate physicians and nursing faculty to staff the clinic, administrators to assist with the design and renovation project, financial assistance in the construction phase, and "deficit funding" to help the clinic meet its operating expenses. More specifically, the university hospital agreed to provide up to $30,000 a year for five years, the school of nursing agreed to contribute $10,000 a year for five years, and the unified faculty practice plan agreed to contribute up to $130,000 over three years. In return, the university would be able to use the clinic as a community-based training site for medical and nursing students, residents, and advanced practice nurses, as a forum for conducting research, and as a source of specialist, diagnostic, and inpatient referrals to the academic health center. The partners agreed that all revenue generated by the practitioners at the clinic would remain with the clinic.

In addition to the referral dollars that the university receives, the academic medical center has benefitted financially in another way. According to Hamilton, the university runs a family medicine clinic across the street from the Center, but it has been operating at capacity. If the Center's clinic hadn't opened the family medicine clinic would have had to expand to provide care to the 1,500 new patients seen at the Center. Additionally, many of those patients are members of the university-affiliated HMO, and the community clinic provides these HMO members another venue for primary care.

The Center's coordination office, organized and staffed by the health department using a federal grant and city funds, is the first office clients encounter when they come into the Center. This office helps clients navigate the services and programs offered at the Center, and provides support services such as translation. It also provides outreach assistance to all of the partner agencies, including home visits for patients who miss appointments or need follow-up; Center-wide and community-wide publicity and marketing of individual agency programs; and a central clearinghouse and resource inventory of health and human-service referrals. The office also provides a forum for identifying and encouraging inter-agency collaborative efforts. "Our approach is not to case manage the clients," said Gross, "but to coordinate the providers, and it seems to be a success story."

As an illustration of how the coordination office can help make connections between agencies, Gross and coordinator Lucretia Sullivan-Wade referred to a problem at the Center last summer. Observing that the waiting room was overrun with unsupervised children whose parents were being seen by providers, the coordination office staff facilitated a Center-wide discussion of the problem. As a result, the Family Enhancement Center and the Junior League proposed a reading program for the waiting area, which was complemented by a story hour run by the library. The coordination office also arranged to have staff from the WIC program provide nutritional displays in the waiting area. "Our piece involves exploring and developing the collaborative opportunities that exist among our partners," said Sullivan-Wade. "It's our job to look out for those kinds of things."

Synergy I-C

Coordinate Services Provided at Different Sites

The third model for connecting clinical, wraparound, outreach, and social services relies less on co-location than on coordinating services provided at different sites. This "integrated system" or "center without walls" approach can encompass a much broader range of services than a one-stop center, since it is not constrained by the space that is available in a particular building. It also can take advantage of the diverse places in the community that people go to meet their health and social needs, assuring that regardless of where an individual shows up, she or he is aware of the full range of services available through the system and has support in reaching and using those services.

The cases in the database that follow this approach involve anywhere from two partners to a large number of private and public organizations. All provide some range of clinical services; many include social supports as well. Partners include:

- entities that provide acute and long-term care at traditional clinical sites, such as mainstream medical practices, community health centers, health department clinics, school clinics, academic practices, emergency response programs, hospitals, nursing homes, rehabilitation centers, family planning clinics, and substance abuse treatment programs

- "health depots" that provide clinical care at nontraditional sites, such as fire houses, community centers, and museums

- programs that provide clinical care where people live through such mechanisms as mobile health units or home health services

- governmental social service agencies

- various community-based organizations, such as meal-delivery services, soup kitchens, food-distribution centers, churches, community centers, and Head Start programs

Hospitals, health departments, and community groups are extremely active in these collaborations. Some partnerships are evolving into Medicaid managed care organizations; a number are part of the Community Care Network program funded by the W. K. Kellogg Foundation.[39-41]

Coordinating services is both the challenge and essence of these collaborations, and the cases in the database use various strategies to accomplish this goal. To track patients through the system and to help assure the provision of needed services, collaborations

- use common intake and risk-assessment protocols;

- employ case managers and care coordinators to facilitate cross-system referrals;

- establish a system-wide program of wraparound and outreach services, including transportation between sites.

To facilitate communication among partners—and between consumers and professionals—collaborations utilize not only newsletters and meetings, but also telecommunications. Some examples are:

- telephone information hotlines

- "on-line" pharmacy services

- system-wide electronic information and telemedicine systems

- Internet patient education kiosks

- wireless computers that connect nurses making home visits to medical records at the practice base

Working as a system, the partners in these collaborations often change the way they do their work. For example, in situations where close proximity of services enhances utilization or health outcomes, the services of one partner are moved to another partner's site. When a particular service can be provided more effectively or efficiently by one partner in the system, contracts are used to delineate this special role. When two or more partners need support that the system as a whole does not provide, they jointly contract for that service. And when the services of two partners actively reinforce each other, arrangements are made to exchange or share staff, or to create joint programs administered by one or both partners.

Not surprisingly, personnel and roles shift from one health sector to another in the course of some of these collaborations. In one case, in which a health department folded its prenatal services into a collaborative program administered by a medical center, the department's entire home health staff became employed by the medical center. Because this occurred in the context of a collaborative process, however, employment and benefits for the staff were guaranteed.

Case Illustration: Synergy I-C

EAST ST. LOUIS HEALTH COALITION (IL)

East St. Louis, Illinois, suffers from a constellation of problems. In 1990, it had four of the poorest neighborhoods in America, a murder rate twice that of Washington, DC, an average infant mortality rate of 20.3 for every 1,000 births, and cerebrovascular, pneumonia, and diabetes death rates among African-Americans twice that of the state rate for African-Americans.

Compounding the community's poor health status was the disarray of the area's health care providers. In 1990, the local public hospital was losing $5 million a year, the health department had 50,000 immunization records waiting to be filed, and the community health center had only four physicians to cover a catchment area of 40,000 patients. There was virtually no communication between the providers; some services were underutilized, others were duplicated. In 1988, an experienced public health administrator, Bob Klutts, M.P.H., was recruited to head the community health center. Within the year, Klutts was asked to head the health department in addition to running the health center. In 1993, in response to mounting taxpayer pressure to take the community hospital off the tax rolls, Touchette Regional Hospital became a not-for-profit controlled affiliate of the community health center. At that point, Klutts was directing the health department, the community health center, and the hospital.

"It was a total mess," said Klutts of the health care system he inherited. "We had no continuity of care. For a teenage girl who got pregnant, the health department had inadequate staff to assure the delivery of prenatal care—we would just give her a list of community physicians. After the pregnancy, we would tell her to come back for contraceptive pills."

Using an administrative strategy known as "matrix management," in which personnel are either shared or co-located, Klutts proceeded to create an "invisible system" of health care among the three providers. In a community of 80,000 people, the three institutions provided a significant proportion of care. They covered nearly all obstetrical and newborn care, three-quarters of pediatric care, and half of all adult medical care. Together, the three institutions formed the East St. Louis Health Coalition. The idea behind the Coalition was deceptively simple: each would do what it did best, and the professional resources that each needed would be commonly shared or contracted. From the community's perspective they appeared as three independent entities, but by entering any one of the community-based sites or clinics an individual could be linked to the providers and programs of all three.

As it turned out, the key was not only coordinating care across the institutions and reducing duplication, it often was as simple as educating clients to each of the partner's programs and resources. For example, pregnant teenagers coming for prenatal care now are enrolled automatically in the WIC program, which is co-located at every obstetrics or pediatric clinic site. "It used to be that the health department thought it was seeing all the eligible WIC clients in the neighborhood," said Klutts. "Since we started referring from the clinics we've seen a four-fold increase in the number of clients served by WIC."

The Coalition coordinates personnel in a variety of ways. Certain administrators, such as Klutts, work part-time on several payrolls, splitting their time among the three institutions. The provider staff of the community health center, including physicians and nurse practitioners, are contracted out to health department clinics addressing sexually transmitted diseases (STDs) and family planning. Designated technical and professional staff at the health department work second jobs at the health center, and a handful of strategic planners and information system specialists work informally across all institutions on a project-by-project basis. The medical director of the health center serves in the same capacity at the health department.

"We allow our professionals to do the things they do well," said Klutts. "Instead of three sets of case managers, the health department does the case management for all the institutions. For our sickle cell program, the health department does the counseling and family education, the health center primary care doctors provide the medical care, and the hospital provides a hematologist and social worker in its clinic." From the patient's perspective, according to Klutts, "it's all seamless. We try to close all the loops." When a physician encounters an STD patient at a health center clinic, he or she can call in a health department communicable disease specialist next door to begin the contact-tracing. It even has made professional recruitment easier. "Most of our young nutritionists want a lot of new experiences," said Klutts, "so not only can we offer them better pay, we can provide them with direct patient care contacts as well as experience with WIC counseling."

The results of this coordination have been significant. The immunization rate, tracked by the shared computerized database, rose from 23 percent in 1988 to 86 percent in 1996. The percentage of low birthweight babies at the hospital dropped by nearly half between 1992 and 1995, from 15.6 percent of all births to 8.6 percent. The health center has seen the number of visits increase over nine-fold in nine years, from 8,600 in 1988 to over 80,000 in 1997, and the number of physician staff has increased from 4 doctors in 1990 to 25 in 1997.

"There's a tremendous economy of scale," said Klutts. "We've even saved a lot of meeting time. It used to be that all three agencies sent one or two people to the same meeting. Now, one person represents all three of us."

Synergy II

Improving Access to Care by Establishing Frameworks to Provide Care for the Un- and Underinsured

Considering the large number of people in the country who lack adequate health insurance and the failure of recent attempts to achieve universal coverage, it is not surprising that many of the cases in the database focus on providing medical care for the un- and underinsured. While some of these cases build on the services that medical and public health professionals provide for individuals (as described in Synergy I), the key reason for combining resources and skills in this type of collaboration is to establish a framework that makes it feasible for the mainstream medical sector to play a more active role in indigent care. Seventy-one cases in the database overcome the logistical, financial, and legal barriers that medical practitioners face in delivering such care through collaborative activities that bring together

- *medical practitioners* willing to provide primary and specialty care for the un- and underinsured

with one or more of the following:

- *administrative services* to plan and coordinate the effort
- *convenient sites* to provide clinical care
- *ancillary staff, supplies, and services* (such as lab, X-ray, pharmacy)
- *screening programs* to identify patients eligible for care
- *referral mechanisms* to link patients with appropriate practitioners
- *immunity from liability* for medical malpractice

THE IMPORTANCE OF WORKING TOGETHER TO CARE FOR THE UNINSURED

In today's environment, a number of factors are compromising the ability of both the public health and medical sectors to provide care for the uninsured. Economic pressures in the health care market are limiting the ability of mainstream hospitals and practitioners to use fees from insured patients to subsidize care for those who cannot pay. As safety-net providers lose Medicaid patients and Medicaid revenue to managed care organizations, they are finding it increasingly difficult to finance care for the uninsured patients who remain.

Taxpayers are unwilling to pay more money for medical care for indigent people. And, although repeated attempts have been made to enact health care reform, it has not been possible to achieve a system of universal coverage in this country.

This environment is creating a crisis not only for uninsured individuals but also for the two health sectors and the community at large. Professionals in both public health and medicine are frustrated with the financial barriers that prevent people from obtaining the most basic medical services, let alone the benefits that the latest biomedical advances can offer. Safety-net providers are becoming increasingly concerned about their economic viability, and if they cannot continue to provide indigent care, private hospitals are likely to face considerably higher uncompensated emergency room costs than they do at the present time. Untreated communicable diseases among the uninsured threaten the health—and health care costs—of insured people in the area. Inadequate delivery of basic clinical services, such as prenatal care, to indigent populations can lead to serious social and economic consequences for the entire community.

If anything is becoming apparent in this crisis situation, it is that the public health sector cannot be expected to care for the uninsured alone. Not only are the available funding streams insufficient, but a substantial number of state and local health departments are attempting to move away from the provision of medical services to individuals in order to strengthen their capacity to prevent or quickly address community-wide health problems. While improving access to health insurance ultimately will require changes in policy, the cases in the database document that, even without such reform, many professionals and institutions in the mainstream medical sector are willing to play a more active role in providing care for the indigent population. The models described below illustrate how collaborative interactions can make it possible for them to do so.

PARTNERS INVOLVED IN THESE COLLABORATIONS

More than any other type of collaboration in the database, cases in this synergy involve individual clinicians. Most likely, that is because the nature of this synergy is to establish a responsive framework that allows primary care practitioners and specialists to provide indigent care without getting bogged down in logistics, becoming exposed to legal risk, or compromising the viability of their own practices. Medical societies also play key roles, lending legitimacy to the endeavors, organizing and running free clinics, and helping to establish referral networks that allow practitioners to provide free care in their own offices. Local health departments participate by organizing efforts, convening partners, performing eligibility screenings, establishing voucher systems and referral networks, conducting mass media campaigns, and contracting with the private sector to provide medical care. State governments provide critical legal supports, such as immunity from liability, as well as funding from indigent care pools. A broad range of organizations—hospitals, managed care organizations, academic institutions, governmental and voluntary health agencies, churches, and businesses—contribute needed facilities, staff, and supplies, and help in obtaining grant support.

While Samaritanism is clearly a driving force in these collaborations, it is not the only one. Contributing to the provision of indigent care helps all partners establish a presence in the community. For medical practices, clinics, hospitals, and managed care organizations, that presence may be helpful in attracting insured patients. As access to primary care for the indigent improves, some hospitals see reductions in uncompensated emergency room costs. Academic institutions participating in these collaborations obtain financial support for faculty members, training sites for students and residents, and opportunities and venues for research. The public health sector benefits from these interactions by obtaining additional personnel to staff its clinics, which allows public health professionals to concentrate their time and resources on wraparound, outreach, and population-based services.

MODELS OF PROVIDING CARE FOR THE UN- AND UNDER-INSURED

The cases in the database use four approaches to provide medical care for the un- and underinsured, which can be distinguished according to whether the collaboration is spearheaded by the medical sector or the public health sector.

- When the medical sector takes the lead, clinicians deliver care through free clinics or referral networks.

- In activities organized by the public health sector, medical practitioners either are recruited to enhance clinical staffing at public health facilities, or arrangements are made to shift patients from public health clinics to mainstream medical settings.

Models Organized by the Medical Sector

Synergy II-A
Synergy II-B

Establish Free Clinics
Establish Referral Networks

In the cases involving free clinics and referral networks, mainstream medical practitioners usually participate on a voluntary basis, building on a long-standing tradition of providing free care to people in need. While clinicians in private practice often are active participants in these collaborations, few have the time, skills, or resources to organize a free clinic or referral network on their own. Consequently, medical societies and institutions are more likely to play a leadership role in these efforts, engaging partners in governmental and voluntary health agencies as well as in the broader community to provide facilities, supplies, and administrative support.

These collaborations capitalize on the influence that medical societies and physician leaders have with their peers, which helps in recruiting local practitioners to the effort. Engaging the local health department in the project is facilitated when a physician leader also has experience in public health. One of the most important roles of government in these collaborations is the protection of participating practitioners from malpractice liability. In one state, for example, legislation was passed that protects physicians providing uncompensated care from malpractice suits by making them agents of the state. In one local community, immunity was achieved by making participating physicians employees of the county.

While some medical practitioners are amenable to working in free clinics, referral networks make it easier for many others to participate. This approach allows clinicians to deliver care to indigent patients in places where they usually work, such as their own offices or hospitals. As a result, they do not have to travel to distant locations or work in unfamiliar practice settings. Since the entity administering the referral network—in our cases usually a local health department or medical society—matches physicians' specialities with the medical needs of patients and screens patients to document that they do not have the ability to pay, participating practitioners are assured that they are seeing patients who really need their care. In cases that use voucher systems, practitioners can control the number of indigent patients they see.

Referral networks allow clinicians to document, and get recognition for, the amount of uncompensated care they provide. Moreover, through the activities of other partners in the collaboration, clinicians often have access to free ancillary services—such as medications, diagnostic tests, and supplies, as well as wraparound, outreach, and case-management services—which are critical in providing effective care for indigent patients. Although practitioners donate their professional time to the collaboration, the practice expense involved in providing services in their usual site of care is frequently quite low. If appointment slots are available, it costs very little for a practitioner to see an additional patient.

Case Illustration: Synergy II-B

ESCAMBIA COUNTY "WE CARE" PROGRAM (FL)

One baby's death in Pensacola, Florida, in the mid-1970s, dramatically changed the shape of indigent care in this port city on the Gulf of Mexico. An obstetrics and gynecology (OB/GYN) resident on call at the public hospital delivered a premature baby on the night shift. There were complications, and the baby died. The award to the baby's parents of over $1 million bankrupted the Pensacola Education Program, which administered the OB/GYN and five other residencies. Subsequently, four of the six residency programs in town closed down. The pediatric and OB/GYN residencies were picked up by a local hospital, but much of the indigent specialty care for adults that had been provided by the three large tertiary hospitals was lost. "We had patients wandering from emergency room to emergency room," noted Reed Bell, M.D., a pediatrician who is a former local health officer and a former president of the county medical society.

In 1992, two of the local hospitals, Sacred Heart and Baptist Health Care, established a joint community clinic to provide for the primary care needs of the uninsured and low-income adult populations. Although this relieved some of the pressure from non-emergency patients overburdening the hospitals' emergency rooms, it still did not address the problem of specialty care for indigent people. In Pensacola and Escambia County, the uninsured population included people who had been downsized out of jobs, proprietors of "mom-and-pop" businesses, homeless adults, and low-wage workers employed in blue-collar and tourism jobs. Many did not seek medical care despite problems of chronic pain or chronic conditions such as hypertension or diabetes, waiting instead for a crisis to develop.

When Bell became the health officer of Escambia County, he was determined to address this specialty care need. Given his standing at the county medical society and his dual directorship of the hospital's pediatric residency program and the Children's Medical Services program, Bell had considerable influence with both the private medical community and the county commissioners. "At least when I came to the floor of the medical society they allowed me a hearing," said Bell.

He knew of a program in Alachua County, Florida, called "We Care," in which volunteer physicians had established a framework for providing indigent care, so he approached the local commissioners to fund a We Care office in the county public health department. At the same time, Bell and his colleague Stuart Shippey, M.D., persuaded the medical society to support the effort by recruiting physicians to participate in the program. "Having physician leadership behind this made all the difference," said Bell of his efforts to recruit volunteer physicians. "Some people we had to coax pretty hard, but most were very willing. A lot of our success is based on peer relationships." In addition to the medical society recruitment effort, the We Care coordinator, Karen Dany, regularly makes presentations at group practices and hospital staff meetings.

In an earlier effort to promote such voluntary care for indigent patients, the local medical societies and the Florida Medical Association had lobbied the state legislature, which passed a "sovereign immunity" law in 1990. As such, physicians treating indigent patients are considered state agents and can only be held personally liable for gross negligence.

There were other elements that helped spur the Escambia We Care project. According to Donna Jacobi, M.D., the current chair of the medical society's Indigent Care Committee, there was an interest in documenting the amount of uncompensated care—particularly specialist care—being delivered in the county. Also, for the community physicians already "writing off" charity care, there were significant benefits to registering their patients in the We Care program—the ancillary services of diagnostic tests, lab work, hospitalization, and medications could be arranged through the We Care office; physicians no longer had to leverage favors from their peers. Moreover, explained Jacobi, the We Care coordinator serves as a master scheduler, assuring that no single physician is unduly burdened by charity care, and counsels her clients to be "more dependable patients."

Coordinator Dany, employed by the health department, maintains a computerized patient-management and tracking system that also tabulates the amount of donated care or services each physician or institution provides. If a patient needs surgery, for example, Dany will arrange for and schedule a surgeon, anesthesiologist, hospital room, and X-ray and blood services as needed. Dany maintains a roster of 260 specialists, including surgeons, cardiologists, and endocrinologists, although some specialties—such as rheumatology and dermatology—are underrepresented despite vigorous peer-recruitment campaigns.

In addition to setting up referrals for specialist care, Dany also works as an *ad hoc* case manager. All of the physicians interviewed attributed much of We Care's success to Dany. Having worked as a volunteer missionary in India and a former Medicaid eligibility specialist, she is someone who can blend compassion with deft bureaucratic coordination. Although her program does not have funds to support services such as transportation, she makes referrals to the county mental health center, discusses finances with patients, and initiates a number of "in-house" referrals to public health programs. "I advocate for the patient for what they need," said Dany, "but I also try to protect the providers."

Over the past five years the We Care program has served over 1,800 patients, and at any given time Dany has a caseload of approximately 350. "Some of our docs like the case management part of it," said the medical society's Jacobi, "and some are just happy that we're finally keeping track of all the indigent care that has been delivered."

Models Organized by the Public Health Sector

Synergy II-C
Synergy II-D

Enhance Clinical Staffing at Public Health Facilities
Shift Indigent Patients to Mainstream Medical Settings

When the public health sector takes the lead in the indigent care cases in the database, the key player usually is a local health department or not-for-profit public health organization (such as a community health center or a school clinic) and its relationship with the medical sector is more often contractual than voluntary. Since the focus of these collaborations is the entire patient base of the public health entity, clinical care encompasses patients on public assistance, such as Medicaid, as well as the uninsured.

In the cases that enhance clinical staffing in public health clinics, the public health facility provides the space, supplies, and support services for indigent care while clinicians from a local medical practice, hospital, managed care organization, or academic medical center oversee the care of clinic practitioners or directly deliver care to clinic patients. In some collaborations, personnel are provided *pro bono* by the medical sector—in return for such benefits as an enhanced community image, an expanded patient or referral base, or the opportunity for students and residents to care for low-income patients in a community-based setting. In other cases, the public health agency pays its medical sector partner for providing care. Motivations behind these types of contractual relationships include a desire to improve access to care, and the quality of care, in public health clinics, and a need for additional funding to support medical faculty.

Rather than enhancing care *in situ*, some health departments see collaboration as a way to move away from providing medical care directly to indigent individuals while continuing to assure the availability of safety-net services. In these cases, contractual relationships are established that shift patients from public health agencies to the mainstream medical sector. Some of the shifts in the database cases are precipitated by crisis situations, such as the loss of essential clinical staff in a public health clinic. Others are stimulated by problems with the quality of care. Most, however, are driven by fiscal constraints and a desire to strengthen population-based services at the health department. Although most of the contractual arrangements have been instituted fairly recently, several cases have documented improvements in patient satisfaction, health outcomes, and the financial status of the partnering health department as a result of the collaboration.

Case Illustration: Synergy II-D

ALBANY COUNTY "HEALTHY PARTNERSHIPS" (NY)

In the capital city of Albany, New York, the county health department ran three primary care clinics, one in a northern "rust belt" community, one in an urban inner-city neighborhood, and one in a rural community. Assuring high quality medical care was a constant struggle for the health department, as was recruiting *per diem* physicians to staff its clinics, arranging for after-hours coverage, and paying malpractice insurance.

In early 1995, Jim Crucetti, M.D., M.P.H., the health department commissioner, tried to contract out for all obstetrical and pediatric physician services. Surprisingly, no one responded to his bid. Crucetti decided to "sweeten the pot" by offering to turn over all clinic management and operations to a successful bidder, including the clinic sites themselves. In addition, the county would supplement payments to providers for any indigent care that exceeded a predetermined limit, and provide community outreach and public health nursing at the site.

Three of the area's largest health care providers decided to bid together for the health department's patients—Seton Health System and St. Peter's/Mercycare Corporation, both

Catholic-run hospital networks; and Whitney Young Community Health Center, a federally qualified health center. They had a number of existing linkages among themselves, and their catchment areas matched the health department sites. The three partners did not anticipate making much profit, if any at all, but each insisted that the collaboration fit into their institutional missions—it met the Catholic health systems' mission of service to the poor and the community health center's mission of caring for the underserved. "It seemed like the right thing to do," said Whitney Young's administrative vice president, Steve Laskoe. "This was not financial but social and health policy activity, and it was important to show that care for these populations is not just a government operation."

The northern rust belt clinic was the first to be turned over. It had been a small operation, with just a physician and a public health nurse working part-time out of the basement of a renovated church, seeing 25 pediatric and obstetric patients each week. The county turned over the clinic, its equipment, and patients to the Seton Health System, and committed the half-time services of a public health nurse and community health worker to the clinic site. They further agreed to pay Seton up to $1,500 per quarter for indigent care. In return, Seton would be responsible for all the health needs of the referred patients. The county was allowed access to all patient clinical and billing records to assure that appropriate medical care and proper accounting practices were being followed. "We run this site just as we do our family care centers," said Pamela Rehak, Seton's Director of Planning and Community Relations, "with the same attention to quality and patient satisfaction."

Over the course of a year, the other public clinics were phased out and the patients were distributed among the partners. Because of the size of their primary care networks, the partners are able to run the system more efficiently than the health department did. At the downtown Albany site, says Joe Pofit, M.S., M.P.H., St. Peter's Vice President of Planning and Communication, "We absorbed the additional volume without having to add staff, facilities or equipment, and we have increased our clinic's productivity and added revenue." The partners have been able to bill the state's Child Health Plus program for pediatric services, which the county health unit is unable to do. They also participate in a greater number of health plans and have more efficient accounting systems. As for the patients, in addition to having access to more primary care sites, they also have far greater access to such hospital system resources as social work, specialty care, and diagnostic services than had been available through the county clinic. A recent patient poll indicated that 98 percent of the former health department clients are happy with the new system.

All told, there were about 1,000 to 1,500 families involved in the shift from the public health department to the partners. Because the hospital systems can tap into a greater number of revenue pools, they estimate that the real number of non-paying patients is 80 percent less than initially thought. They also have discovered other efficiencies as a result of their partnership with the health department. By using the community health worker to follow up on missed appointments with home visits, St. Peter's already has begun to see its "no-show" rate drop considerably.

The health department has undergone substantial personnel restructuring in light of the partnership. Crucetti and nursing director Peggy DiManno, R.N., M.S., have taken three nursing positions that had been devoted to serving the clinics and reassigned them to population services—one to STD and TB services and clinic oversight; one to expand the immunization program to include hepatitis B, travel, and other adult immunizations; and one devoted to working with community groups on problems such as domestic violence and teen pregnancy. Having been "cross trained" for a number of different functions and programs, the entire nursing staff is now taking on multiple roles rather than being dedicated to a single office or program. Crucetti said this has added a great deal to the health department's capacity without having to approach the county executive for additional funds. The health department has broken even on its primary care operation; the lost revenue from Medicaid and indigent care dollars has been offset by savings on *per diem* physician and malpractice costs.

The primary care collaboration among the health systems and the health department has also stimulated a "Healthy Communities" project spanning three counties and dozens of providers. The health system executives, who each refer to Crucetti as a visionary for his mediating role in a very competitive marketplace, have clearly been changed by the experience. "Not one of us is good at doing all of this," concluded St. Peter's Joe Pofit, "but if each of us does a little bit we can accomplish a great deal."

Synergy III

Improving the Quality and Cost-Effectiveness of Care by Applying a Population Perspective to Medical Practice

The cases described thus far document how the two health sectors can reinforce each other by coordinating what they do for individuals. A distinctly different way of collaborating is to bring the individual and population perspectives of medicine and public health together. Seventy-four of the cases in the database apply a population perspective to medical practice in efforts to improve the quality and cost-effectiveness of clinical care, as well as to ensure the economic viability of medical professionals and institutions. These collaborations combine

- *medical care for individuals*

with one or more of the following:

- *population-based information*, such as data about the prevalent health problems and health risks for a particular population; the underlying causes of health problems; the risks, benefits, and costs of various approaches to diagnosis and treatment; and health resources available in a geographic area

- *population-based strategies*, such as community-wide screening, outreach, and case finding

- *population-based analytic tools*, such as practice-based risk assessment, cost-effectiveness analysis, and the measurement and evaluation of performance

THE VALUE OF APPLYING A POPULATION PERSPECTIVE TO MEDICAL PRACTICE

Although the concept of "population medicine" has received widespread attention only recently, population-based thinking has played an important role in medical care for quite some time. For much of the century, however, this population perspective has been subtle, undergirding the information and decision-making process that clinicians use to diagnose and treat the symptoms of patients. Data drawn from populations are the foundation for epidemiologic research, which elucidates underlying causes of disease as well as the normal ranges for laboratory tests. They also are the basis for public health reports, which alert practitioners to health problems in the community.

Clinical trials study populations of patients to ascertain the effectiveness of medical interventions. Evidence-based medicine and community-oriented primary care apply epidemiologic tools directly to clinical medicine.

In the current health system, the medical sector's attention to populations is becoming considerably more explicit and more important than it has been in the past. With the growth of managed care, risk-bearing organizations are becoming responsible for providing clinical services to defined populations—the particular group of people cared for by a medical practice or enrolled in a managed care organization. As physician practices, integrated systems, and managed care organizations take on financial risk, they are under pressure to provide these services for a fixed price. With the increasing emphasis on performance measurement, they also are expected to document that particular clinical services have been delivered to their populations and that specific health outcomes have been achieved.

Success in this environment depends, to a large extent, on the medical sector's ability to obtain and make use of population-based information, methodologic tools, and strategies in their practices. On the one hand, medical professionals need ways to keep up-to-date with the rapidly expanding base of research knowledge and to understand and use that population-based information effectively in decisions related to particular patients. They also need to be able to collect and analyze data about their practice populations—and obtain information about the broader community—in order to anticipate health service demands, identify and implement cost-effective practices, and assess and improve performance. As medical practices and plans seek to expand their patient base and to meet performance goals, they need population-based strategies to identify patients who can benefit from the services they provide but who do not take the initiative to obtain that care.

Repeatedly in the focus groups conducted around the country, medical professionals described the public health sector—particularly governmental health agencies—as a potentially valuable source of health information. Nonetheless, they often expressed frustration with the public health data they received. Many of the health problems that clinicians care about are not reportable diseases, yet few clinicians know how to make health officials aware of the types of information they would find useful in practice or how to obtain that information from health departments in a timely manner. While large practices and managed care organizations can meet some of their data and analytic needs on their own, a number of factors are making at least some degree of collaboration with the public health sector essential. The costs of data collection and analysis are extremely high; many analyses require personnel with formal training in biostatistics or epidemiology; some enrolled populations do not have a stable relationship with any particular practice or health plan; and meaningful information about certain health measures requires denominators larger than any single practice or managed care organization can generate on its own.

For the public health sector, working with the medical sector along these lines also makes sense. The collection and analysis of population-based data are, perhaps, the quintessential functions of public health.[103] Yet in the current environment, health departments have limited funds to support these endeavors, and they are losing certain sources of data as a greater proportion of the population moves to managed care. Public health professionals are continually seeking—but have difficulty finding—effective ways to translate important epidemiologic findings into clinical practice. In addition, if public health screening programs are to be a cost-effective strategy, governmental and voluntary health agencies need mechanisms to assure that patients identified as having health problems through these programs actually receive follow-up care. This objective is complementary to the medical sector's need to bring patients with health problems to their offices. The models described below illustrate how collaborations geared toward bringing a population perspective to medical practice can address these issues.

PARTNERS INVOLVED IN THESE COLLABORATIONS

Depending on the model, collaborations in this synergy involve either: (1) a broad range of professionals and community organizations; (2) agencies and associations limited to medicine and public health; or (3) one or more public health professionals (usually epidemiologists or biostatisticians) working within a medical setting. The latter situation, involving only one organization, may not be perceived to be a collaboration at all by the organization involved.

When agencies and associations in medicine and public health work together in this type of collaboration, important relationships are established between academic institutions and governmental health agencies, between academic institutions and medical practices, and between medical associations and governmental and not-for-profit health agencies. In these relationships, partners in medicine and public health contribute what they do best: their scientific and methodologic expertise; their knowledge of medical or public health practice; their influence with peers; and their contacts with other sectors in the community. The most important characteristic of these relationships, however, is that they establish a dialogue between the two health sectors. As a result, what each sector knows and does becomes considerably more responsive to the needs of the other.

MODELS FOR APPLYING A POPULATION PERSPECTIVE TO MEDICAL PRACTICE

The cases apply a population perspective to medical practice in three ways:

- by using population-based information to enhance clinical decision-making

- by using community-wide screening to "funnel" patients with health problems to appropriate providers of medical care

- by using population-based information and analytic tools to support the management of medical practice

Synergy III-A   Use Population-Based Information to Enhance Clinical Decision-Making

Efforts to provide the medical sector with up-to-date public health information can be extremely valuable to clinicians by helping them readily identify new knowledge that is relevant to their practices and, at the same time, cope with information overload. That benefit has not been fully realized, however, in part because the medical and public health sectors have tended to work independently in these endeavors, with public health professionals preparing informational materials and medical practitioners receiving (but not necessarily paying attention to) the information that is produced. The cases in the database demonstrate that a collaborative approach can make this traditional method for bringing a population perspective to medical practice considerably more effective. By working together, the two health sectors can assure that the content and presentation of informational materials will be meaningful in clinical practice. Collaboration also can legitimize public health information for medical practitioners, helping it reach a wider audience, and making it more likely that the materials actually will be used.

The collaborations of this type that we have collected take place at national, state, and local levels, bringing together governmental public health agencies, medical societies and associations, and academic institutions. For the most part, they address topical issues of importance to both health sectors, such as communicable diseases (HIV/AIDS, STDs, TB, Lyme disease, and antibiotic resistance), chronic diseases (cardiovascular disease and diabetes), and clinical preventive services (screening for breast and cervical cancer and for lead toxicity). The information is presented to health professionals through a range of media, including professional journals and monographs, professional meetings and seminars, multi-state teleconferences, and the World Wide Web.

Depending on the case, partners in the two health sectors work together in the development and/or dissemination phase of these activities. By cosponsoring meetings, coediting journals, and coproducing materials with the medical sector, public health professionals are better positioned to present information in places where medical practitioners are likely to see or hear it (i.e., the "right" journal or meeting), and in a way that grabs their attention. These collaborations also are helpful in assuring that the material that is presented is up-to-date, scientifically sound, applicable to the realities of clinical practice, and approved for continuing medical education credit. In the dissemination phase of the project, medical leaders and professional associations play important roles by publicizing the material or event, and by providing their endorsement. In some instances, this type of endorsement is helpful in overcoming some physicians' distrust of government, which can make them wary of information promulgated by departments of public health.

Case Illustration: Synergy III-A

GEORGIA HIV/AIDS GUIDES (GA)

The face of HIV/AIDS was dramatically changing in Georgia in 1987. Over a third of new HIV infections were being diagnosed outside of metropolitan Atlanta, in rural and isolated areas. In these communities, physicians often were unfamiliar with HIV/AIDS resources and emerging clinical options such as zidovudine (AZT), which could potentially delay the progression of HIV to AIDS. Joseph Wilber, M.D., head of the state health department's infectious disease program, recognized the need to educate doctors to their evolving role in treating HIV/AIDS. As it was, he, others in his division, and the district health officers were fielding calls regularly from clinicians in practice who needed guidance. "How should I treat my HIV-positive pregnant patient?" "Where can I send patients who want to be tested?" "What types of follow-up and specialist care do my HIV- positive patients need?" "In many towns," recalled Wilber, "there was no place for the patients to go. We needed to get the private physicians up to speed."

Wilber, who had spent 30 years as an internist before joining the health department full-time, approached the Public Health Committee of the Medical Association of Georgia about a joint project. He proposed collaboratively writing a clinician's guide to HIV/AIDS and distributing it to all the primary care doctors in the state. Notwithstanding earlier differences of opinion between the state health department and the medical society over issues such as informed consent for HIV testing, the Public Health Committee was eager for a resource that could support practicing physicians. Staff members were assigned to the project—Camilla Grayson, M.S.W., from the medical society, and Diana Kirkpatrick, M.P.H., C.H.E.S., from the health department—and using a Wisconsin clinical guide as their model, Wilber, Grayson, and Kirkpatrick outlined their book.

Relying on research material from the Centers for Disease Control and Prevention (CDC) and input from an advisory board of HIV/AIDS clinicians and infectious disease specialists, the writing group described the clinical elements of care for an HIV-infected patient: the diagnostic process, treatment options, and follow-up guidelines. "The medical aspects were approached from the practicing physician's perspective, which involves the scientific and clinical angles of dealing with individual patients" said the medical society's Grayson. What Wilber and Kirkpatrick brought from public health, stated Grayson, "was that they made us look at HIV/AIDS in a broader context and consider how physicians could treat a patient and spread a message. They raised the issue of doing better testing and the value of reporting and surveillance. As a health educator, Diana was very helpful in finding the best method to present the messages in ways that were sensitive to a number of audiences."

Published in 1988, *The Clinician's Guide to AIDS and HIV Infection in Georgia*[72] provided a resource inventory of specialist care, community organizations, and laboratory resources, and a section on Georgia laws involving testing and counseling, patient confidentiality, reporting requirements, and informed consent. It also included a chapter on the epidemiology of AIDS in Georgia. "Small town doctors were surprised to see the number of cases in their area," said Wilber. Grayson noted that the group also was "trying to encourage physicians to become more knowledgeable, to be able to talk to groups about AIDS, particularly in the rural areas."

The Guide was jointly published using funds from the two partner agencies as well as monies solicited from the four medical schools in Georgia, the state hospital association, the Southeastern AIDS Training and Education Center, and the Burroughs Wellcome pharmaceutical company. The full printing of 14,000 copies of the book was distributed to all primary care physicians in the state, and to specialists in emergency medicine, obstetrics and gynecology, infectious disease, and pediatrics, every public health department, and every medical and public health school. The group followed this up with a second edition in 1992, and Wilber's successor at the health department, Kathleen Toomey, M.D.,M.P.H., supported the publication of a pediatric guide in 1996.[98] "We wrote the pediatric guide with the infectious disease clinic at Grady Hospital," said the health department's Kirkpatrick, "and we also worked with social workers from Grady to cover the psychosocial aspects of HIV/AIDS." Based on feedback from practitioners, the writers expanded the treatment guidelines in the pediatric guide, said Kirkpatrick, "so that the book tells clinicians what to expect and what should be done for children at different stages, from newborn up." The book includes chapters on safe sex counseling for adolescents, crisis intervention for children affected by HIV/AIDS, and specific nutritional needs of children with HIV/AIDS.

As with the development of the first two guides, the writing group used the medical society's Public Health Committee, composed of public health physicians and private practitioners from around the state, as a sounding board to oversee the tone and utility of the book. One of the book's "side effects" was the education of the Committee members themselves, particularly regarding public health funding needs for surveillance and prevention activities. "This prompted us to support more of what public health was doing, and vice versa" said Grayson, who is in charge of health policy for the medical society. "We had been polarized over some issues, but this allowed public health to see what medicine could offer, and it has helped improve our relationship."

Wilber, who has since retired from the state health department and is currently developing a free AIDS clinic in a rural Georgia town, said the books represented "good science and good medicine. It was a wonderful collaboration, and it was a bit unusual. But it was the best way to reach the rural and small town doctors—through the state medical association."

Synergy III-B   ## Use Population-Based Strategies to "Funnel" Patients to Medical Care

Another way to bring a population perspective to medical practice is by linking clinical care to population-based screening strategies. Although public health screening programs always have been dependent on medical care to obtain follow-up diagnosis and treatment services for persons with abnormal results, today's performance pressures and market forces are making medical practice dependent on effective screening strategies as well. In this context, it is not surprising that "screen and treat" collaborations are well represented in the database.

A broad range of partners are involved in these cases, including health departments, other government agencies, voluntary health organizations, managed care organizations, hospitals, medical practices, academia, community-based organizations, business, the media, and religious organizations. Combining their diverse resources and skills, these partners strengthen the traditional "screen and treat" strategy in two ways: by improving the effectiveness of the screening process itself, and by assuring that all individuals identified as having problems on screening tests receive appropriate follow-up care. Both health sectors benefit as a result of these collaborations. Progress is made toward achieving important HEDIS [126] and *Healthy People 2000* [179] performance targets. The cost-effectiveness of public health screening programs is improved by assuring that screening leads to medical care that improves health outcomes. Medical organizations and institutions attract new insured patients. And needed medical services are provided to the uninsured.

The cases in the database address a spectrum of health problems that can be detected through population-screening programs. Most are diseases that cause serious damage before patients develop symptoms, such as hypertension, diabetes, hypercholesterolemia, breast and cervical cancer, and lead toxicity. Others are conditions for which some people do not seek care, such as pregnancy, vision impairment, or domestic violence. In certain cases, screening programs are used to identify people who are well but who have not received important preventive services, such as immunizations. Others screen a population to identify individuals who are engaging in behaviors that put them at risk for developing serious health problems in the future.

Regardless of the particular health problem being addressed, the cases use similar types of strategies to enhance the effectiveness of the screening process. Since these strategies have the potential to reinforce each other, most of the collaborations pursue a number of them at the same time. For example, partners

- conduct education and media campaigns to enhance awareness of the targeted health problem among the public and medical practitioners;

- establish reward systems such as free meals at local restaurants to encourage community workers to refer patients to screening or treatment programs;

- publicize screening activities by writing articles, distributing fliers, and donating free advertising;

- contribute space, staff, and supplies to screen people at schools, churches, museums, firehouses, and other convenient places;

- provide incentives and support services—free gifts, refreshments, and child care, for example—to encourage people to participate in screening events;

- engage clinicians to perform or interpret screening tests that require medical expertise such as mammography or Pap smears.

Of even greater value is the connection these collaborations make between screening and follow-up medical care. In some of the cases, funding for the project is dependent on establishing such linkages. To be eligible for breast and cervical cancer screening funds in some states, for example, local health departments are required to enlist the cooperation of the medical sector to ensure that all women—those who are indigent as well as those with the ability to pay—receive follow-up diagnostic and treatment services if they need them.

Medical societies, using a good dose of peer pressure, play important roles in getting mainstream practitioners involved in these programs. Participation does not need to be a financial burden for these practitioners, since many of the patients identified through screening programs are covered by public or private insurance. In a case that identified untreated cataract as the leading cause of blindness in an inner-city population, for example, most of the affected individuals were beneficiaries of the Medicare program.[158] When the number of indigent patients identified through a screening program is significant, referral networks (as described in Synergy II-B) are sometimes established to assure that the distribution of insured and uninsured patients is evenly weighted across practitioners. Clinicians either receive a discounted fee or provide services *pro bono* when they care for indigent patients. In return, some receive important practice supports, such as free medications and supplies, or access to wraparound, outreach, and social services (as described in Synergy I).

Case Illustration: Synergy III-B

MONROE COUNTY "WOMEN'S HEALTH PARTNERSHIP" (NY)

After several years of funding hospital-based breast cancer screening programs, in 1992 the New York State Department of Health determined it was not reaching people it needed to reach—the uninsured and underinsured, and women in minority populations. So the state appealed to the local health departments to serve as conveners in their communities. In turn, the state would provide funding to networks of community agencies and health care providers to promote cancer screenings, knock on doors to persuade the unpersuaded, and link women to diagnostic and treatment services as needed.[172]

As it happened, Monroe County, New York already had much of this community apparatus in place. Coming off a successful four-year influenza vaccination project (illustrated in Synergy IV-C), the Monroe County Health Department had a web of contacts in the practice and academic communities, and it had on staff an experienced project director,

Bonnie Lewis, who had orchestrated a clinical prevention campaign through doctors' offices. Their first task of "persuading the unpersuaded" actually involved bringing the two competing cancer advocacy groups, the American Cancer Society and Cancer Action, together in the coalition. "It was the first time they sat willingly at the same table," marveled one participant.

Under the direction of the deputy health department director, Nancy M. Bennett, M.D., M.S., the Partnership included the Monroe County Medical Society (which initially served as the fiscal agent for the project's funding), several University of Rochester medical school departments involved in data analysis and evaluation activities, the American Cancer Society and Cancer Action, the faith community, a number of community-based organizations, and a service-delivery component that involved radiologists and several hospital-based women's centers. The Partnership developed a series of committees to oversee components of the work—such as evaluation, publicity, professional education, and physician recruitment—and to coordinate the 41 Partnership agencies and over 110 providers to perform the screenings and provide necessary treatment.

At the heart of the Partnership is the office run by Lewis. "Our strategy," said Lewis, "is that we don't take credit for things. We're the workhorse that drives the operation." Her staff of three operates on a $469,000 annual budget, of which 40 percent is spent on clinical services, 10 percent on data analysis and evaluation, and half on outreach, advertising, and coalition staffing. The office oversees budget management, data collection, scheduling and case management of 2,500 clients, report writing, and the coordination of at least eight monthly committee meetings. The Partnership is funded by the state health department, the Rochester Primary Care Network (a not-for-profit foundation established by a local managed care organization), and a Johnson & Johnson Community Health Award.

The Partnership uses media and community events to publicize the breast and cervical cancer screenings and promotes the screenings as pathways for women into primary care. The Partnership office will determine a woman's eligibility for the program over the phone, with no documentation required, and schedule an appointment with a medical practitioner of her choice. "If she doesn't have a provider we find her one and pay for her initial exam," said Lewis. Almost half of the women have some type of insurance, although they may have a high deductible or no coverage for mammograms. In the case of Medicare patients, who are covered for bi-annual breast exams, the Partnership pays for the exam in the "off" year.

Through the medical society's and the Partnership's ties to the practice community, they have recruited every radiologist in the area to participate. The negotiated rate of $62 for a mammogram and breast exam, which is the Medicare reimbursement rate, is higher than some managed care rates. As for treatment, according to Lewis, "the surgeons are accepting our rate of $290 for an incisional biopsy where they would normally get $800. They come to the table because they know that their input is valued. The burden of uncompensated care is lightened when shared by many providers. And peer pressure does help."

The Partnership extends itself beyond its conventional bounds as well. When a local gynecologist had a patient who needed follow-up counseling, and who had already broken nine appointments, the physician called the Partnership offices for help. Although the patient was not a Partnership client, Lewis immediately dispatched the patient educator to the woman's home. The educator explored what was bothering her and eventually persuaded the reluctant patient to visit her doctor. Likewise, the Partnership provides a number of support services, such as child care and transportation, to assist women in overcoming barriers to making and keeping their appointments.

The Partnership's bureaucratic flexibility and broad community reach has paid off. Since the Partnership's community-wide campaign began, mammography rates for women ages 50 to 74 in Monroe County have increased from 43 percent to 62 percent, with the greatest improvement in those neighborhoods with particularly low rates at baseline. As a result, breast cancer increasingly is being diagnosed at earlier stages. Of the 2,500 clients served by the Partnership thus far, 10 women have been identified with cancer, and 9 have accepted treatment.

"The role of the health department as convener of the coalition has been critical," said Bennett. "Although we're sometimes overlooked as a player, we are perceived as being neutral. We're not in competition with the providers in the community because the health department does not provide primary care except to children in foster care. These days, there's a real risk of splintering care in the community, and the potential for a lot of competition. We need to step into the role of holding the system together—by sharing data, and by helping people to collaborate."

Synergy III-C	## Use Population-Based Analytic Tools to Enhance Practice Management

In the third model for bringing a population perspective to medical practice, a variety of analytic tools—clinical epidemiology, risk assessment, cost-effectiveness analysis, and performance measurement—are used to support the management of medical practices and organizations.[22,43,136,156] Partners in these collaborations include academic institutions, hospitals, group practices, health departments, and managed care organizations. In most of the cases, the partners bring their methodologic, practice, and management skills to the table. Some collaborations also involve data sharing; those that focus on data systems and data collection are described in Synergies IV and V. The relative paucity of reports involving managed care organizations may reflect the fact that these organizations commonly employ professionals skilled in biostatistics and epidemiology and consequently do not have to go outside of the organization to carry out these activities. When they do, it is to get special expertise that they do not have in-house or to address problems that require analysis of more than their own patient data.

To a large extent, the cases we have collected use population-based methodologic tools to support medical sector organizational planning and management of financial risk. Toward that end, analyses focus not only on the practice or enrolled population but also on the broader community. For example, information about health status, health risks, and health service needs in a practice or enrolled population is used to inform decisions about the locations of practice sites, the services to be provided at each site, practice staffing patterns, and the need for patient education programs. Information about disease prevalence, risk factors, and health service utilization in a particular area is used to help clinics, practices, and managed care organizations decide whether they can afford to take on financial risk for a new population. Information about health problems and available health resources in a community is used to justify the need for new health facilities and services in that area.

A number of cases in the database also use these tools to support quality improvement and performance measurement in medical practice. In these collaborations, the two health sectors work together not only on data analysis but also in providing feedback to medical professionals about the results of that analysis. Some of the cases evaluate the outcomes of clinical protocols— around the treatment of drug-resistant TB, for example. Others analyze the causes of poor health outcomes, such as high rates of perinatal mortality. In other cases, the purpose of the collaboration is to develop indicators to measure performance or to analyze why certain performance targets are difficult to meet.

Case Illustration: Synergy III-C

PARKLAND COMMUNITY-ORIENTED PRIMARY CARE CLINICS (TX)

The day that Parkland Memorial Hospital's newly renovated and constructed facilities were opened in Dallas, Texas, in the mid-1980s, noted CEO Ron Anderson and senior strategist Paul Boumbulian, they were "at capacity." According to the executives of the public hospital, "the recession [in Texas] had increased demand beyond projections."[5]

By 1985, Dallas county officials recommended that Parkland consider decentralizing its overcrowded facilities and moving its high-volume primary care practice to community-based centers. After an intensive review of various ambulatory care models, the Parkland executives decided to develop a network of Community-Oriented Primary Care (COPC) clinics. Based on the work of South African physician Sidney Kark and the early U.S. community health centers, Parkland's COPC clinics were designed to assess and treat both the community and the patient. Key to the organization of clinical services were population data—knowing a market, the health needs that could be addressed by clinical or community programs, and the clinical staffing requirements. The hospital employed such population sciences as demography, epidemiology, and sociology, among others, to analyze the effects of socioeconomic factors and health utilization on its clinical practice needs. The clinics grew from these population analyses.

"In Dallas, we're the only hospital taking a close look at the uninsured population," said health planner Michelle Tietz of Parkland's Department of Strategic Planning and Population Medicine. "Other hospitals tend to be more physician-oriented, asking whether the community can support another orthopaedic practice. We look at the health of the population, where they are, what their housing stock is, where they're moving." In their first community assessment in 1986, the planners analyzed internal data from their three ambulatory clinics and emergency department to determine where their patients were coming from. "To everyone's surprise a suburban zip code popped up," said Tietz. A further analysis of census data and vital statistics revealed pockets of poverty and housing transiency in this suburban neighborhood. As a result, a COPC clinic was planned for the community.

Parkland's planning department has evolved as a multidisciplinary team, led by Boumbulian, who has a doctorate in public administration and a masters degree in epidemiology, and staffed by Sue Pickens, a veteran hospital health planner pursuing a doctorate in medical sociology, and Tietz, an M.B.A. In addition, the group has enlisted the help of a doctoral student at the University of Texas at Houston School of Public Health and a noted community researcher, Lu Ann Aday, Ph.D. Parkland also recently hired the woman who ran the county health department's AIDS registry and an urban sociologist to help with HIV/AIDS planning.

The department uses a mix of primary and secondary data sources to create a data map of 79 neighborhoods in Dallas County that combines sociodemographic and health information. They buy mortality and natality data from the state health department and hospital discharge data from the hospital association. For sociodemographic and economic analyses, they purchase census data. In order to measure the health of the population, the strategic planning group uses morbidity data from its clinics and emergency department, reportable disease data from the county and city health departments, and information they collect from telephone surveys of their patients, the population in the clinics' catchment areas, and the larger county population.

What sets the Parkland planners apart is their use of the data they collect and analyze. The information gleaned is applied directly to clinical and programmatic services. It also serves as the foundation for community organizing around health and social issues. During one recent community survey, for example, the department found a high prevalence of hypertension, diabetes, and hypercholesterolemia, so they facilitated a community-wide effort to address these problems. They organized a community task force, led by the County Judge (the highest elected official in the county) and the president of the Dallas-Forth Worth Business Group on Health, to educate the community about the consequences of these conditions and to encourage affected individuals to seek appropriate care. The planning group also is analyzing the data for differences among ethnic groups so that they can more effectively target the community campaign.

In another example, the planning group noticed that in one year over 1,000 women from Garland, a community twenty miles away from the hospital, were giving birth at the hospital without having received prenatal care. They concluded there was an urgent need for prenatal, obstetric, and pediatric services in Garland. "That got picked up by a Garland newspaper," recalled Boumbulian, "and I got a phone call from the local health department director and medical officer there. I thought they were going to read me the riot act. Instead, they told me it confirmed what they suspected, and that it matched their utilization data for certain public health services—data we didn't have." Together, Parkland and the Garland Health Department worked to establish a COPC clinic in the neighborhood, with the city of Garland donating the land to the project and adding police services so the hospital did not have to employ its own security personnel.

"Our COPC clinics are not designed with a cookie cutter," said Boumbulian, "they're developed specifically for each community." His data team also supports a number of community-assessment projects in the clinic neighborhoods, convening forums with residents and community leaders to help identify health priorities. "If you look at what determines health," said Boumbulian, "you would see that 80 percent of it is largely outside the health care delivery system. We follow the two principles of COPC. The first is doing an assessment; that's where you start. The second is a dialogue with the community. By working together we can develop a healthier neighborhood."

Synergy IV

Using Clinical Practice to Identify and Address Community Health Problems

Collaborations that bring together the individual and population perspectives of medicine and public health can proceed in one of two ways. They can either apply a population perspective to medical practice (as described in Synergy III), or they can take advantage of the opportunities inherent in medical practice to achieve community-wide goals of public health. Eighty-three cases in the database demonstrate the power of the latter approach through interactions that combine

- *clinicians' access to and influence with individuals*

with one or more of the following:

- *community-wide frameworks* for collecting health-related information

- *population-based strategies* to facilitate the delivery of clinical services in mainstream medical practices

- *community programs* to address health risks in the social and physical environment

THE IMPORTANCE OF USING CLINICAL PRACTICE TO ADDRESS COMMUNITY HEALTH PROBLEMS

Although public health focuses predominantly on populations, the medical sector's encounters with individuals—the building blocks of populations—have always been relevant to public health's mission. Historically, public health has relied on, and often has mandated reporting of, information obtained through patient encounters to support functions that are important to the broader community (such as surveillance, vital statistics, disease registries, and tracing of communicable disease contacts). Clinicians also notify public health officials when patients in their practices present with unexplained constellations of symptoms. These alerts have drawn the attention of researchers and government agencies to newly emerging health problems, such as toxic shock syndrome, Lyme disease, and HIV/AIDS.

Clearly, medical practitioners' encounters with patients can be a valuable source of information about health risks and health problems in the community—information that the public health sector needs to detect and address threats to health at an early stage. Equally important, medical practice can contribute to the implementation of public health strategies. For example, as documented by the U.S. Preventive Services Task Force,[180] clinicians can deliver preventive and treatment services to individuals in their practices, thereby helping to assure the health of the broader community. By diagnosing health problems in particular patients, they can target environmental or infection control interventions to prevent the exposure and development of disease in others. Also, by providing counseling and educational materials to the individuals in their practices, they can reinforce community-wide efforts to promote behavioral change. These types of activities allow clinicians to address underlying causes of disease in their patients and to apply what they learn in their practices to a broader population.

In the past, a variety of factors—including the lack of universal health insurance, limited coverage and payment for preventive care, and logistical and cultural barriers—have made it difficult for public health agencies to rely on the medical sector in achieving clinically oriented health objectives. Consequently, public health programs focusing on particular health problems or on particular segments of the population have played a central role. Changes in the current environment, however, are making it essential for the two health sectors to work more closely in these endeavors. Clinical preventive services increasingly are being covered by private health insurers and the Medicare program. Through state managed care contracts and "medical home" initiatives, clinical services for Medicaid recipients are moving from public health clinics to the mainstream medical sector. Incentives to stay "in network" are limiting the options of the growing number of managed care organization enrollees to receive care in public health clinics. Report cards are assessing the extent to which medical practices, managed care organizations, and health departments achieve important health goals.

These changes are disrupting connections between clinical and population-based services that previously had been established through public health programs and clinics. In addition, they are making the medical sector responsible for delivering, rather than just offering, clinical services that are critical to the entire community's health. In this environment, public health agencies have little choice but to work with and through the mainstream medical sector to assure the delivery of clinical preventive and treatment services. And mainstream medical practitioners need the support of population-based strategies and information systems to meet performance goals.

PARTNERS INVOLVED IN THESE COLLABORATIONS

As with other cases in the database, these collaborations involve a broad range of partners, each contributing what it does best or can do most efficiently. State health departments play essential roles by providing the policy framework for statewide information systems. That is probably the reason they are more involved in these cases than in any other type of collaboration in the database. Hospitals and managed care organizations, driven by cost and performance pressures, contribute valuable infrastructure support, personnel, grant-writing skills, and/or funding to many of the collaborations. Academic institutions play central roles by bringing technical expertise to information system design and by participating in the design and evaluation of collaborative strategies.

Medical practitioners are a key target of these activities—the goal, after all, is to take advantage of what mainstream clinical practice can contribute to public health objectives. Toward that end, clinicians bring their practical experience to the design phase of the collaboration, and provide individual-level care. Medical societies are effective in encouraging physician participation in these endeavors. A broad spectrum of community partners—including local health departments, other government agencies (such as the police), community-based organizations, businesses, the media, and religious organizations—are involved in the population-based strategies that "funnel" individuals to clinical settings, and in the community-based programs to which patients in medical practices and hospital emergency departments are referred.

As has been noted previously, what each partner contributes to the project depends, in part, on local circumstances. This can be illustrated by two collaborations that engaged the medical sector in addressing the underlying causes of lead toxicity in children. While, in both cases, chelation therapy for lead toxicity was provided by the medical sector, the environmental intervention was handled quite differently in each. In one case, a managed care organization contracted with the local health department to carry out the environmental intervention. This approach made sense since the local health department already was involved in lead abatement and the managed care organization did not have the expertise or volume of affected children to make such activities worthwhile. In the other case, by contrast, a medical center spearheaded the environmental intervention. This decision reflected quite different local circumstances: in this community, the medical center treated the vast majority of children with lead toxicity and therefore had a sufficient volume of patients to warrant engaging in an environmental program. Moreover, while the health department was involved in regulating housing, it had neither funding nor programs directed toward lead abatement.

MODELS FOR USING CLINICAL PRACTICE TO ADDRESS COMMUNITY HEALTH PROBLEMS

The collaborations in the database harness the public health potential of medical practice in three distinct ways:

- by using clinical encounters to build community-wide databases
- by capitalizing on clinicians' access to individuals to identify and address underlying causes of community health problems
- by engaging diverse partners in the community to achieve clinically oriented health objectives

While all of these approaches build on past relationships between the two health sectors, the interactions of the partners are modified in important ways.

Recognizing the clinical encounter as a public health opportunity, the collaborations are structured in such a way that it becomes worth the clinician's time and effort to realize this potential. Equally important, the collaborations make it feasible for the public health sector to involve medical practitioners more closely in its work.

Synergy IV-A   Use Clinical Encounters to Build Community-Wide Databases

Historically, the reporting of clinical data to city, county, or statewide agencies has constituted one of the most common types of interactions between medicine and public health. Aggregated in various types of vital records, registries, and surveillance systems, these data have been used by health professionals and government agencies to monitor the incidence and prevalence of disease, to formulate population-wide policies and campaigns, and to support epidemiologic and biomedical research. While clinically based information systems have been of obvious value to the research and public health communities, practitioners caring for individual patients have not perceived them to be particularly useful. At best, clinicians who provide the data for these systems have received feedback only indirectly, through articles published in medical journals or public health alerts. Since reporting is time-consuming and, in some cases, raises concerns about patient privacy, the medical sector's responsibility for providing certain types of information has had to be mandated by law. Even so, legal requirements have had limited success in assuring complete and up-to-date databases.

In today's environment, the direct usefulness of community-wide data systems to medical practice is increasing. The instability of some enrolled populations—particularly in the Medicaid program—coupled with the need to meet HEDIS performance targets is making it essential for medical practices and managed care organizations to have access to information systems that go beyond their own patient populations. As more and more of the medical sector takes on financial risk, there is a clear need for community-wide information systems that can identify costly but preventable health problems at an earlier stage than would be possible with data limited to any one practice or enrolled population. In this context, it is not surprising that a substantial number of the cases we have collected bring the medical and public health sectors together to develop community-wide frameworks for collecting clinical information.

Collaborations of this type encompass a broad range of data systems, including:

- vital records, such as electronic birth certificates

- surveillance systems targeted at communicable diseases, antibiotic resistance, or behavioral risk factors

- registries centered around such health problems as cancer, trauma, asthma, tuberculosis, or immunization

The clinical data in these systems derive from encounters with individuals in medical practices, clinics, managed care organizations, hospitals, or clinical laboratories. In some cases, clinical data are linked to information from public health departments and other government agencies (such as the medical examiner's office or the justice or transportation departments).

While, in some of the cases, the purpose of the collaboration is limited to encouraging clinicians to provide information to a public health database, the majority—and more interesting—of the cases show how collaboration can make an information system more useful to professionals and organizations in both health sectors. In these instances, practitioners in medicine and public health work together in the design and implementation phase of the project, creating systems that are interactive or, at the very least, those in which the information flow is two-way. Since these systems are actively used by the medical sector in clinical and organizational decision-making, the clinical data contained in them are likely to be more accurate, complete, and up-to-date than data populating noninteractive systems. As a result, public health analyses based on the same information are likely to be more reliable as well.

Medical and public health sector input into the design of a community-wide framework for collecting health information is obtained through consultations or focus groups with the types of professionals who ultimately will be using the system. These discussions are helpful in identifying the needs of practicing clinicians—such as accurate information, quick response from the database, and easy-to-use computer programs—and the ways in which the system is likely to be used in a medical setting—for example, which support staff would utilize the database, what additional software would be useful, and how the database might be integrated into practice or institutional operations. Input from public health practitioners is valuable in elucidating how the information in the system would be used to monitor health outcomes, to determine where clinical services are being delivered, or to target outreach efforts and media campaigns.

Input from clinical practices has a substantial impact on the design of the information systems.

- In some of the immunization registries, for example, access to the system proceeds through multiple channels: modem, Internet, fax, or phone.

- Inquiries about the immunization status of a particular child can be made through a variety of identification numbers (registry, WIC, AFDC, or Medicaid) as well as "sound-alike" spellings of children's and parents' names.

- To meet medical professionals' requests for practice supports that enhance clinical decision-making and facilitate the timely delivery of vaccinations, some immunization registries have the capacity to generate computerized reports of the immunization status of all of the children in the practice; information about different types and lots of vaccines; "tickler files" identifying children who need to come into the office for vaccinations; and phone-call lists, recall notices, and patient reminders—all personalized to the clinician's practice—to facilitate outreach to particular children.

- To meet more general needs of medical practices, some registries come with clinic management and record-keeping software. Others use the registry's electronic platform for multiple purposes, such as a lead-screening database, a communicable disease registry, a tuberculosis-tracking system, and an "emergency response outbreak system."

Whereas collaboration in the design phase, in and of itself, is beneficial in facilitating subsequent implementation, some cases involve users actively in the implementation phase as well. In one case, for example, a select group of private physicians—those serving children at highest risk for not being immunized—were provided with all of the necessary hardware and software to connect to the registry, with training in the use of the registry for themselves and their office staff, and with ongoing technical support.

Case Illustration: Synergy IV-A

NEW JERSEY INFORMATION SYSTEMS (NJ)

In the late 1980s, the hospitals and the state health department in New Jersey each wanted a reliable perinatal database, although admittedly for different reasons. To support epidemiologic analyses, the health department wanted the capacity to monitor and record prenatal and birth events electronically. Hospitals wanted to be able to submit paperwork electronically, to reduce the collection of redundant information, and to have more prenatal and medical information about pregnant women before they presented in labor at the emergency room. The state hospital association wanted a more accurate research database in order to analyze epidemiologic trends, assess risk in different hospital markets, and obtain reliable data for negotiations with insurers. Since it seemed that a single information system might work for all the parties, the state's Director of Maternal and Child Health, George Helpin, M.D., convened an advisory group of state personnel and hospital representatives to consider their mutual needs.

The group initially struggled with their competing interests. "We had many, many disagreements," recalled the health department's Virginia Dato, M.D., M.P.H., a pediatrician finishing her preventive medicine residency who was assigned to the project. "There was little trust." When a vendor involved in the project agreed to meet everyone's needs simultaneously, however, the project quickly evolved into a technical problem-solving exercise. The group's "product" was an electronic birth certificate that would provide the state health department with aggregate statewide data to support surveillance, vital registries, and epidemiologic investigations. Each hospital, however, could customize the birth certificate to meet its own needs.

Similar electronic ventures emerged in New Jersey throughout the 1990s—an interactive immunization registry, a laboratory-reporting system for multidrug-resistant pathogens, and an environmental emergency-notification system, among others. As the technology blossomed, each of the autonomous projects has been joined into a single overarching electronic network that supports a variety of medical and public health objectives. The goals of all of these projects are similar—to simplify (or automate) the reporting of key events or incidents; to create reliable databases that can provide useful information for clinical, epidemiologic, and policy-planning purposes; and to provide meaningful feedback to providers that will help guide clinical decision-making and support more effective medical practice.

In the electronic birth certificate project, the working group acknowledged the specific needs of all partners. They designed the system so hospitals could add modules to gather data that would not be forwarded to the state. According to Rona Remstein, R.N., B.S.N., of the New Jersey Hospital Association, some hospitals wanted to monitor breast-feeding patterns, others wanted to track high-risk babies, and still others wanted to monitor Caesarian section rates and induction indicators. In turn, the health department added reporting forms that could be folded into the electronic birth certificate. They designed modules that automatically registered low birthweight babies for newborn hearing-screening exams, and added a parentage certificate that could be printed and signed by the baby's mother and father. The working group's attention to each partner's particular interests clearly paid off. Within two years of its implementation, all the hospitals in the state were voluntarily registering their births electronically, and the comprehensive birth data were being used to populate the immunization database.

When New Jersey suffered a major measles outbreak in 1989–91, it spurred a number of immunization efforts. One strategy was to create a centralized computer database that integrated immunization data from a number of sources, such as WIC, AFDC, clinics, providers, and hospitals, so that any authorized health care provider could access a child's immunization history. In 1993, The Robert Wood Johnson Foundation awarded the Department of Pediatrics at the University of Medicine and Dentistry of New Jersey $3 million to develop the database over three years. The pilot study to test the interactive registry took place in Camden, an impoverished urban area in southern New Jersey, and it involved the major providers of pediatric care in that community.

"Before we had software we had input from providers," said Ruth Gubernick, M.P.H., the Camden County health department's immunization coordinator, who was recruited to serve as a project director. "We assessed different provider practices to see how they did business. We looked at every site to see if they wanted to use the registry on-line, as a part of the registration process, in batch mode at the end of the day, or through a service bureau such as the Camden Area Health Education Center, which provided off-site data entry and reminder/recall functions for private providers." In addition to analyzing the process of how providers would interact with the system, the designers solicited the input of the physicians and clinical office staff for what would be useful to them in their particular clinical settings.

A number of practice supports were added to the basic immunization registry as a result of discussions with providers. The system provides clinicians with immunization status reports for individual patients, and it has the capacity to identify children in the practice who need to come in for vaccinations. It can generate phone call or home-visit lists, as well as recall notices and patient reminders that can be mailed to patients on the provider's letterhead. The registry also generates standardized epidemiologic reports for the practice as a whole, such as the proportion of children who are up-to-date with their vaccinations. Some practices have found that up-to-date immunization rates drop for the 15-month-old age group, prompting them to revise their outreach strategies for reminding parents to bring their babies in for vaccinations. Going beyond immunization, the registry also will include a lead-screening field.

The registry has had a secondary effect of improving the relationship between the private practitioners and the local public health department. "The physicians used to think that the public health immunization clinics were pulling paying patients away from their practices," said Gubernick. "Now they can see that only 2 percent of private patients in Camden are picked up at the health department clinics. Also, they now have a better understanding that the health department clinics keep pointing the child back to their primary care provider." In addition, providers are utilizing the health department outreach workers more often to assist with hard-to-reach patients. "This can't just be public health telling providers what they have to do," offered Gubernick, who has many years of public health experience, "for this to work, it has to be cooperative."

Synergy IV-B · Use Clinical Opportunities to Identify and Address Underlying Causes of Health Problems

Clinical encounters provide valuable opportunities for identifying and addressing underlying causes of health problems. Information can be elicited—about health risks, for example—that goes beyond the particular symptoms or disease with which a patient presents. Connections can be made to a patient's social or physical environment to test an infectious disease contact or a potentially toxic worksite or home. In addition, individuals can be provided with targeted counseling or educational materials about personal behaviors, such as smoking, a sedentary lifestyle, or heavy drinking, that are detrimental to their health. Patients engaging in such behaviors can be referred to appropriate programs in the community.

Medical practitioners generally acknowledge that such activities can be useful in identifying and addressing underlying causes of health problems. Moreover, a recent survey documented that primary care physicians believe it is their responsibility to engage in some of these activities, particularly patient education and counseling, which have been shown to be effective in promoting more healthful behaviors.[186] In practice, however, encounters with patients rarely are used in this way. Many clinicians feel inadequate in providing such counseling and educational services, largely because they have not had adequate training in doing so. Even more important, economic and professional incentives have not been supportive.

In the cases of this type that we have collected, changes in the practice environment, and benefits of collaboration *per se*, are making it more worthwhile for clinicians to engage in these activities. For the most part, these collaborations focus on health problems with prominent environmental, social, and behavioral risk factors, such as lead toxicity, asthma, domestic violence, tobacco use, diet, and STDs. In some of the cases, financial risk taken by physicians or managed care organizations is making it more cost-effective for the medical sector to support public health prevention strategies than to treat—often repeatedly—individuals who suffer preventable diseases or injuries. The investment required by the medical sector is low in collaborations in which its role is limited to obtaining information from patients and referring them to programs implemented and financed by the public health sector. In other cases, capitated payments that encompass more than the services that clinicians themselves provide make it possible for the medical sector to finance nonclinical interventions. In one example in the database, savings achieved through changes in lead-toxicity treatment protocols were used to finance environmental strategies that reduced the need for medical treatment.

In all of the collaborations, a close working relationship between medicine and public health creates a "link to action" that justifies using encounter time with patients to address underlying causes of health problems. Because public health professionals, organizations, and agencies are active partners in these interactions, medical practitioners know that something will be done with the information that they obtain from patients, that individuals identified as having a problem will be referred to appropriate community-based programs, and that their "one minute of counseling" will be reinforced by community-wide strategies that make it easier for patients to follow that advice. Equally important, the collaborations often provide medical professionals with valuable practice supports—such as counseling guides, patient education materials, and resource directories—that minimize the time and effort involved in engaging in these activities. In return, health departments receive valuable clinical support in achieving their objectives, and governmental and not-for-profit public health organizations see enhanced utilization of their services.

Case Illustration: Synergy IV-B

KENNEDY KRIEGER INSTITUTE LEAD PROGRAM (MD)

For the older eastern cities of Baltimore, New York, Philadelphia, and Boston, the problem of lead poisoning poses as great an economic and political challenge as it does a health risk for children. In Baltimore, where over half of the city's housing has lead problems, two parallel activities occur when a child is diagnosed with lead poisoning—a health department case manager is assigned to oversee the clinical course of treatment, assuring that the child has adequate primary care and follow-up blood screening as required by CDC protocol, and an environmental inspector evaluates the house and issues a lead violation notice to the landlord.

Several problems arise. First, tenants often refuse access to health department workers. They don't want the health department issuing a lead violation notice to their landlord because it may result in their eviction despite consumer protections to the contrary. Second, in many cases the health department has no means of access because the tenants—who may lead transient lives—have moved.

For the landlords, the cost of remediation may be more than the house is worth. According to the CDC's Harold Knight, posted to the Baltimore City Health Department, it is possible to pay $20,000 for lead abatement in a house that is worth only $15,000. One option for the landlord is to evict the tenants and board up the house. This further diminishes the available housing stock in an inner city already suffering from a dearth of affordable housing. The landlords know their political leverage and often feel free to ignore the compliance order. The houses that remain on the market continue to be contaminated with lead, and children may return to physicians two or three times with elevated lead levels. Knight estimates that the lead-toxicity recidivism rate was 54 to 60 percent in 1994.

One of Baltimore's largest medical providers of lead treatment is taking an innovative approach to break the lead-poisoning cycle, using capitated payment to finance environmental solutions. The Kennedy Krieger Institute, a private center for children with brain-based disabilities, sees between 80 to 90 percent of the lead-poisoned children in Baltimore, including 600 patients at one clinic alone.[97] Traditionally, its lead-toxicity treatment protocol has involved removing the child from the house, hospitalizing him or her for a lengthy course of chelation therapy, and reporting the incident to the health department for monitoring of lead-abatement efforts. According to neurologist Gary Goldstein, M.D., the Institute's president, Kennedy Krieger was limited by a very restrictive reimbursement structure—it had to hospitalize each child even if it was cheaper to house him or her in a hotel, and such supportive activities as social work counseling and housing support were not reimbursed.

In 1994, Kennedy Krieger recruited a professor of public health policy, Mark Farfel, Ph.D., to investigate the most cost-effective ways of abating lead. With funding from the

Department of Housing and Urban Development and the Environmental Protection Agency, the Institute began a clinical trial—still ongoing—which involved hiring commercial vendors to do a $1,000, $3,000, or $5,000 abatement of randomly assigned lead-contaminated houses, and then following the houses for subsequent cases of lead poisoning.

At about the same time, Kennedy Krieger approached a number of managed care organizations and insurers about capitating the Institute's fees for lead-toxicity treatment, using a sliding scale that provided higher capitation payments for more severe cases of lead poisoning. For approximately one-third less money than it had received on a cost basis, the Institute was now free to structure its treatment in any way it wanted, with the proviso that it was responsible for the care of the child for one year. The interim strategy employed by Kennedy Krieger was to stop using the hospital and instead to move the children being treated, generally ages one through four, into a residence Kennedy Krieger owned. Since the Institute wanted to be able to move the children and their families back into lead-safe homes in the community, however, it also established a registry of lead-safe housing that it had inspected and certified. Instead of housing the children at the Kennedy Krieger house to conduct the chelation therapy, the Institute now moves the family directly into a lead-clean environment, which allows it to provide the therapy on an outpatient basis. The Institute pays the family's moving costs and supports any other financial needs they have in the move. This often includes paying overdue utility bills, laying out money for utility deposits, and occasionally paying rent if a family falls behind. "It costs more to treat them in the conventional way than it does to move them," noted Goldstein. In addition, the Institute treats the now vacant homes and adds them to their housing registry.

The landlords have been happy to enter their lead-clean houses on the registry because it assures them of tenants and provides them the financial "back-up" of the Institute. Kennedy Krieger, in turn, is able to deploy a social worker to assist the families, and it has a network of referral links with community-based tenant and housing organizations. The Institute also participates actively in a number of community lead awareness and prevention activities.

The lead program is having the additional consequence of working as a community redevelopment effort (albeit on a very small scale) in assuring stable housing and encouraging landlords to comply with lead-poisoning notices. Kennedy Krieger acknowledges the program's limitations—there may be houses that still generate a number of lead-poisoned children, and the most that Kennedy Krieger can do is report the recalcitrant landlords to the health department.

According to Goldstein, the Institute now spends more on community services than it does on medical services, and this has proven to be a more cost-effective way of treating and preventing lead poisoning in children. Moreover, its recidivism rate, once 50 percent, is now zero.

Synergy IV-C   **Collaborate to Achieve Clinically Oriented Community Health Objectives**

A substantial number of collaborations in the database center around the delivery of clinical preventive and treatment services to individuals.[180] For some of these objectives, such as immunization and the treatment of communicable diseases, the health of the entire population depends on the delivery of individual medical care. For other objectives, such as prenatal care, promoting the health of individuals also contributes to the economic well-being of the community. In spite of the importance of delivering these services, however, the country is far from meeting target goals. According to the latest update of *Healthy People 2000*, two-thirds of noninstitutionalized people 65 years of age and older have not received influenza vaccine; over 25 percent of children ages 19 to 35 months are not up-to-date with their vaccinations; and nearly one out of every four pregnant women receives no prenatal care in the first trimester.[177] In each case, the rates are considerably worse in certain geographic areas and for particular population subgroups.

The collaborations in the database that address clinically oriented health objectives focus primarily on childhood and adult immunizations, EPSDT exams, prenatal care, dental care, mammography, Pap tests, retinal screening tests for diabetes, control of hypertension, and treatment for STDs and tuberculosis. Most of these cases move beyond traditional interactions in which public health agencies recruit medical practitioners to provide clinical services in community settings—through mass immunizations in schools, for example. Instead, they are structured to work in the current environment through strategies that optimize the delivery of clinical services in mainstream medical settings. Many of these strategies build on synergistic interactions that have been described previously.

In collaborations involving a broad range of partners—encompassing not only the health sectors, but also other government agencies, businesses, religious organizations, the media, and schools—various approaches (similar to those presented in Synergy III-B) are used to "get the message out" and to "funnel" people into medical offices. Education campaigns, for example, are instituted to make members of the public and health professionals as well more aware of the need for particular clinical services. Media used to publicize the issue include billboards, newspaper articles, mailings, fliers distributed on the street, and the Internet. Telephone hotlines are set up to answer questions and provide people with additional information. Letters are sent to insured and practice populations informing them of the value of the particular service and directing them to appropriate providers in the area. In some campaigns, clinicians are given posters on which they can graphically chart their rates of service provision.

Outreach services (as described in Synergy I) are important components in many of these collaborations as well, helping to address logistical barriers that patients face in obtaining clinical care. Some projects supplement care in medical offices by offering clinical services in convenient locations, such as churches, malls, and schools. In others, home visits are arranged to provide needed services to hard-to-reach patients of medical practitioners. Many cases provide transportation services to help patients reach clinicians' offices.

Practice supports—particularly the interactive information systems discussed above—are common features of these collaborations. These systems provide clinicians with better information about the rates at which services are being provided in a given practice. In addition, they identify patients in need of services and automatically generate reminder letters to be sent to them. Other supports provided through the collaborations include free vaccines, medications, and supplies for patients in need, and help with claims processing for health professionals.

Case Illustration: Synergy IV-C

MONROE COUNTY "McFLU" CAMPAIGN (NY)

In the mid-1980s, the CDC and the Health Care Financing Administration (HCFA) selected Monroe County, New York as one of ten sites to evaluate the cost-effectiveness of influenza vaccine among elderly patients. In part, Monroe County was chosen on the strength of the University of Rochester Medical Center, home to a leading vaccination epidemiologist, William Barker, M.D. In part, it was chosen because it is an ideal community to "test market" a health planning approach. Monroe County is a mature health care market, with a mix of urban and suburban populations, and a history of collaborative health planning dating back to the 1950s. "There's a cooperative spirit," said Barker. "You don't have to build everything *de novo*." Barker and his colleagues dubbed their project "McFlu."[7–9,27]

Although a relatively benign winter ailment for most of the population, influenza often proves devastating for seniors, particularly if it leads to life-threatening pneumonia. Although available vaccines reliably decrease the chance of seniors coming down with influenza, many are not immunized. One baseline study of Monroe County physicians found some practices with only 35 percent of their older patients vaccinated. Clearly, access to a medical practitioner was not the problem, since virtually all of the seniors were covered by Medicare. The CDC and HCFA wanted to see if Medicare reimbursement for influenza vaccination would lead to a rise in immunization rates, and if this, in turn, would lead to a decrease in influenza-associated morbidity and mortality. Equally important, they wanted to see if the cost of providing vaccinations would be less than the cost of treatment and hospitalization for influenza. The CDC had a secondary interest as well—to see if it was possible to create a partnership between public health agencies and the practice community, with an academic medical center supporting the research infrastructure. In addition to conducting the cost-effectiveness study, the researchers in Monroe County proposed other activities to enhance the reimburse-ment effort: broadcasting a community-wide and senior-specific message encouraging influenza vaccination, increasing the awareness and interest of the medical community in providing immunizations, and directing seniors to physicians' offices for the reimbursable service.

From the outset, each partner's role in McFlu was well defined. The health department would distribute and track the influenza vaccine and recruit providers and patients; the university would conduct surveillance and coordinate the entire demonstration project, including running monthly meetings of McFlu's partners; a number of medical institutions (4 hospitals and 32 nursing homes) and medical practices would participate in lab-collection activities and provider recruitment as well as immunizations; and the practice community would immunize their Medicare patients. "It wasn't a huge amount of money," said Barker of the $8 per shot the providers received, "but it was a lot of patients." By the end of the McFlu demonstration, over 83 percent of all eligible physicians in the county were participating in the project.

In the second year of the collaboration, the project assigned the health department's Bonnie Lewis to coordinate the effort. "They needed systems development," recalled Lewis, "public relations, provider enrollment and reimbursement, data management, and the tracking of 80,000 immunizations." The innumerable details of the complex project were all organized through Lewis' office.

There were several "adjustments" to the demonstration project over its four-year life span. After a number of incomplete Medicare claims were returned to physicians, the health department took on the role of central claims processing. As a result, the "return rate" dropped from 25 percent to 2 percent of all submitted claims. The McFlu investigators also made two other efforts to boost physician participation. They experimented with a financial incentive, in which physicians received up incremental bonuses in payment as their immunization rates approached 90 percent. And they started a poster program that documented practice immunization rates on poster boards hung in doctors' offices. Both of these programs proved significantly effective.

Overall, McFlu increased immunization rates from 45 to 75 percent of the eligible population and decreased pneumonia hospitalization rates and nursing home outbreaks. There were several indirect consequences of the McFlu project as well. According to Barker, McFlu prompted "physicians to think about their practice as a population rather than just as individual patients." When first approached to participate, doctors commonly insisted they already were vaccinating most of their Medicare patients and therefore McFlu wouldn't make much of a difference. "We pulled the medical records and computer billing records," recalled Barker, "and physicians were astounded to find out that their rates were much lower than they thought."

A second consequence was the strengthened link between the University of Rochester Medical Center and the local health department. "McFlu was a prototypical community health study," said Barker, "and it has served as a model for developing a center at the university to jointly conduct public health research with the health department. Clearly, the health department is accountable, but it doesn't have the capacity of the university to conduct the research and evaluation."

On a national level, the results of McFlu and other influenza demonstration projects around the country led HCFA to amend Medicare reimbursement. Since 1993, annual influenza immunization has been a covered benefit under the Medicare program.

Lastly, McFlu provided a demonstration of community-based strategies that would prove useful in other collaborative efforts, most notably the Women's Health Partnership profiled earlier in Synergy III-B. "McFlu brought an idea to life on which public health, academia, and the practice community could work together to improve the community's health," said deputy health department director Nancy M. Bennett, M.D., M.S. "The local health department traditionally has been marginalized—thought of as a safety net. Projects like McFlu help to clarify an emerging role for public health agencies. We certainly don't have to lead everything, but we do have to be at the table when the health of the community is at stake."

Synergy V

Strengthening Health Promotion and Health Protection by Mobilizing Community Campaigns

All of the collaborations described thus far involve medical care as one of their components. By linking clinical practice to other individual-level services and to population-based strategies, these collaborations enhance the practice of medicine, address determinants of health that go beyond medical care, and support the achievement of clinically oriented health objectives. Another way for the medical and public health sectors to collaborate is by working together on population-based strategies that protect and promote community health. This type of interaction occurs in over 150 cases in the database, including some of the collaborations described in Synergies III and IV. By working together on population-based strategies, professionals and institutions in medicine and public health address underlying causes of some of the most pressing health problems Americans face—such as tobacco use, poor diet, inactivity, injuries, and violence—and strengthen essential functions of public health. They do so by bringing together two or more of the following non-clinical resources:

- *influence with peers, policymakers, and the public*
- *legal authority*
- *convening power*
- *information*
- *scientific and technical expertise*
- *advocacy, lobbying, and public relations skills*

THE VALUE OF COLLA-BORATING AROUND HEALTH PROMOTION AND HEALTH PROTECTION

Historically, the medical and public health sectors have worked together around a number of health protection and health promotion issues. Examples include sanitary reforms of the 19th century, fluoridation of the water supply, the identification and reduction of risk factors for cardiovascular disease, the enactment of seat belt and helmet laws, and the adoption of policies to discourage the use of tobacco. For the most part, however, the medical sector has viewed its involvement in these issues as an optional or "extracurricular" activity—unrelated to clinical practice and otherwise "taken care of" by public health.

In the current environment, the two health sectors have much stronger reasons to collaborate around health protection and health promotion than they have had in the past. On the one hand, today's health professionals are confronting an extremely difficult set of health problems, which neither sector can address alone. Problems such as violence, substance abuse, teenage pregnancy, sexually transmitted diseases, chronic disease, and environmental and occupational hazards lead to an enormous burden of illness and disability. Medical practitioners see patients suffering from these conditions everyday. Yet, addressing the behavioral, social, and environmental causes of these problems requires strategies that go beyond the biomedical model. Identifying and dealing with such factors is central to the mission of public health, through population-based strategies that include surveillance, health assessment, public education, outreach and screening, laws and regulations, and environmental detoxification. The public health sector needs a broad range of community partners to carry out these activities, however. Budget constraints and shifting Medicaid financing streams have left many health departments without sufficient resources to take effective action by themselves. Moreover, public health agencies and voluntary health organizations are limited in their ability to act directly on many health determinants.

A second impetus for this type of collaboration—perhaps even more compelling than the first—is that today's economic pressures are making the prevention of health problems important to the medical sector as well as to the public health sector. As managed care organizations and capitated practices take on financial risk, they bear the costs of treating the expensive sequelae of preventable health problems. Consequently, they are financially dependent on the capacity of communities to identify and address the root causes of health problems, to control the spread of communicable diseases, and to protect the food and water supply. In this context, the medical sector has a stronger incentive to pay attention to the effectiveness and funding of agencies carrying responsibility for health protection and health promotion, and to provide support for their population-based activities.

PARTNERS INVOLVED IN THESE COLLABORATIONS

These cases involve community groups to a greater extent than any other type of collaboration in the database. In some of the cases, in fact, community groups play the leadership role, and professionals and organizations in medicine and public health participate as partners in a much larger process. Because of this dynamic, campaigns to protect and promote community health illustrate not only how the skills and resources of the medical and public health sectors can reinforce each other, but also how the combined assets of the two health sectors can be reinforced by other public, private, and not-for-profit organizations in the community.

The central role of community-based organizations, businesses, unions, schools, churches, and the media in these collaborations reflects their importance in developing and implementing population-based strategies. The objective of such strategies is to improve the health of some or all of the inhabitants in a community. Community groups not only represent various components of this population, they also have access to people in places where they live, learn, pray, and work. Consequently, community partners are valuable in obtaining input from different groups of residents, assuring that priorities reflect community concerns, and that interventions are responsive to community values and needs. They can facilitate efforts to communicate, reach, and influence these populations in culturally appropriate ways; they can help identify opportunities and obstacles to achieving desired objectives in different neighborhoods; and they can contribute a range of other important resources to the collaborations, such as data, media connections, and funding.

MODELS FOR COLLABORATING AROUND HEALTH PROMOTION AND HEALTH PROTECTION

In the cases in the database, collaborations around health promotion and health protection take five forms:

- community health assessments
- public education campaigns
- health-related laws and regulations
- community-wide campaigns to achieve health promotion objectives
- "Healthy Community" initiatives

The first three models bring partners together around a single population-based strategy. In the other two, various population-based strategies are combined.

Synergy V-A

Conduct Community Health Assessments

Many collaborations in the database involve community health assessments. That is not surprising, since the identification of health problems is the starting point for action in both medicine and public health. Moreover, the process of conducting an assessment provides a good medium for bringing diverse community partners together.

In some of the cases collected, the focus of the assessment is narrow, concentrating on one issue or one segment of the population (for example, access to medical care, use of tobacco and alcohol in Latino youth, or motor vehicle injuries). In others, the focus is broader, encompassing a wide range of factors that determine the health of a geopolitical population as well as the resources that a community can muster to respond to health needs. Regardless of focus, the community health assessment either can be an end in itself, or it can be the first step in a collaboration that leads to community-wide interventions.

Although community health assessments sometimes are performed by one sector alone, the cases document good reasons to involve others in the effort. One motivating factor is the requirement for institutions or organizations in both sectors to perform these assessments. The emphasis on community health assessment by JCAHO, and the fact that local health departments often need to carry out similar activities to obtain state funding, may explain the prominent involvement of hospitals and local health departments in many of the cases. Obviously, efficiencies can be achieved by working together rather than by duplicating each others' efforts.

A second reason to work together is that information obtained through community health assessments—and the process used to obtain that information—often is valuable to partners in both sectors. Data about health problems and health resources in a community are helpful in

- identifying and prioritizing community health problems;

- planning and justifying the need for health programs and health services (whether in medicine or public health);

- assuring that programs and services offered are responsive to community needs;

- determining how to allocate limited resources;

- supporting training, evaluation, and research.

In some cases, these data are used to rally community concern around a problem or to provide valuable ammunition for advocacy and lobbying efforts. In others, participation in a community-wide health assessment helps health organizations and institutions develop stronger community ties. These factors may account for the active role of integrated systems (especially the Community Care Network and Community-Oriented Primary Care models), academic institutions, and a broad range of community-based organizations in many of these collaborations.

Additional incentives to collaborate relate to improving the quality and usefulness of the assessment and to reducing (or sharing) overall costs. Community health assessments usually are more robust if they aggregate data from multiple sources—for example, quantitative data derived from surveys and administrative databases, and qualitative information drawn from community meetings, interviews, and focus groups—and if they analyze those data from multiple perspectives. In the cases collected, the expertise and connections of a broad range of professionals and community leaders have been helpful in

- designing the assessment instrument;

- obtaining access to existing data;

- collecting new information;

- analyzing the data that are gathered;

- writing, producing, and disseminating the report;

- obtaining financial support.

Access to diverse sectors of the community also is valuable in obtaining input and endorsement. The practical experience of community partners gives people beyond medicine and public health a voice in defining health problems and in planning and modifying health services. The authority of various partners lends legitimacy to the project with health sectors as well as community groups. The greatest benefit of garnering broad community involvement in a health assessment, however, may be to assure that something is ultimately done with the product. If partners frame the issues together—by doing the assessment as a collaboration—they may be more likely to take action on the results.

While community assessments often simply confirm partners' previous perceptions about health problems, in some instances they lead to surprising results. One case, for example, documented that a significant portion of inner-city residents lacked access to primary care in spite of an adequate supply of physicians in the area, the presence of a large medical center, and a progressive health department. This assessment led to the development of a collaborative health center, which brought together an array of individual-level services as described in Synergy I. In other cases, assessments revealed problems that residents were not aware of, such as teenage suicide. In some, they identified community perceptions, such as the importance of literacy to health, that differed from those of medical or public health professionals.

Case Illustration: Synergy V-A

CLARK COUNTY COMMUNITY HEALTH ASSESSMENT (WA)

In 1992, a small group of community residents protested the addition of several service programs in their neighborhood in Vancouver, Washington. The Southwest Washington Medical Center was thinking of adding social services and a health department WIC clinic to their behavioral medicine program. Kaiser Permanente was considering co-locating a clinic at the site as well. Given the community's environment—generally run-down, with pockets of high unemployment, and a large number of clients using mental health, drug treatment, and other social services—the agencies' planners thought new services would be warmly embraced, or, at the very least, accepted. When instead they were greeted with a "Not In My Back Yard" (NIMBY) outcry, it brought them up short. It also prompted the director of the health department, the executive director of the medical center, and the vice president for community affairs at the Kaiser Permanente health plan, to reconsider their approach to community health planning.

It had taken the three organizations several years of negotiations—against a backdrop of statewide health reform—to even include one another in their strategic health planning, and now the three executives acknowledged that their mutual involvement had not been sufficient. They needed to bring the community into their assessment activities, and it paid to think broadly about the health needs of the entire Clark County. Using their organizational contacts, the three raised over $100,000 from the hospital, the managed care organization, the city and county government, the CDC, and the local health department to hire a facilitator to lead a community-involvement process. In addition, the health department created a Division of Assessment and Epidemiology to help focus its own institutional resources.

At the health department's prompting, a community partnership group was formed. Called Community Choices 2010 (CC 2010), it was composed of residents (including those neighbors whose initial protests spurred its creation), agency leaders, health care providers, local business people, and representatives from such governmental entities as the school district, the sheriff's department, the transportation department, and the economic development agency. The group's goals were to evaluate the health of the community and to prioritize its health needs.

The health department contributed its epidemiologic staff to CC 2010 to help assemble and analyze data. They collected morbidity and mortality data from the state health department—birth and death records, reportable disease data, and prenatal and maternity data. They also reviewed the state's hospital discharge data, culled census data from the county's planning unit, and obtained educational achievement data and dropout rates from the school district. In addition, a number of the partners around the table tapped their own institutional databases: crime data were provided by the sheriff; economic data came from the state employment service; and both Kaiser Permanente and the medical center contributed data on uncompensated emergency room care. CC 2010 also commissioned a series of focus groups in the community and scheduled a number of community presentations.

"The trick," said Bonnie Kostelecky, M.S., M.P.A., R.N., director of the health department's assessment and epidemiology unit, "is that you have to make the data sing for people. We made connections to their lives and their school systems, and we brought it down to their neighborhoods. When we talked about causes of death we didn't just look at rates. We looked at a neighborhood—how it had a lot of elderly—looked at how far they were from services and at where the bus lines were. Once we got them hooked on the stuff, the data were very powerful. It got people to think about the 'upstream' causes of health problems." What began as a finding of high lung cancer and cardiovascular disease rates, for example, led the group to consider possible anti-smoking campaigns, and ways of shaping teen attitudes toward smoking.

After a year-long assessment process, the community partnership settled on six "upstream" domains in which to intervene: youth and families, economic opportunity, access to health and social services, health and safety practices, positive community norms, and education. The facilitator urged the group to identify strategies that addressed each. In particular, she asked the group to think about which agencies and individuals in the community already were committed to these issues. The implementation of these prioritized strategies evolved into a "Healthy Communities" project (profiled in Synergy V-E), involving over 400 people on committees, subcommittees, work groups, and in informal discussions.

The health department, the medical center, and the managed care organization have made a variety of programmatic changes as a result of the health assessment. The health department has focused greater attention on anti-smoking campaigns and has boosted its public funding requests for community-wide health promotion activities. The medical center has used some of the data for targeted market analyses, and has reconfigured some of its patient health education efforts. Kaiser Permanente, involved in a statewide campaign to increase immunization rates, has used the data to target its immunization efforts, particularly in emergency room settings where unexpected "immunization opportunities" arise.

As for the initial NIMBY problem, although the health department agreed to move its WIC and immunization clinics to another neighborhood, the mental health campus and some of the drug treatment programs remain. Not every problem can be resolved with such a community planning process, noted the health department's Kostelecky.

Synergy V-B   Mount Health Education Campaigns

Once a community health problem is identified, public education campaigns can be a powerful strategy for making the public more aware of the issue and for highlighting the role that individuals and community groups can play in addressing it. These campaigns support health promotion by providing individuals with information that can help them modify their own risk behaviors, and by blanketing the community with messages that establish a more supportive social environment.

Cases in which the medical and public health sectors collaborate around health education campaigns are common in the database. Partners include government agencies, medical societies, academic institutions, managed care organizations, insurers, hospitals, businesses, community-based organizations, labor organizations, churches, and schools. Some of the projects are comprehensive in scope, such as a "Take Care of Yourself" book distributed to managed care organization enrollees who work for large employers, or a series of television programs on a broad range of health issues. Others focus on specific health issues that may be health priorities in the community. These educational materials sometimes are organized around the prevention or management of a particular disease (most commonly an infectious disease, chronic disease, or cancer). Another approach is to concentrate on personal behaviors related to health, such as smoking, substance abuse, sexual activity, diet, physical inactivity, drinking and driving, or the use of bicycle and motorcycle helmets. Information about environmental issues, such as hazardous wastes, lead poisoning, and fluoridation, is provided in some materials. Others provide a list of available health resources.

The cases elucidate a variety of ways that collaboration can strengthen health education campaigns. Most important, perhaps, is the value of bringing medical and public health professionals together with community groups in crafting and delivering the message. People are more likely to pay attention to health education campaigns if the message is credible and the messenger is respected. In some of the cases collected, the two health sectors work together to develop a scientifically valid message, based on a careful review of existing data. Health educators, behavioral scientists, and representatives of the target audience work to make sure that the material reflects people's concerns, is understandable (in terms of language and educational level), and is culturally acceptable. Physicians known to the target group often are used as spokespersons.

Collaborations that bring together the resources and expertise of a broad range of partners are helpful in financing the project and in making sure that the message is received by the intended audience. The choice of medium in many cases capitalizes on the connections of one or more of the partners, as well as on their combined knowledge as to what medium will be most accessible to the people they are trying to reach. In some campaigns, the partners publish books, brochures, fact sheets, or directories. When distribution is a collaborative effort—either through mailings to partners' constituency groups, or by making materials available in such places as doctors' offices, pharmacies, schools, churches, nursing homes, libraries, businesses, workplaces, soup kitchens, and homeless shelters—the message can reach a very broad (or targeted) audience. In telecommunications campaigns, the partners get the message out through television programs, videos, radio shows, telephone hotlines, World Wide Web sites, and multimedia information kiosks. Advertisements, billboards, and posters also are used in some cases, as are face-to-face approaches, such as meetings and seminars in the community, theater groups, fairs, door-to-door canvassing, mobile vans, and peer support groups. Interactive events provide opportunities to discuss information and to answer individual questions.

Case Illustration: Synergy V-B

HAWAII "HEALTHSCOPE" TV SERIES (HI)

In the spring of 1993, the Hawaii Medical Association (HMA) approached several local television stations in Honolulu about producing a health education series. They were referred to an independent television producer, Christopher Conybeare, whose wife, Kathryn L. Braun, Dr.P.H., is an associate professor of health education at the University of Hawaii School of Public Health. Together, they persuaded the local NBC-affiliate to air a weekly Friday night series called HealthScope during their ten-week summer period.[24] The group was given two months to prepare the show to air.

According to Braun, Hawaiian physicians "knew that managed care was coming down the line, and they wanted to project their presence in primary care and preventive medicine." The format of the show was designed to disseminate a public health message about the community's leading health risks through HMA physicians, to offer specific cues to viewers to act on these messages through HMA-physician-staffed phone banks, and to use the mainstream media to engage the viewers. Secondarily, the group wanted to promote a better image of HMA physicians and to educate the local television news professionals about public health and disease prevention.

Two major sponsors were recruited to the effort—the Hawaii Medical Services Association (HMSA), a Blue Cross/Blue Shield insurance provider; and Long's Drug Stores, a local pharmacy chain. They each contributed $30,000 to the show's production and advertising costs, and in return they received prominent billing on all advertising fliers, health promotion materials, and three minutes of advertising time during the show. A planning committee organized by Braun and Conybeare included staff and professional members of HMA and HMSA's director of health education. The committee selected the ten topics for the show. "The topics had to work from the producer's perspective on what would 'sell,'" said John Wan, the HMA's executive director, "but we depended on Kathryn to provide the public health perspective on what the community needed to hear." Braun detailed the principal community health risks based on epidemiologic data, focusing in particular on preventable causes of death more prevalent among certain ethnic groups. The committee picked appropriate physicians to appear on-air with the show's host, a local news anchor, and designed a community-wide health promotion campaign to accompany the show.

Each show was tightly scripted by Braun and Conybeare. Guided by Braun's use of the health-belief model, which relates individual health behaviors to a person's values and expectations, the planning committee used physician and patient role models from the community with whom viewers could identify. The majority of the patients were native islanders, selected on the basis of a health problem's prevalence within a given ethnic community. Each show opened with a segment focusing on the prevention and treatment of that week's health problem, followed by an interview with an expert physician and then a profile of a patient. These profiles explored patients' feelings, fears, and coping strategies, and addressed common barriers to prevention and treatment. One show devoted to breast cancer featured a native Hawaiian woman as the patient, since that group has particularly high rates of breast cancer. A show on skin cancer included a segment at a beach featuring a famous lifeguard and surfer with malignant melanoma. Prior to each show, 50,000 fliers advertising the show and promoting the recognition, treatment, and prevention of the "disease of the week" were distributed. Through an associated contest, people correctly answering a quiz could win a vacation package. During the airing of the ten-week series, which followed the popular "Wheel of Fortune" on Friday nights, five to eight HMA physicians staffed a phone bank to answer viewers' questions.

The series was a hit, rated as the number two show in its time slot. The phone bank fielded an average of 86 calls for each show, and the physicians manning it even identified several emergency health problems that required immediate attention. HMSA, which offered a phone line for health education tapes, reported a surge of demand for tapes on certain topics (particularly the socially sensitive ones involving STDs, HIV, and substance abuse), and over 700 people entered the sweepstakes with correct answers to the health promotion quiz.

Because of a large audience response and the sponsor's support, the television station rebroadcast the show in the fall, making money on the project. The partners also achieved two additional objectives. They educated certain media professionals about public health issues, and they helped people to think "epidemiologically" about diseases prevalent among various ethnic groups.

The HMA and its physicians were especially pleased with the exposure. A number of physicians have continued to show videotapes of certain shows in their waiting rooms, particularly those dealing with asthma and pregnancy. "People listen to doctors," noted Braun, "especially in a culture where authority is so respected. The doctors brought authority to the public health message, whether it was about nutrition or exercise or breast self-exam. And it provided a nice forum for them to demonstrate their public health knowledge and their interest in the community."

Synergy V-C   Advocate Health-Related Laws and Regulations

Another strategy for addressing health problems in communities is the adoption of laws and regulations that create social conditions more conducive to safety and health. These laws and regulations *protect* the health of the population by assuring the safety of its air, water, food, drugs, and modes of transportation. They also *promote* community health by

- limiting access to harmful products (through tobacco taxes, for example, or through restrictions on the sale of cigarettes, alcohol, and firearms to minors);

- reducing inducements to engage in unhealthful behaviors (through restrictions on tobacco advertising, for instance);

- requiring or prohibiting certain types of behavior (through such means as seat belt and helmet laws, speed limits, and smoke-free zones);

- providing people with information that allows them to make healthful decisions (for example, through food labeling in restaurants and supermarkets).

In the cases in the database that bring the medical and public health sectors together in these endeavors, the issues are usually tobacco, fluoridation, vehicular injury, and gun control. The types of partners most active in these collaborations include government agencies (particularly departments of health, justice, and transportation), medical societies, hospital emergency departments, community-based organizations, and the research community.

All of these cases center around advocacy and lobbying, which capitalize on the scientific expertise of the two health sectors, as well as on the influence and authority they have with the general public and policymakers. Public health professionals play important roles in data collection and analysis, which help to identify policy opportunities and to provide evidence to support a policy position. The capacity to gather policy-relevant information—through such means as surveys, aggregation of data from different sources, and community profiles—is strengthened by the involvement of a broad range of partners. Physicians appear to be very effective in making the case to the public and to policymakers, not only because their views carry substantial weight with these audiences but because they can describe in vivid terms the medical consequences of taking the "wrong" policy action. Although the collective influence of the partners in these collaborations is sometimes insufficient to overcome opposition from strong special interests, in most of the cases in the database it made a difference.

Case Illustration: Synergy V-C

EMORY UNIVERSITY CENTER FOR INJURY CONTROL (GA)

Every year in the Georgia statehouse the "biker lobby" reemerges, intent on repealing the state's motorcycle helmet law. In the past few years the biker lobby has gained confidence from their success in repealing other states' helmet laws. The lobbyists' positions coalesce around two central arguments—that the data used to support helmet laws are inaccurate, biased, and unreliable; and that the law encroaches on an individual's personal freedom. "The biker lobby argued that the helmets actually cause neck injuries and that helmet advocates have manipulated the data," said Arthur Kellermann, M.D., M.P.H., director of the Emory University Center for Injury Control and chief of the medical school's Division of Emergency Medicine. "This is absurd. The battle over motorcycle helmet laws represents a classic paradigm of public health versus personal freedom—telling someone what they can or cannot do—whether it's tobacco or seat belts or motorcycle helmets."

For Kellermann, this annual event boils down to making complex data believable and compelling, as well as spearheading the lobbying effort to counter an increasingly invigorated anti-helmet campaign. Emory's Center for Injury Control, which was developed in 1993 by the Rollins School of Public Health, has served as the multidisciplinary platform to mount the counter-campaign. "A doctor at the legislature carries ten times more weight than a paid lobbyist," noted Kellermann. "You can speak with a moral authority because you speak for the patients. It's part of the magic of being a doctor—particularly if you're testifying about a public health issue and not a pocketbook issue. In emergency medicine we see the consequences of inadequate prevention."

The Center covers a broad range of injury research and policy development issues, including firearm safety, helmet advocacy, and child safety. The Center is led by emergency physicians cross-trained in public health, and is supported by staff members with public health or research training in epidemiology, surveillance, technology assessment, and program evaluation. Its affiliate faculty on the campus includes professors of psychiatry, engineering, biomechanics, architecture, epidemiology, health policy, behavioral science, surgery, and pediatrics; its off-campus affiliations include public safety grassroots groups and law enforcement agencies. The Center sees itself as an interdisciplinary bridge, according to Kellermann, and it even has helped to develop an undergraduate violence study program at the university.

In keeping with his belief that "knowing how to frame an argument that will persuade the public" is as important a public health skill as running an epidemiological investigation, Kellermann developed a course in the Health Policy Division of the School of Public Health, "Legislative Advocacy for Injury Control," to teach M.P.H. students the "art and science of legislative advocacy." This past semester the students worked on two pending legislative actions—a package of teen-driving initiatives and the motorcycle helmet repeal. While the first sailed through the legislative process, the second involved carefully assembling unassailable statewide motorcycle injury data from the National Highway Traffic and Safety Administration (which refuted the "neck injury" claim posed by the biker lobby) and closely tracking the legislative process. To present the clinical and social consequences of motorcyclists' head injuries, the Center worked with several groups to coordinate the testimony of emergency physicians, paramedics, and hospital administrators. These concerted actions were successful—the bill to repeal the law was decisively defeated in the state senate. "What tipped the scales," said Kellermann, "was the power of the data, and the adverse financial impact of the repeal on taxpayers."

While the Center researches and develops injury control programs—such as an electronic firearm injury surveillance system, nicknamed "Cops and Docs," which links emergency department data from a five-county area in metropolitan Atlanta to police reports and medical examiner data—a good deal of its work is dedicated to policy development. The Center is experimenting with engineering a "child-proof" gun, and is collaborating with justice groups to mandate that American handguns meet the same safety standards as imported handguns. As part of an evaluation project being conducted in collaboration with the local U.S. Attorney, the juvenile courts, and the Atlanta police department, the Center also is proposing a crackdown on illegal gun-carrying by juveniles and the prosecution of adults who supply guns to children.

Across all of these projects, several common themes emerge. One is the interdisciplinary nature of the Center, which bridges the public and private sectors, and brings together groups and individuals with expertise in emergency medicine, public health and safety, law enforcement, and engineering. Another is the intersection of medicine and public health personified by the Center's director and assistant directors. The Center's ability to combine clinical and population perspectives is particularly effective in legislative advocacy efforts. "I can speak as chief of emergency medicine, as a clinician who sees an immediate impact on his patient," said Kellermann, "and I can speak as a public health expert, translating population-based data so it's accessible to legislators and the public. What we do as advocates is blend passion with data."

Synergy V-D   **Engage in Community-Wide Campaigns to Achieve Health Promotion Objectives**

Achieving the benefits of health promotion requires action on the part of individuals. In some situations, like those described in Synergy IV, that action relates to obtaining a clinical preventive service, such as immunization, cancer screening, or prenatal care. In others, the action involves making choices about a personal behavior—such as smoking, driving while intoxicated, engaging in regular physical activity, or using seat belts—that has an impact on health. Although individuals ultimately are responsible for their own actions, choices about personal risk behaviors are not made in a vacuum. Social conditions and norms—including the laws and regulations discussed above—determine the extent to which individuals have access to harmful or addictive products. They also determine the pervasiveness of inducements that encourage individuals to behave in ways that are deleterious or beneficial to their health.

Community-wide health promotion campaigns seek to influence individual behavior by making the environment more conducive to choices that foster health. By doing so, these campaigns reinforce—and are reinforced by—individual-level interventions to influence behavior (such as counseling, nicotine patches, or smoking cessation programs). In numerous cases in the database, partners in medicine and public health, as well as in other sectors in the community, work together to achieve health promotion objectives. For the most part, these collaborations use a multipronged approach—involving a broad range of partners, and combining various types of population-based and individual-level strategies. While any one partner or strategy can make a contribution by itself, there is a cumulative power in approaching a health promotion objective from multiple, reinforcing avenues.

Although details vary, depending on the partners involved and the particular health objective being addressed, in most cases the population-based building blocks of the multipronged approach are similar.

- Community health assessments are used to identify a behavior-related problem that is having a substantial impact on the health (and health care costs) of the community, to identify obstacles to and opportunities for changing that behavior, and to formulate interventions that are congruent with community perceptions and values.

- Health education campaigns are launched to make people aware of the consequences of certain risk behaviors and to persuade them to stop that activity—or not to start in the first place.

- Laws and regulations are adopted, or voluntary community initiatives are implemented, that make it easier for individuals to translate health promotion messages into healthier behaviors.

While legal actions modify social conditions by establishing penalties for engaging in or promoting unhealthy behaviors, voluntary initiatives use an "empowering" approach. Some strive to change expectations of peer groups by influencing what children or teenagers consider "nerdy" or "cool," for example.

Others provide increased opportunities for people to make healthy choices by adding low-fat and low-calorie options to restaurant and school menus, or by creating safe and convenient opportunities for physical activity in places where people live, learn, and work. Still others focus on overcoming financial and logistical obstacles that some people face in attempting to change their behavior, by reducing the cost or increasing the availability of bicycle helmets, for example.

Case Illustration: Synergy V-D

SEATTLE BIKE HELMET CAMPAIGN (WA)

In 1985, the newly created Harborview Injury Prevention and Research Center in Seattle was searching for a kick-off campaign. Several of the pediatricians affiliated with Harborview's trauma center noted that as many as 200 children were being seen each year with bicycle-related head injuries. "It was the logical campaign to do," said Center director Frederick Rivara, M.D., M.P.H. "This was a big problem, and there was a reasonable intervention—one with a single solution."

The solution: bike helmets for kids.[12,48,140,167–170] "This was a relatively inexpensive campaign," said pediatrician Abraham Bergman, M.D., "and as an injury-prevention effort you get a winner right away." The project directors modeled their efforts on Swedish injury-prevention projects, which involved broad-based coalitions. "This was a 'mom-and-apple pie' project," said Rivara. "We persuaded our partners to join the campaign because it made eminent sense, it could be effective, and it could generate good press."

Based on survey research data, the campaign organizers identified three barriers to bike helmet use: (1) parents were unaware of the risks of unhelmeted cycling and the consequences of a bike-related head injury, (2) children's helmets often were more expensive than the bikes themselves, and generally available only at specialty stores, and (3) children were unwilling to wear the helmets because it was "uncool." The Harborview planners wanted to address all three barriers—to persuade parents to buy the helmets, to make the helmets less expensive and more available, and to encourage children to wear the helmets. The medical community could be tapped to persuade the parents, the cycling community could produce and market cheaper helmets that still met safety standards, and the media could help broadcast the message to parents and children. All partners would be involved in publicizing the campaign.

Each of the 16 coalition partners was picked for the resources they could contribute to the campaign. The state medical society promoted the campaign to its physician membership, raised money and maintained a toll-free hotline for educational material, and contributed the use of their advertising agency. The Seattle/King County Health Department produced bike helmet brochures, disseminated educational materials and helmet-manufacturer coupons through its clinics, and organized bicycle rodeos at which helmet coupons were distributed. The Cascade Bicycle Club provided community promotion, contributed a health educator during the summer cycling season, and mounted a school-based campaign featuring a masked (and helmeted) Sprocketman. Group Health of Puget Sound approached the bike helmet campaign as a "clinical preventive service"; its physicians counseled parents and children and distributed discount coupons for helmets. Several helmet manufacturers agreed to produce and mass market discounted children's helmets in the Seattle area. A local television station, KOMO-TV, also joined the campaign, sponsoring events and providing a mass media outlet for the campaign's message. In addition, several prominent professional athletes participated in advertising campaigns that promoted helmets as part of a bike rider's "uniform," just as they are for baseball batters and football players.

Despite all the planning and research, "We did flounder for our first two years," said Bergman, "Our success came in hiring a full-time coordinator during the bicycling sea-son who had the time and skill to bring people together, to make sure material was available, and essentially to bird-dog everyone to make sure they were doing their job." Since most of the campaign was funded through in-kind contributions and money from an insurance company for the development of educational material, the cost to the Harborview Injury Prevention Center was only $15,000 for part-time staff support. "Each partner had to contribute something to the campaign," said Rivara—either money or in-kind support, "but the key was the coordinator. You can't depend on volunteerism alone. Plus, when you show people it's successful, it's easier to keep them on the bandwagon." Using rigorous observational studies to compare helmet usage rates among 5- to 15-year-olds in Seattle with peers in a control community, Portland, Oregon, the researchers documented an increase in helmet use in Seattle from 5 percent in 1987 to 16 percent one year later, rising to 40 percent in 1992. By contrast, Portland's helmet use rate increased from 1 percent in 1987 to 3 percent one year later.

The researchers at Harborview's Injury Prevention Center demonstrated other important results as well. Overall, the helmet coupons were redeemed at a 5 percent rate, considered very high by industry standards. Physician-distributed coupons, however, were redeemed at a 12 percent rate, suggesting the powerful influence of physician counseling. Group Health monitored both the injury rates and the helmet campaign's cost-effectiveness. The rate of head injury in ambulatory care and emergency department settings dropped by two-thirds, and the researchers estimated that a helmet subsidy of $5 to $10 cost less than the medical treatment and hospitalization that would have been incurred in unhelmeted children.

The campaign organizers attributed their success to the simplicity of the campaign, the narrowness of its focus (they did not attempt to persuade teens to modify their behavior, only younger children), the broad base of their partnership, the use of mass media, and the lowering of helmet costs. As for the campaign's "persuasiveness," Bergman credited two forces—the clinical authority of physicians and other health care providers, and the compelling stories of head-injured patients and their families broadcast widely on television. "That was the most powerful educational tool we had," said Bergman.

Synergy V-E   Launch "Healthy Communities" Initiatives

Healthy Communities projects—and related initiatives—are community-wide efforts that bring the public, private, and nonprofit sectors together to develop solutions to community health problems and to improve the quality of life.[59,76] These projects go beyond categorical health promotion activities by establishing a broad-based process to deal with multiple community health issues over a prolonged period of time. Reflecting community perceptions of health problems, and recognizing the importance of socioeconomic determinants of health, these initiatives address issues that go beyond the traditional purview of the health sectors, such as jobs, education, parenting, housing, and poverty.

In the Healthy Communities-type collaborations in the database, professionals and institutions in medicine and public health are partners—but often not leaders—in the endeavor. Some of these cases have gone no farther than conducting a community health assessment and writing an action plan. Others are using these data to design specific interventions and to evaluate health outcomes. The key differences between projects that focus on assessment and those that move on to interventions may be the stage of the process, the past history of collaboration among the partners, and the influence and resources that the partners bring to the enterprise. In other words, how a community health assessment is ultimately used may be related to the commitment of the partners and to the sustainability of the larger effort.

In general, the Healthy Communities-type projects in the database proceed in seven stages.

- A coalition representing key stakeholders, or those who can implement change, in the community is established.

- A community health assessment is conducted by one or more partners.

- A task force is convened to draw up an action plan based on the assessment.

- Funding is obtained for the project.

- Volunteers are recruited.

- Specific interventions in the action plan are implemented.

- The impact of the interventions is evaluated and additional strategies are introduced.

Case Illustration: Synergy V-E

CLARK COUNTY "COMMUNITY CHOICES 2010" (WA)

Moving from health assessment to action has been a stumbling block for many community groups. When the Clark County, Washington, Community Choices 2010 (CC 2010) completed its year-long health assessment in 1994 (profiled in Synergy V-A), it existed as a loose-knit partnership of community residents, business people, municipal representatives, and health and human service providers. Although CC 2010 had formed in response to a call by the area's three major health institutions—the local health department, the medical center, and the largest managed care organization—to join in a community planning process, the partnership had developed a life of its own. The members had identified a number of areas in which government, business, and neighborhood groups could make a difference in the community's health, and they were eager to oversee the implementation of their plan. With the financial support of the Southwest Washington Medical Center and Kaiser Permanente, each of whom agreed to contribute $50,000 annually to CC 2010, the Healthy Communities project joined the Vancouver Chamber of Commerce in January 1995 as an affiliate.

According to Bonnie Kostelecky, the health department's Director of Assessment and Epidemiology, the group needed to be a formal, independent entity apart from its sponsors. That way, she said, the community process wouldn't be abandoned, it wouldn't be subject to political or institutional whims, and the group could maintain its neutrality. "They also needed someone to facilitate this very complex process on an ongoing basis," said Kostelecky.

With their start-up money, CC 2010 hired an executive director and signed a contract with the Chamber of Commerce. The Chamber provided space, a part-time administrative assistant, and a media/marketing coordinator. The original community partnership evolved into a 24-member Steering Council, and the six health priority areas they had identified turned into work groups with subcommittees and strategic work plans. According to CC 2010 director Lynne Conner, she now coordinates the work of over 350 volunteers and a number of funded projects in a "strategic planning and response model" in which community members select a particular problem, gather and analyze data, and then promote a collaborative solution.[42]

As part of the initial health assessment, the group had focused on analyzing the "upstream" causes that resulted in poor health. Recognizing that many of the determinants of health involve social or economic forces, CC 2010 focused on community efforts to enhance "economic opportunity, education, youth and family, and positive community norms." Strategies implemented by the group include mentoring programs for young men and teenage boys using clergy and police officers, anti-violence campaigns disseminated in the workplace, and efforts to promote affordable housing, among others. Only two of the priorities were explicitly directed at health and human services—"health and safety," which spurred strategies aimed at teen smoking and employment smoking policies, and "access to services," which has focused on reducing barriers to services and creating "workfare" jobs in anticipation of welfare reform changes.

Given its assessment function, and the fact that many residents and professionals in the county consider CC 2010 the central data clearinghouse, the group sometimes resembles a regional planning council. At other times, the group serves as the broadest of community advocacy groups. The group holds public forums, and publishes community report cards and assessment reports that are developed and produced through the work of other partners at the table, including the health department's Division of Assessment and Epidemiology. Government, private agencies, and businesses contribute to the collection of this information and use it extensively for program planning. When the health department was thinking of opening a weekend WIC clinic, it turned to CC 2010 for advice on how the clinic could relate to other community efforts. One local business solicited CC 2010's help in planning its employee wellness program.

"All the incorporated cities in the county use our assessments for deciding how to allocate funds," said Conner, "and every city has adopted the issues of affordable housing and family wage jobs as their priorities." CC 2010 has made recommendations to the city and county commissioners in the arenas of education, employment, and juvenile justice, and has participated as a coordinating council for a number of activities, particularly those addressing high school dropout rates, youth violence, domestic abuse, and drug and alcohol education. The group also identified cardiovascular disease as a major health problem. "Since we found out we were the county with the highest smoking rate in the state," said Conner, "we're planning a tobacco summit in the spring."

Although community "health" is the group's focus, medical and public health professionals constitute only one piece of CC 2010's broad-based approach. The group's ambitious goals are to "create and sustain a healthy community" through the tools of assessment and advocacy, using the levers of voluntary action and civic responsibility rather than government regulation. "We identify a problem," said Conner, "we convene the community around a strategy, and then we continue to measure the problem—and publicize the strategy—to see if things are getting better or worse."

Synergy VI

Shaping the Future Direction of the Health System by Collaborating Around Policy, Training, and Research

All of the collaborations described in the preceding synergies center around some aspect of medical or public health practice. Collaboration also can provide a means for shaping the practice environment. The cases in the database that take this approach do so by influencing health system policy, by educating the future generation of health professionals, or by expanding the knowledge base that supports health professionals' work. Although these types of collaborations are quite distinct (and will be discussed separately below), they all are based on combinations of two or more of the following skills and resources:

- *influence with peers, policymakers, and the public*
- *practical experience*
- *scientific expertise*
- *pedagogic skills*

Synergy VI-A Influence Health System Policy

Although the medical and public health sectors have differed on health system policy issues in the past—especially those related to patient care—areas of common ground are beginning to emerge as market forces take on a greater role in the American health system. In the current environment, both health sectors share concerns about the direction in which the health system is evolving, particularly in relation to access to care for the un- and underinsured, the impact of economic pressures on the quality of care, and the assurance of important public goods, such as payment for uncompensated care, the delivery of essential population-based public health services, health professions education and training, and health-related research.

At the same time as their agendas are coming closer together on these issues, both health sectors are concerned about their ability to have an impact on policy decisions—at organizational as well as governmental levels. Physicians, especially those in subspecialties, are experiencing diminishing power and income. Managed care organizations and insurance companies are becoming more involved in clinical decisions, fueling a backlash that has led to efforts to legislate medical care. Also, as managed care organizations take over some of the clinical aspects of public health—and governments are under pressure to downsize and privatize programs—public health agencies are under fire to justify the need for what they do.

In this context, it is not surprising that health system policy is a focus of 63 cases in the database. While most of these collaborations address governmental policy issues, particularly at the state level, some relate to organizational policy as well (for example, the establishment of the AMA Section Council on Preventive Medicine, which has influenced AMA policy positions). Depending on the case, the two health sectors work together on one or more of the following steps of the policy process:

- identifying and framing the policy issue

- gathering and analyzing data to inform decision-making

- developing and evaluating policy options

- advocating preferred options to important constituents and decision-makers

- implementing the adopted policy

Based on the case reports, there are a number of benefits in collaborating around these steps of the policy process. Most important, perhaps, collaboration is a way for the two health sectors to identify areas of common concern and to harness sufficient power and skills to do something about them. By combining their authority and influence around health systems issues, the medical and public health sectors not only can be more influential than either can be alone, they also can deflect perceptions of self-interest. Because cross-sectoral collaboration brings science and practical experience to bear on the policy-making process, it also provides a mechanism for promoting the development of sounder and more feasible policies. Finally, working together on the development of policies can facilitate their subsequent implementation, both by promoting the endorsement of health professionals and organizations in each sector and by assuring that proposals actually will work in the real world.

A range of partners is involved in these types of collaborations. Governmental public health agencies play key roles through their convening power, analytic expertise, regulatory authority, and ability to represent the "public good." Professional associations also are prominent. They lend legitimacy to the endeavor; use their authority to influence peers, the general public and policymakers; provide public relations support; and facilitate the involvement of practitioners in the field. Individual health professionals participate through their influence with patients and their practical medical and public health experience. Academic institutions enhance the policymaking process by contributing scientific and analytic expertise.

Overall, the cases in the database address five types of health system policy issues:

- access to care for the un- and underinsured

- provider payment and insurance benefits

- the quality of medical care

- the regional organization of health care delivery

- the organization and financing of public health programs

Not surprisingly, quite a few of these collaborations focus on access to care for the un- and underinsured. Some of the cases provide policy support for the collaborations described in Synergy II, primarily through legislative initiatives that give medical practitioners immunity from liability when they provide indigent care. Others leverage public funds to support safety-net facilities, through tobacco taxes or city tax levies, for example. Another approach is to provide insurance coverage to the un- or underinsured—either directly, through the establishment of public or private insurance plans, or indirectly, through tax incentives for employers who expand insurance coverage.

The two health sectors also work together to influence provider payment policies and insurance benefits. One case, for example, rationalized Medicaid payment for pediatric office visits, reducing program outlays for expensive emergency room use. In another case, described under Synergy IV, cost-effectiveness analysis influenced the 1993 federal decision to cover influenza vaccinations as a Medicare benefit. Collaborative efforts also have convinced a number of states to use the U.S. Preventive Services Task Force guidelines[180] as a basis for Medicaid benefits.

In cases concerned with the quality of medical care, the two health sectors collaborate around quality assurance standards (for mammography screening or diabetes care, for instance), performance measures for managed care organizations, and requirements for managed care organizations to participate in certain public health activities. The focus here is not only on fostering accountability for services important to individual and community health, but also on assuring that the use of quality assessment tools will not penalize good practitioners. In cases in which health departments are involved in oversight or quality reviews of the medical sector, the involvement of respected medical reviewers with practice experience makes the process more helpful and palatable.

Policy collaborations concerning the regional organization of health care delivery have a long history, dating to the regionalization of perinatal care in the 1960s and, subsequently, to the regionalization of trauma services. With the emergence of managed care, a number of health departments are revisiting these issues, involving the medical sector in decisions about the organization and financing of these systems as well as the designation process for regional centers.

In policy collaborations in the database that focus on the organization and financing of public health, the medical sector usually advises federal or state health agencies about particular public health programs (such as maternal and child health, adolescent health, health promotion and disease prevention, environmental health, or mental health). In some of these cases, advisory bodies are asked to develop recommendations on programmatic and fiscal matters and to elicit public comment on these recommendations. In others, the collaborations are oriented toward enhancing physician involvement in public health programs, both by educating mainstream practitioners about programs and by providing them with support services (as described in Synergy I).

Collaborations around the organization and financing of public health take other forms as well. In some cases, the two health sectors collaborate on policies that reorganize state and local health departments, or that transfer or privatize certain public health functions. In others, statutory connections are established between health departments and medical associations, frequently via the board of health.

Case Illustration: Synergy VI-A

STATE OF FLORIDA DEPARTMENT OF HEALTH (FL)

In 1975, Florida undertook an experiment in public administration on a grand scale. The state legislature reorganized the public health and welfare systems into a single "super-agency," the Department of Health and Rehabilitative Services (HRS). Under the premise that poor and needy individuals often require a combination of health and social services, the state planned to coordinate all its programs through a single agency. The policy had implications at all levels. Since the agency was built around a "case management model,"[84] administrative "generalists" drawn mostly from the social service ranks replaced specialized health professionals at managerial, regional, and executive levels. The state health officer—the highest ranking public physician—no longer held a cabinet-rank or had any formal direct involvement with county health officials, and instead reported to an assistant secretary of planning.

A number of public health professionals in the health department were frustrated with the change, and many rebelled against the integrated structure or left the department. Equally unhappy was the Florida Medical Association (FMA), which had a longstanding relationship with the public health department and was concerned about the devalued role of health professionals. "What was absent," said E. Russell Jackson, Jr., FMA's executive coordinator, "was not only physician influence but public health influence as well." Jackson knew the territory. He had served as a senior health department official in the 1970s and 1980s; his father also had served the health department as a senior administrator in the 1940s and 1950s.

"We were continually getting dragged down in social service and child-welfare issues," said deputy state health officer Richard Hunter, Ph.D., who joined the department in 1989.

"People didn't understand the word 'Health' in our name. We were having problems getting funding for our budget—especially prevention programs—in an overall budget that included welfare and food stamps. Individuals and families superseded us, and community prevention just kept getting pushed down. We couldn't get our labs funded. Public health was being identified as indigent care only."

During the 1990s, the state moved a series of programs away from the public health component of HRS, including environmental and food service programs, transferring them to other state departments such as Agriculture, Environmental Protection, and Business Regulation. According to Marc Yacht, M.D., a county health officer and former president of the Florida Public Health Association, at this point, "Health professionals envisioned the complete assimilation of public health as an arm of social services." Even as the public health functions were being lost, the agency grew to 40,000 employees, the largest state governmental entity in the country.

In 1995 and 1996, the medical association spearheaded a coalition led by Alvin Smith, M.D., FMA president, that included the state public health association, the state nursing association, and the state environmental health association in a coordinated lobbying effort to reorganize the HRS. The partners drafted a joint resolution calling for a single health agency distinct from social services. Their efforts were reinforced by a series of widely publicized child-welfare "blunders" in which children either were not protected in time or removed too hastily from their parent's care. The state legislature, according to Jackson, was disenchanted with the "super-agency" and receptive to the coalition's proposal to split out public health.

As it happened, the FMA presented the strongest "public health" voice in the state, according to most observers. The public health professionals within the department were restricted in lobbying against their own parent agency, so the FMA became the coalition's principal standard bearer. The FMA lobbyists, who had considerable influence with state legislators, pressed the case. Several political forces also made it an opportune time for reorganizing the department. The Democrats held a marginal majority in the state house of representatives, and the Republican-controlled Senate was keenly sensitive to "doing something for the doctors," according to a key legislative staff member. Governor Lawton Chiles had been stumping for several years for a "reengineered government" that would be smaller in size and more efficient, so he was at least willing to entertain the idea of splitting up the HRS. At the end of the legislative session, the two houses unanimously passed the bill reorganizing the health department and welfare agencies, and the governor signed it into law.

There were several immediate results of the change: the newly created cabinet position of Secretary of Health was filled by a physician; additional money was made available to the new Department of Health for staffing and for prevention programs; and the county health units again were named "county health departments," with a clear line to the state administrators. There were also political compromises. The Agency for Health Care Administration, which governs a number of programs affecting physicians, including Medicaid, practice guidelines, and disciplinary actions, was not folded into the new health department as the coalition had proposed, nor were mental health services. Whether the reborn state health department emerges as an administrative success story remains to be seen. Still, "this has been a real shot in the arm for public health workers," said Bob Harvey, director of the Florida Public Health Association. "We're in the process now of trying to rebuild the county health departments, and we're getting back to the point where health professionals are governing health professionals." As far as the health department's Hunter is concerned, the support of the state medical association was the deciding factor: "The FMA was clearly the leader. This just wouldn't have happened without them."

Synergy VI-B

Engage in Cross-Sectoral Education and Training

Health professionals, particularly those in training, are beginning to recognize the new career niches that are developing in the health system, as well as the new skills and relationships that can help them succeed in the changing environment. Appreciating the growing importance of analytic, management, and financial skills to clinical practice (as described in Synergy III), medical professionals are seeking to become more proficient in these areas themselves or to develop relationships with experts in the public health and business sectors. A basic understanding of epidemiology, risk assessment, cost-effectiveness analysis, and performance measurement is valuable here, as are specific clinical applications of these methodologies, such as evidence-based medicine, outcomes research, practice guideline development, and quality assessment. Economic and performance pressures also are making certain individual-level services—such as wraparound, outreach, and social services—and population-based strategies considerably more relevant to clinical practice (as described in Synergies I through V). Consequently, medical professionals benefit from exposure to public health practice in the community, particularly to models that link the activities of the public health sector to mainstream clinical care.

Looking at the current environment from the point of view of public health professionals, many of the same points apply. Training in clinical applications of public health methodologies is becoming increasingly valuable as managed care organizations, integrated systems, and large group practices seek to hire or contract with professionals who have such expertise (Synergy III). Management and business skills are needed to restructure not only governmental health agencies, but also voluntary public health organizations. Familiarity with mainstream medical practice—and proficiency in developing partnerships with the medical sector and other groups in the community—is becoming a critical component of public health practice (Synergies I through V). In this context, exposure to effective collaborative models is as important to public health professionals as it is to medical professionals. Moreover, both sectors can benefit from training in the interpersonal and management skills that are integral to collaboration.

While students, residents, and faculty in health professions institutions participate in many collaborations in the database (in all six synergies, in fact), only a portion of these cases bring the two health sectors together for the explicit purpose of improving education and training. Nonetheless, almost 100 collaborations fall into this category, involving a variety of approaches that can be used to broaden the perspective of

- students in degree-granting programs;
- residents and fellows in postgraduate training programs;
- professionals in active practice.

Some of these cases are associated with national initiatives, such as the Health of the Public Program, Community-Campus Partnerships for Health, and Interdisciplinary Congresses held by the Association of Academic Health Centers. It is important to point out, however, that educational initiatives focusing on one sector alone (such as those establishing a closer relationship between schools of public health and public health practice sites) are *not* included in the database. All cases were required to involve interactions between medicine *and* public health.

The vast majority of database cases targeted at degree programs focus on changing the educational experience of medical students. The extent of influence of these programs ranges from marginal to substantial. Some schools offer students opportunities to participate in extramural community service volunteer opportunities, for example, or establish elective courses and rotations to which only a small proportion of students are exposed. Others, by contrast, incorporate a broad perspective in the school's mission or structure, instituting courses, rotations, or practica that are required of all students.

Four models of collaboration are used in these cases:

- intra-institutional curriculum changes
- dual-degree programs
- connections between schools or programs in the two sectors
- initiatives involving academia, medical and public health practice sites, and the broader community

In the first model, which could be termed "adopt a perspective," a medical school incorporates public health skills or perspectives in its curriculum without interacting with schools or programs in public health or with public health practice sites. The medical school faculty involved in these initiatives, however, usually have formal training in public health. The second model is the dual-degree program, commonly giving students either an M.D./M.P.H. or an R.N./M.P.H. degree. This model may or may not involve much interaction between the schools or programs in different sectors.

Collaboration is more pronounced in the third model, which connects faculty and students in different schools and departments. In these cases, faculty have dual appointments in schools in both sectors, for example, in a school of medicine or nursing and a school of public health, and they teach courses in each school—either alone or together. In one example, an interdisciplinary course entitled "Community Voices: Partners in Health" brings together faculty and students from schools of medicine, public health, social work, and pharmacy. This type of collaboration also leads to the development of cross-sectoral centers for research and training in areas such as nutrition, injury control, infectious diseases, and cancer.

The fourth model establishes connections not only between the two health sectors' schools and departments, but also between academia, medical and public health practice, and the broader community. When dual appointments occur in this model, the health professional often serves as a faculty member at a school of medicine and as an official in a local health department. Cross-sectoral links between academia and practice also are spurred by requirements that faculty members devote a proportion of their time to community projects, or that students rotate through health departments, community health centers, or COPC practice sites.

In some of these cases, students from a range of schools, such as medicine, public health, nursing, and allied health, work together in interdisciplinary teams, sometimes for prolonged periods of time. These teams rotate through settings that coordinate individual-level services (as described in Synergy I). They also participate in projects to assess and address community health problems (as described in Synergies IV and V). By working in teams, students see first-hand what professionals in the other health sector can offer, and how that expertise is relevant to their own work. This experience helps to promote respect and understanding among professionals in different health sectors; it also provides the students involved with valuable contacts for the future.

Rather than focusing on students in training, some cases use collaborative approaches to broaden the perspective of health professionals in the field. In a sense, all of the cases in the database fall into this category since professionals in both health sectors gain valuable on-the-job experience when they participate in any of the collaborations that have been described. The training objective is more explicit, however, in collaborations that provide medical professionals with population-based information (as discussed in Synergy III), and in collaborative conferences focusing on the interaction between medicine and public health. At a formal level, a number of academic institutions are offering M.P.H. programs geared to medical professionals who are actively in practice. In addition, some managed care organizations are establishing "managed care colleges," which provide their medical professionals with practical population-based skills as well as interdisciplinary team experiences.[190]

Case Illustration: Synergy VI-B

NORTHEAST OHIO UNIVERSITIES COLLEGE OF MEDICINE (OH)

In September 1975, the dean and the provost of the Northeast Ohio Universities College of Medicine (NEOUCOM) enrolled the first class of their newly established medical school. It was a bit of a gamble, considering they had no medical school faculty, no buildings, and no campus. They did have a vision of a "community-based medical school," and they had a bit of breathing room. The medical school, a consortium run by Kent State University, Youngstown State University, and the University of Akron, was designed as a six-year B.S./M.D. curriculum in which students spend their first two years in an accelerated premedical curriculum and the subsequent four years learning the basic medical and clinic sciences. The administrators of this fledgling medical school figured they had until 1977 to fully assemble all the medical pieces.

One of the very first faculty members recruited in 1975 was C. William Keck, M.D., M.P.H., whose charge was to develop a broader "community orientation" than just working with community hospitals. At the time, Keck—an alumnus of the Case Western Reserve University School of Medicine, the Harvard School of Public Health, and the Peace Corps—was on the medical school faculty at the University of Kentucky, teaching in the Department of Community Medicine. He also was the health officer for a district health department he had consolidated from six local county health departments.

The NEOUCOM dean was joined in his recruitment effort by the Akron Board of Health. Together, they offered Keck a joint appointment as the Akron health director and as a medical school faculty member. The medical school contributed an additional 20 percent to the salary to make the position more financially attractive. The unique organization of the school—with three academic divisions: Basic Medical Sciences, Clinical Sciences, and Community Health Sciences—also was a draw. Keck, who directs the Community Health Sciences Division and reports directly to the dean, said, "That Division gave us some prominence in the school. We weren't going to be buried in the structure."

Keck began the students' "community" education in the summer of 1976 by developing a required eight-week practicum, a course still taught today between freshman and sophomore years. Students work in small teams, guided by a community preceptor from a local agency and a medical school methodologic faculty member. Each team's objective is to develop problem-solving skills by analyzing a community problem, gathering relevant data, and developing a program to address the problem. After a few years Keck added a new twist: the teams competed for block grant money in a mock legislative hearing presided over by actual state legislators. "People remember this practicum," said Keck, "because it's often the first time they've had to problem-solve, particularly in front of a legislator." Keck also wanted to impress the relevance of a community orientation and the value of community teachers on the young medical students—most of whom were only 18 or 19 years old—"before they got too old and cynical."

The other major community piece instituted by Keck is a required community medicine clerkship in the medical students' senior year. As with the practicum, the clerkship links small teams of students with a community preceptor and methodologic faculty member. Unlike the practicum, where students always start at square one, senior clerkship students in this real situation begin where previous groups have left off. The projects may be organized around community health campaigns, or around the coordination of individual services. One recent student team worked with the fire department to analyze residential fire deaths, and then developed a targeted campaign using epidemiologic techniques to identify high-risk neighborhoods. The next team of students developed a fire prevention "game" for children that is now disseminated throughout the schools. Another student team worked with clients of a homeless shelter to help them navigate a mandatory Medicaid managed care program by learning how to select the most appropriate managed care organization for them.

Keck maintains that there are a number of valuable lessons from these community experiences that medical students can apply to later practice: the relevance of community resources; the value of working with public health agencies; a better understanding of how clinicians can influence individual behavior, particularly in concert with community-based strategies; and a notion of how the population sciences of epidemiology and biostatistics can be used to evaluate and enhance clinical practice. Taken together, the community courses "make teachers of community-based health professionals, firefighters, judges, nurses, health department directors, educators, and physicians," noted Keck. "And it links them directly with our methodologic faculty in teaching teams that are proving to be very powerful." Faculty are required to devote one-third of their time to community service, which is then factored into promotion and tenure decisions.

The community links have benefitted the medical school and health department as well. Two other medical school faculty, in addition to Keck, split their time between the university and the health department, one serving as the disease control officer and the other providing medical direction for the breast and cervical cancer screening programs. As for the medical school, "The Division of Community Health Sciences has built a broader constituency for the medical school in the community," added Keck. Not only has the medical school fulfilled the community promise made by its new dean to the state legislature almost 25 years ago, suggested Keck, it also has assured the political support of the community should it ever need it.

Synergy VI-C   Conduct Cross-Sectoral Research

Research plays an important role in many of the collaborations in the database, both in establishing the need for joint projects, and in contributing to their design and evaluation. This role is usually supportive, however, and the research often is conducted by investigators in only one of the health sectors. In 31 cases, by contrast, cross-sectoral research is the focus of the collaboration; the explicit purpose of bringing medical and public health professionals together is to strengthen the research enterprise.

Most of the cases that take this approach do so by establishing a cross-sectoral research center. While some of these centers bring together diverse types of professionals within a single school, others connect various schools within an academic health center, or connect academic institutions with health departments and other government agencies. The scope of these research centers varies substantially, ranging from a particular health problem, like cancer or violence, to a specific policy domain, as in New York's Center for the Study of Issues in Public Mental Health (described in the case illustration below), to a comprehensive agenda, as in a Center for Community Health Improvement.

Case reports reveal significant benefits from engaging in cross-sectoral investigation. At the earliest stage of the research process, the involvement of investigators with backgrounds in diverse disciplines can be useful in identifying important questions. Working together, the members of a cross-sectoral team can see a problem from a "big picture" perspective, taking into account health determinants ranging from molecular mechanisms to environmental and behavioral factors, and considering the full spectrum of individual and population-based interventions. This type of perspective is illustrated by a nutrition center that concentrates not only on biological mechanisms, but also on the epidemiologic relationship between diet and disease, the elucidation of strategies to modify diets in individuals and populations, and the development of practice-based skills for delivering nutrition information to the community and to individuals. To the extent that partners beyond the academic community are involved in these centers, research questions can be identified that are relevant to practitioners in both health sectors and to people working in other sectors in the community. An example along this line is a center established to identify the costs and risk factors associated with violence in a particular area.

A cross-sectoral approach also can be valuable in designing, implementing, and disseminating research findings. Investigators with expertise in medicine and public health often have complementary methodologic skills, which can strengthen the team's capacity to investigate complex problems. Moreover, with a broad range of professional and organizational connections, a cross-sectoral team is in a good position to encourage the participation of subjects and health professionals in its research, and to know about and obtain access to relevant data already being collected in the public and private sectors. The power of a number of centers stems, in part, from their ability to combine data obtained through the medical sector with data collected by an array of government agencies. After the investigation is completed, strong connections can facilitate broader dissemination and action on research findings (through the types of mechanisms described in previous synergies). As part of its work, one center even studies the effectiveness of different methods of dissemination.

Important financial benefits of cross-sectoral centers also are documented in some cases. Academic institutions report that these centers are more competitive in obtaining grant funding than individual departments working alone, that the productivity of investigators working in the centers is higher, and that establishing the centers reduces expensive duplication of resources. For health departments involved in these activities, collaboration provides valuable support in measuring the health status of residents, in identifying effective strategies for improving community health, and in performing evaluations of public health interventions.

Case Illustration: Synergy VI-C

THE CENTER FOR THE STUDY OF ISSUES IN PUBLIC MENTAL HEALTH (NY)

Finding the most appropriate housing for the thousands of mentally ill, homeless residents of New York City is an incredibly difficult challenge. All too often, despite the best intentions of case workers and policymakers, a mentally ill person leaves his or her residence to return to the streets. Many of these individuals carry the dual diagnosis of mental illness and drug addiction. When they become homeless, medication compliance and drug-treatment programs often are abandoned along with their housing.

In 1996, New York's Center for the Study of Issues in Public Mental Health was approached by the Deputy Commissioner of Health and Mental Health Services for New York City's Human Resources Administration and the executive director of a not-for-profit housing agency. "They had two separate datasets from a program to develop community beds for the homeless mentally ill," said Carole Siegel, Ph.D., the Center's director and a biostatistician. "They had data on who gets into the beds, and separate data on the housing. They wanted us to help them understand which populations were being triaged into this housing, and whether the triaging was successful."

As a research partner, the Center provided the city commissioner and the housing director with a unique resource. The four-year-old "center without walls" is a cross-sectoral research enterprise that supports mental health policy decisions by using New York State and its counties as its laboratories. The Center draws researchers statewide from the clinical and basic sciences, such as medicine, pharmacology, nursing, and bio-chemistry, and the public health and social sciences, including biostatistics, epidemiology, ethnography, economics, psychology, sociology, and health law. Formally, the Center links the Nathan Kline Institute, a state-funded psychiatric research facility affiliated with New York University, with the New York State Office of Mental Health, and with the Rocke-feller College of Public Affairs and Policy at the State University of New York at Albany. In return for addressing issues relevant to policy and program needs, the researchers are given access to comprehensive datasets previously beyond their reach.

In this case, the city commissioner, himself a psychiatrist, and the housing director, a social worker, needed help in understanding how an individual's environment—specifically, the specialized housing—affected his or her psychological stability and consequently the ability to stay in a safe, supportive setting. The Center assigned a statistician and a public policy analyst to work on the project. The team examined multiple levels of data, accounting for the effects of housing policies, housing conditions, and each individual's unique characteristics. Working with the commissioner and the housing agency director, the team merged the disparate datasets, and focused on the factors that led to an individual staying or leaving housing.

"I think the commissioner and the director of the community organization learned a few things about the housing they didn't know," offered Siegel. Among the team's findings was the effect of certain housing policies—such as zero drug tolerance—in propelling mentally ill residents who relapse back onto the streets rather than addressing their substance abuse problem. The researchers also pointed out that a large number of people who were placed in these beds directly from hospitals may not have been given appropriate discharge planning, and, as a result, often reverted to unstable housing conditions or homelessness. Furthermore, even in congregate housing with very structured environments, too little attention may have been paid to medication compliance.[106] Taken together, the findings prompted the commissioner to suggest a number of programmatic changes and to create new housing options.

The Center's approach to the city's housing problem illustrates its multidisciplinary perspective and capacity. As one of only five such centers funded by the National Institutes of Mental Health (NIMH) to focus on adult mental illness, the Center's mission is to "close the gap between research, policy, and services," said Dixianne Penney, Dr.P.H., the Center's assistant director. "Before the Center existed," said Siegel, "we would read the literature and the journals to generate research studies. No one was saying, 'This is very important, perhaps we could develop a program around it.' Now we're conceptualizing problems that people are interested in. Having this close connection to policy allows our portfolio to be relevant and not generated from an academic ivory tower."

Currently, with NIMH's funding of $3.5 million over five years, the Center has almost 30 inter-institutional research projects underway. One project is examining the decision processes used by physicians in the treatment and disposition of mentally ill patients who show up at psychiatric emergency rooms. Bruce Way, Ph.D., and his research team discovered very little agreement among psychiatrists at four hospitals on a number of important dimensions. With the assistance and support of one of the emergency department directors, the researchers are developing practice guidelines for psychiatric emergency clinicians and general emergency physicians. This "decision model" has been designed as a computer program, and currently is being pilot-tested in a psychiatric emergency room.

The Center's researchers also have become increasingly involved in studies examining managed care and mental health, including a project to evaluate a managed care plan for New York State Medicaid recipients discharged from state psychiatric centers, and the development of rate-setting methodologies to account for the "risk" of mental illness among various populations. "What's exciting about the Center," said Siegel, "is that it comingles researchers, policymakers and planners with the opportunity of working with the primary office of mental health in the state. We're not inventing projects—as real-world problems, they're calling out to be researched."

Structural Foundations of Medicine and Public Health Collaborations

The preceding sections described various ways that professionals and institutions in medicine and public health can combine their resources and skills, and the synergies that can be achieved by doing so. Carrying out these collaborations, however, requires structural arrangements that allow partners from the two health sectors—as well as from the broader community—to work together in a common enterprise. While some of the cases in the database rely on friendships or informal meetings to achieve this objective, formal structures, which can institutionalize collaborative relationships, more commonly are employed.

Below, we discuss five types of structural foundations that are used in the collaborations in the database:

- coalitions

- contractual agreements

- administration/management systems

- advisory bodies

- intra-organizational platforms

The first three structures support the coordination of activities carried out by independent professionals or organizations in different sectors. The fourth, advisory bodies, provides an organization in one sector with input from other sectors. The last structure allows a single organization to expand its perspective by bringing in professionals with the skills and expertise of another sector.

These structural arrangements are not the only types observed in the database of cases. Others, however, occur too rarely to be analyzed adequately. A small proportion of cases, for example, incorporate features of a joint venture, in that a new legal entity is established in which some or all of the partners share profits, losses, or control. Very rarely in the cases we have collected, collaborations use some form of merger to achieve their goals. When this occurs, the merger tends to be partial: one partner takes over ownership and control of only a portion of the activities of another partner, such as home health services.

Coalitions bring representatives of autonomous organizations together to address a specific problem or need that is important to all partners but that cannot be addressed through the influence, skills, and resources of any one partner alone. Historically, coalitions have been used frequently in advocacy and community-wide health campaigns. It is not surprising, then, that coalitions are common in cases that bring different sectors together to conduct community health assessments and health education campaigns (Synergies V-A and V-B), to advocate health protective laws and regulations (Synergy V-C), to engage in community-wide efforts to achieve health objectives (Synergies IV-C, V-D, and V-E), to implement "screen and treat" strategies (Synergy III-B), and to influence key stakeholders and decision-makers on health system policy issues (Synergy VI-A). The suitability of coalitions for the activities described in these synergies relates to three factors.

- All of the collaborations involved benefit from the participation of a broad range of community partners.

- All tolerate limited and variable commitment from partners.

- None require close coordination of partner activities (in other words, the success of the collaborative enterprise is not very dependent on what any one partner does).

Coalitions are good platforms for bringing together a broad range of partners and perspectives because they provide a neutral meeting ground for potentially competitive member organizations, and they do not require partners to sacrifice much autonomy or control. The authority, responsibility, and capacity to take action lies within the coalition itself rather than in any one partner or external body. Consequently, the members of a coalition collectively shape all aspects of the collaborative enterprise—including the process for group decision-making and the mechanism for mediating problems or concerns among partners—and they do not need to be concerned about an external system being imposed on them. The risk to any organization participating in a coalition is usually small: there are no binding contracts; large investments rarely are involved; and few changes are required in partners' day-to-day activities.

The power of a coalition derives from the influence of the group as a whole and from its capacity to carry out multipronged strategies. Clearly, coalitions have more influence if they represent a spectrum of important constituencies. Toward that end, coalitions in the database pay attention not only to the number and breadth of their member organizations, but also to the extent to which the individuals representing those organizations can make resource and policy commitments. It is also important to consider the particular skills and expertise of each partner. The willingness of partners to participate in a coalition often hinges on how much they are asked to do. Consequently, coalition campaigns are more likely to be successful if partners are chosen whose contributions can complement and reinforce each other, and if the coalition structure can provide the necessary administrative support to transform these isolated activities into a coherent strategy.

A key attribute of coalitions is that they do not require equal or consistent involvement on the part of all partners: each member organization can participate to a degree (and for a duration of time) consistent with its own level of interest. This is advantageous in that a coalition can benefit from the limited contributions of partners who are unable or unwilling to give the enterprise a large commitment. It also means, however, that structures other than (or in addition to) coalitions should be considered when the activities of different partners in a collaboration are complex or closely interdependent. Indeed, some coalitions in the database—for example, the cases used to illustrate Synergies III-B, IV-C, V-D, and V-E—created administrative/management systems when the need became apparent.

Case illustrations involving coalitions:

Synergy III-A	Georgia HIV/AIDS Guides (GA)
Synergy III-B	Monroe County "Women's Health Partnership" (NY)
Synergy IV-C	Monroe County "McFlu" Campaign (NY)
Synergy V-A & V-E	Clark County "Community Choices 2010" (WA)
Synergy V-B	Hawaii "HealthScope" TV Series (HI)
Synergy V-D	Seattle Bike Helmet Campaign (WA)
Synergy V-IA	State of Florida Department of Health (FL)

CONTRACTUAL AGREEMENTS

A contract is a binding agreement that commits one party to carry out a function or to provide a service for another party. Contracts explicitly delineate each party's roles and responsibilities in the arrangement, as well as any exchange of funds or resources that may occur. In many situations, contractual agreements are formalized in legal documents. They also can take the form of memoranda of understanding or verbal agreements.

In the database of cases, contractual agreements are particularly common in Synergies I and II—collaborations in which partners provide a range of services to individuals, including the un- and underinsured. The success of these collaborations often depends on certain interactions between partners. Consequently, contracts are used to clarify partners' roles in these critical interactions and to assure that they are carried out.

In most cases, contractual agreements specify an exchange of resources, such as money for services, space for services, or services for services. Examples include collaborations in which a health department hires medical practitioners to work in its clinic; a hospital houses the home-visiting staff of a local health department in exchange for home visits for its patients; or medical practitioners willing to care for Medicaid patients in their offices receive free support services from public health nurses. Contracts also are used to assign (or waive) liability for acts undertaken as part of the collaboration. Protection from malpractice liability through such means is a key component of collaborations that engage medical practitioners in indigent care.

Contracts are common in collaborations in which health professionals play multiple roles, as in the joint appointments described in the case illustrations for Synergies I-C and VI-B. These agreements also are common in collaborations that involve a change in roles of organizations in the two health sectors. When the provision of a certain service, such as home health services, moves from one sector to another, contractual agreements assure continued employment and benefits for qualified individuals. Contracts also are valuable when health departments move from providing services directly to assuring the delivery of services. Through contractual agreements, a health department can assign a particular activity to a partner better able to carry it out, yet still maintain responsibility and oversight authority for the contractee's activities.

Case illustrations involving contractual agreements:

Synergy I-A	South Carolina "Partnerships for Children" (SC)
Synergy I-C	East St. Louis Health Coalition (IL)
Synergy II-D	Albany County "Healthy Partnerships" (NY)
Synergy IV-A	New Jersey Information Systems (NJ)
Synergy VI-B	Northeast Ohio Universities College of Medicine (OH)

ADMINISTRATIVE/ MANAGEMENT SYSTEMS

Administrative/management systems are structures that closely coordinate the activities and resources of the partners in a collaboration. While all collaborations require some degree of administrative support (often considerably more than the partners initially anticipate), more elaborate management structures are needed in collaborations that require a significant amount of central organization or control. In the cases in the database, these structures are common in collaborations in which numerous partners provide highly interdependent services, or in which partners pool certain resources to improve the cost-effectiveness of their combined activities.

Administrative/management systems run some or all aspects of a collaborative enterprise. Depending on the work involved, the "system" may be a full-time staff person or an office or division within a new or existing entity. In some of the cases in the database, one of the partners in the collaboration takes responsibility for carrying out this support function. In others, the partners create a new structure explicitly for this purpose. Regardless of the approach, the administrative/management system reports to the partners as a whole, although it usually is delegated responsibility for day-to-day operational decision-making.

The establishment of an administrative/management system frees most or all partners from the burdens of running the collaboration—although that benefit comes with the loss of a certain amount of control. When a new office, division, or center is established for this purpose, the administrative/management system exists beyond the hierarchy and bureaucratic structure of any partner organization. One advantage of this approach is that none of the partners needs to modify an internal administrative structure to participate in the collaboration. More important, a separate "management control center" is likely to have greater flexibility than an office constrained by the limitations of a partner organization, and is more likely to be perceived as being neutral by all of the partners involved.

The focus and scope of administrative/management systems in the database are quite diverse, reflecting the nature of the collaborative enterprises themselves. Some "one-stop centers" (Synergy I-B), for example, establish coordination offices to help clients navigate the center, to centralize outreach services of partner agencies, and to identify and address problems, often through new collaborative activities. Integrated systems (Synergy I-C) sometimes institute "matrix management" strategies to make functional connections among partner organizations and to maximize their resources. These platforms support sharing of personnel, co-location of services, common contracting for services, centralized purchasing, or system-wide services and information systems. By administering the integrated system as a whole, the partners in these types of collaborations reduce duplication of services, improve utilization of needed services, and achieve economies of scale. In Synergy II, administration/management systems are particularly prominent in cases that involve the establishment of referral networks to provide care for the uninsured (Model II-B). Critical support functions carried out by network offices include patient eligibility and screening, referral of patients to participating practitioners, management of voucher systems, documentation of uncompensated care, and arrangements for ancillary services, medications, and supplies.

As mentioned earlier, coalitions sometimes find it necessary to establish formal administrative structures, primarily because their activities become too complex or longstanding to run without such support. In the Monroe County "Women's Health Partnership" (Synergy III-B case illustration), for example, the coalition created and funded the position of project director to manage a partnership that encompassed 41 organizations, interacted with 110 community physicians, and maintained a database of clients, activities, and outcomes. In this case, administrative support was provided by a project director rather than by one of the partners in the coalition for two reasons: to overcome bureaucratic limitations of the health department, and to avoid escalating tensions among member advocacy groups. In Clark County's "Community Choices

2010" (Synergy V-E case illustration), the decision to make the coalition an affiliate office of the Chamber of Commerce was spurred by a desire to institutionalize an ongoing process and to keep the endeavor neutral of government and private special interests.

In some cases in the database (Synergies V and VI), collaborations involve the establishment of new centers, which manage the interactions of professionals in different government agencies, or in different academic schools and academic departments. In these cases, the academic health center or the state government can be viewed as a "meta" support system for the collaboration, providing the platform that makes it possible for the partners in the enterprise to work together.

Case illustrations involving administrative/management systems:	
Synergy I-A	South Carolina "Partnerships for Children" (SC)
Synergy I-B	South Madison Health and Family Center (WI)
Synergy I-C	East St. Louis Health Coalition (IL)
Synergy II-B	Escambia County "We Care" Program (FL)
Synergy III-B	Monroe County "Women's Health Partnership" (NY)
Synergy IV-A	New Jersey Information Systems (NJ)
Synergy IV-C	Monroe County "McFlu" Campaign (NY)
Synergy V-C	Emory University Center for Injury Control (GA)
Synergy V-D	Seattle Bike Helmet Campaign (WA)
Synergy V-E	Clark County "Community Choices 2010" (WA)
Synergy VI-C	The Center for the Study of Issues in Public Mental Health (NY)

ADVISORY BODIES

All of the preceding structural arrangements are used in collaborations that coordinate activities across organizations. Not all collaborations work in this way, however. In certain instances, the collaborative enterprise is geared toward providing an organization in one sector with input from other sectors. To support this type of endeavor, cases in the database usually employ some form of advisory body.

Similar to contractual arrangements—but in contrast to coalitions and administrative/management systems—advisory bodies support the functions of a parent organization rather than the collaboration itself. Advisory bodies often are created by, and are responsible to, a government agency, or they serve as an arm of a research entity. The tasks of advisory bodies include informing the parent organization, making recommendations, and building support for decisions among important stakeholder groups. Although an advisory body may deliberate independently in constructing its recommendations, it does not have the authority to make operational or policy decisions, nor to take action to carry out its recommendations. The principal function of the advisory body is to harness the expertise, practical experience, and influence of professional leaders and external groups for the decision-making entity.

In the cases in the database, advisory bodies vary widely in their formality, and in the scope and focus of their work. Examples include not only officially appointed bodies, but also *ad hoc* groups. The groups contribute to the development of cross-sectoral information systems (Synergy IV-A) and provide input on a broad range of policy issues (Synergy VI-A).

In many cases in the database, advisory bodies provide a good structure to support collaboration. They are formed around policy issues that have a direct impact on stakeholders in multiple sectors, or around the development of information systems that need to accommodate diverse users in the field. They are comprised of individuals who not only can convey the concerns and perspectives of key stakeholders, but who also can build constituency support. And they are run so that stakeholders have genuine input on policies or systems that will affect them. Toward this end, a number of cases incorporate hearings, workshops, or focus groups to obtain input broader than the membership of the advisory group itself. Some commit substantial resources and staff to the process, facilitating the capacity of the advisory body to make informed recommendations.

Even if the above-mentioned criteria are met, however, there is no guarantee that the work of an advisory body will have much impact. For that to occur, the parent organization must really want the input it is obtaining, and be willing to let the recommendations of the advisory group influence its decision-making process. Problems occur when the advisory process is highly politicized or when recommendations engender opposition by strong and vocal special interest groups.

> Case illustration involving an advisory body:
>
> Synergy IV-A   New Jersey Information Systems (NJ)

INTRA-ORGANIZATIONAL PLATFORMS

While the majority of cases in the database cross organizational boundaries, a small proportion of collaborations bring the medical and public health sectors together within the confines of a single organization. Usually this occurs when a medical organization adopts a perspective outside its "traditional" bounds by bringing in professionals with public health skills and expertise. Examples are common in Synergy III-C, especially in cases in which managed care organizations, integrated systems, or large group practices hire epidemiologists and biostatisticians to apply population-based analytic tools to medical practice.

Isolated examples also occur in other synergies. When Baltimore's Kennedy Krieger Institute (Synergy IV-B case illustration) moved to capitated payment, getting involved in housing programs to prevent lead toxicity became more economical than repeatedly providing lead-toxic children with chelation therapy. Application of this platform to Synergy VI-A is illustrated by the AMA's formation of the Section Council on Preventive Medicine in 1975, an organizational move that encouraged the adoption of a number of prevention-oriented policies by the House of Delegates. Northeast Ohio Universities College of Medicine (Synergy VI-B case illustration) uses an intra-organizational platform to support educationally oriented medicine and public health collaboration.

Cases illustrations involving intra-organizational platforms:

Synergy III-C	Parkland Community-Oriented Primary Care Clinics (TX)
Synergy IV-B	Kennedy Krieger Institute Lead Program (MD)
Synergy VI-B	Northeast Ohio Universities College of Medicine (OH)

Strategies for Successful Partnerships

Collaborations in the case database are not always successful, and those that are usually have weathered difficult, stormy periods. While collaborations fail for a variety of reasons, it is fair to say that most problems revolve around the relationships of the partners involved. Cross-sectoral collaborations bring together a broad range of individuals and organizations, not only in medicine and public health, but often from other sectors in the community as well. Many of these partners are separated by deep cultural differences; some are competitors; few have any history of working together. Viewed in this context, there would seem to be daunting barriers to getting potential partners to acknowledge their mutual interests in collaboration, let alone to establishing working relationships that allow them to put their ideas into action.

The cases in the database suggest that for collaborations to succeed, partners must perceive a compelling *need* to work with professionals or organizations in other sectors and be *willing* to do so. To some extent, the willingness to participate in a collaborative enterprise depends on whether potential partners give it a high priority. That decision, in turn, relates to whether the expected benefits appear to be worth the investment and commitment, and whether the project is likely to be feasible and well run. Willingness to participate also hinges on relationship issues. Unless potential partners have confidence and trust in the leaders of the enterprise and the other participants, they are unlikely to get involved in a meaningful way. If confidence and trust dissipate after the project gets started, it is difficult, if not impossible, to sustain a collaborative partnership.

Quite a few of the cases in the database—successes and failures—describe how the collaboration deals with partnership issues. In addition, there is a growing body of literature around cooperative behavior and interorganizational relationships, particularly in the business sector.[2,70,94,95,123,191] While considerably more needs to be learned about the determinants of successful cross-sectoral partnerships, the following eight strategies gleaned from the case reports and the literature may be helpful to people who are considering engaging in or leading medicine and public health collaborations:

- build on self-interests as well as health interests

- involve a "boundary spanner" in the project

- seek out influential backing and endorsements

- don't expect other partners to be like you

- be realistic

- pay attention to the process

- ensure adequate infrastructure support

- be "up-front" about competition and control issues

BUILD ON SELF-INTERESTS AS WELL AS HEALTH INTERESTS

While virtually all of the collaborations in the database address important health issues—of individuals and/or populations—many do so indirectly, by enhancing the capacity of professionals and organizations in the two health sectors to do their work. In the current environment, with everyone under siege, few health professionals have the time or energy to engage in "extracurricular activities." Consequently, to make the collaboration a high priority for participants, most of the successful cases in the database focus on pressing problems that partners face, and provide them with external resources and skills to address these problems. By participating in such enterprises, health professionals and organizations are better able to achieve their missions, to meet economic and performance pressures, and to maintain, or even extend, their stature and sphere of influence.

The problems that partners face, and the benefits that each seeks to achieve through collaboration, are frequently different. Consequently, most of the collaborations in the database are less accurately characterized as partners working together toward a common goal, than as partners working together in a common enterprise to achieve benefits that are important to each of them, but which none can achieve alone. Successful collaborations do not shy away from acknowledging the motivating power of this self-interest. Quite the contrary, they recognize that since collaboration is hard work, partners need to obtain benefits that are valuable to them. Moreover, they recognize that these benefits often provide the means for improving the health status of individuals and populations.

Two additional points about self-interest are worth noting. First, not all partners are intuitively aware of how a collaboration can further their own interests. In the South Carolina "Partnerships for Children" (Synergy I-A), for example, few pediatricians anticipated the considerable impact that public health nurses would have on their practices—in expanding their patient base, in decreasing "no-show" rates, in improving immunization rates, and in enhancing revenues and productivity. This inability to foresee benefits is not surprising since many health professionals are unaware of how the other health sector—or groups in the broader community—can contribute to their work. In South Carolina, the successful experiences of the five pediatricians who participated in the pilot program convinced many other pediatricians around the state of the value of these partnerships.

Second, the pursuit of self-interest within the context of the collaborative enterprise needs to be limited: benefits for one partner cannot be achieved at the expense of others. In some cases, this rule of conduct extends beyond the activities of the collaboration itself. As partners begin to appreciate, and rely on, each others' resources and skills, they have an incentive to ensure that organizations other than their own remain viable.

INVOLVE A "BOUNDARY SPANNER" IN THE PROJECT

A key strategy to making many collaborations work is the involvement of a health professional who understands and can bridge the cultures of medicine and public health. Alter and Hage refer to such individuals as "boundary spanners."[2] In the cases in the database, boundary spanners include professionals with formal training in clinical and public health disciplines, as well as professionals who have experience working in both sectors. Most commonly, physicians—particularly those with backgrounds in preventive medicine, pediatrics, and emergency medicine—nurses, nutritionists, social workers, health educators, and administrators play this role.

Boundary spanners are valuable in collaborative activities for a number of reasons. All have connections in both worlds, so they often know "whom to call" to get the project going. Their credibility with professionals in both sectors helps to give potential partners the confidence and trust they need to enter new relationships. This is especially true when a boundary spanner plays leadership roles in multiple partner organizations, as the East St. Louis Health Coalition illustrated (Synergy I-C). Equally important, the ability of boundary spanners to see the collaborative enterprise from multiple perspectives simultaneously—medical practice, public health practice, and often academia as well—makes them good leaders and facilitators. Because they understand the language of different partners, they can be helpful in promoting effective communication. Their knowledge of common requirements in different sectors—for instance, around community health assessments or performance measures—can identify important collaborative opportunities. And their awareness of the concerns and needs of both sectors often makes the process and product of the collaboration more responsive to everyone involved.

SEEK OUT INFLUENTIAL BACKING AND ENDORSEMENTS

Many cases in the database find endorsements advantageous in bringing potential partners to the table, in building trust among people in the field, and in obtaining meaningful commitments from organizational partners. The backing of professional associations, for example, legitimizes collaborative endeavors and makes members aware of what such projects can accomplish for themselves and the people they serve. The endorsement of governors, mayors, health officials, and legislators gives a number of collaborations critical political support. In collaborations involving organizations, support is often sought from each partner's chief executive and board of trustees. Memoranda of understanding also are used to ensure that institutional commitment to the project extends beyond the tenure of particular individuals. These organizational endorsements are crucial not only in giving staff the permission and support they need to participate in the collaboration, but also in sustaining that participation over the "long haul."

DON'T EXPECT OTHER PARTNERS TO BE LIKE YOU

All collaborations have some common ground. At the very least, partners agree that the enterprise is a valuable undertaking, although the particular benefits each partner seeks to obtain may be quite different. In some cases, partners need to share additional characteristics as well. For example, it is unlikely that Albany County's "Healthy Partnerships" (Synergy II-D) would have gone forward if all of the partners had not been committed to serving the poor.

In spite of this common ground, however, the success of cross-sectoral collaboration depends on differences among partners. These enterprises work because partners contribute complementary resources, skills, and expertise to the endeavor. By bringing diverse "building blocks" together, the group as a whole is able to achieve results that no single partner could achieve alone.

Tensions can develop when partners have different "languages" and values as well as different resources and skills. In these situations, the viability of the collaboration depends on its capacity to foster tolerance, respect, and trust. While communication and boundary-setting strategies are important here (both are described in more detail below), it also is essential to help partners recognize that they do not have to agree about everything—or even most things—to work together on a circumscribed project. Differences in political and economic values may be important in some venues, but they often are not directly relevant to the partnership's activities.

BE REALISTIC

A prominent characteristic of successful collaborations is their "down-to-earth" point of view. These enterprises recognize the inherent difficulties in getting a cross-sectoral collaboration to move forward. Consequently, they seek to achieve an early success, and then build on that success to extend the project or to initiate further collaborations.

Cases that bring together partners who are very foreign to each other, and who have not worked with each other before, stress the importance of engaging in a narrowly focused, noncontroversial project that can lead to short-term—and, if possible, financial—benefits. The Seattle Bike Helmet Campaign (Synergy V-D) is a good example along these lines.

Successful collaborations also pay attention to the burdens that are imposed on participants. On the one hand, this means assuring that the financial contributions expected of each partner are realistic, that administrative support is adequate, and that partners take on roles that reflect what they do best and most efficiently. On the other hand, it means using the collaboration to make the lives of medical and public health professionals more rewarding, pleasurable, or efficient. Toward this end, collaborations seek not only to reduce paperwork and bureaucracy, but also to obtain sufficient input from the field so that their products will be useful to people in practice (for examples, see Synergies II-B, III-A, and IV-A).

PAY ATTENTION TO THE PROCESS

Cross-sectoral collaboration is a complex undertaking. In most cases, it involves the creation of functional relationships among numerous people from diverse backgrounds who work at various levels in different organizations. Needless to say, the process by which these relationships are promoted has a profound effect on the success of the collaboration.

Nearly all of the cases in the database that address the process of collaboration emphasize several common points.

- All partners should be involved in the enterprise from the planning stage. Successful projects rarely are designed by one partner who, after all decisions are made, brings the other partner(s) in.

- It is important to clarify each partner's roles and responsibilities early in the endeavor, specifying what each is expected to contribute and what each will get in return.

- It is extremely valuable to identify a neutral convener and a skilled facilitator who has the trust and respect of all partners.

- The process should be flexible and responsive to partners' needs, identifying ways to sidestep organizational bureaucracies.

While these factors are important, the most critical elements in the collaborative process are

- adequate administrative support;

- effective strategies for promoting understanding and communication.

Good channels of communication—at every level and phase of the collaboration—are needed to build a common language among partners; to foster trust and mutual respect; to support group decision-making; to keep partners fully informed about what is going on; to enable them to learn about each others' concerns, values, and work; to air disagreements; and to provide them with avenues to respond to changes and emerging problems. Successful collaborations provide numerous and diverse opportunities for communication among partners, including meetings, conference calls, faxes, e-mail, and co-location of staff. The types of mechanisms employed, however, are probably less important than the example set by the leadership of the partnering organizations. If the people spearheading the collaboration trust, respect, and understand each other, it is more likely that others involved in the enterprise will do the same.

ENSURE ADEQUATE INFRA-STRUCTURE SUPPORT

All successful collaborations require adequate funds and in-kind contributions to support the administration and implementation of the project. The particular needs and sources of support in each collaboration are quite variable, however, depending on the nature of the enterprise and the partners involved. Some of the successful cases in the database obtain grants from federal, state, or local government agencies and/or from national or local foundations. Often these funds are used to support the construction of buildings or the development of information systems. Other collaborations are supported entirely by partner income or investments. One of these cases cited the *lack* of external support as a factor contributing to the success of the project since it led to a greater degree of commitment from the partners involved.

Several characteristics of successful collaborations make them particularly well suited for obtaining external funds. On the one hand, collaboratively developed grant proposals often are more robust than what any partner could prepare alone. In addition, collaborations often employ financial strategies that capitalize on the complementary strengths of each partner. Hospitals, for example, are well positioned to raise money for capital expansions. Federally qualified health centers, which receive cost-based reimbursement, can maximize a collaboration's revenues for primary care. State health departments can tap into public funding streams to support the collaborative development of information systems. The East St. Louis Health Coalition (Synergy I-C) is a good example of this type of leveraging. Finally, some collaborations lead to the formation of centers to provide a good conduit for external funding (Synergy V-C and VI-C case illustrations).

It is important to point out that not all successful collaborations require additional investments, either on the part of the partners involved or external funders. Highly structured collaborations, for example, frequently expand the number and effectiveness of services that partners provide for a given investment, or, in rarer cases, achieve cost savings. Their capacity to do so is related to the control of the collaboration's administration/management system over purchasing, contracting, location of partner services, and connections between services. In quite a few cases, one or more partners participating in successful collaborations see significant increases in their revenue. This is particularly true when the collaborative enterprise expands their insured patient base or grant funding.

BE "UP-FRONT" ABOUT COMPETITION AND CONTROL ISSUES

Partners enter cross-sectoral collaborations with legitimate fears. They are concerned about losing control—over their own professional and institutional destinies, over the direction of the collaboration, and over the limits of their participation in the collaboration. They also are concerned that the collaboration *per se*, or one of its partners, will compete with them or attempt to take them over. These fears are exacerbated because partners from the two health sectors rarely enter collaborations on an equal footing. In many cases, the power, prestige, and resources of medical partners are considerably greater than those of partners in public health (some have compared this relationship to the "lion laying down with the lamb"). In other cases, the regulatory authority of a governmental health agency makes it the dominant partner. Regardless of who has the upper hand, competition and control issues are a major problem in collaborative endeavors, and a key reason for their early or late demise.

The successful collaborations in the database use one of two strategies to deal with the competition issue. The first strategy is to avoid it. When partners are competitors in certain areas (for patients or for funding, for example), many collaborations set clear boundaries making these areas "off limits." The Monroe County "Women's Health Partnership" (Synergy III-B), for example, would not have gone forward without an agreement that the coalition would not compete with its partners by conducting independent fundraising. In other cases, by contrast, competition among partners ends as a result of the collaboration. In the Albany County "Healthy Partnerships" (Synergy II-D), for example, the local health department contracted with other health systems to take over its Medicaid and indigent care activities. In many of the integrated systems cases (Synergy I-C), certain activities are taken over by one partner in the collaboration.

Control issues within collaborations depend on the structural arrangement involved. In collaborations using advisory bodies, control is in the hands of the parent organization, although the other partners have relatively little to lose by participating in the enterprise. In contractual arrangements, both partners negotiate the terms of their relationship. Administrative/management systems work for the collaboration as a whole, although, in some cases, partners give up considerable control over their day-to-day activities in order to achieve benefits they desire. In coalitions, the partnership has control over the direction of the project, although it has little recourse if any particular member of the coalition bows out. The key to dealing successfully with intracollaborative control issues centers around choosing the right structural arrangement for the task at hand, and in making potential partners aware of the implications of that arrangement.

It is important to point out that while health professionals entering into collaborative relationships are commonly concerned about *losing* control, in most of the successful cases in the database, working with others actually *enhances* partners' control over their professional destinies. Some of these collaborations strengthen health professionals' input into policy decisions (Synergy VI-A) or into the design of information systems (Synergy IV-A), giving them considerably more control than they previously had over their working environment. Others enhance the ability of health agencies and institutions to minimize disruption of services for their clientele, and to assure continued employment for qualified staff or faculty (Synergies I and II). Virtually all of the collaborations give health professionals and institutions greater control over their ability to achieve their practice, teaching, and research missions.

Part III

Conclusions and Next Steps

The Benefits of Collaboration in Today's Environment

Health professionals in America today are working in a chaotic and anxiety-provoking environment. For both the medical and public health sectors, change is the only predictable aspect of that environment, and change is accelerating, making it apparent that working in traditional ways is no longer a viable option. The health professionals and organizations engaged in the collaborations we have described have taken a proactive approach to dealing with these challenges. By reshaping the relationship between medicine and public health, they have found ways to take charge of, and thus to shape, their own professional futures. Their collaborative strategies enhance not only the health of the individuals and populations they serve, but also their own effectiveness, influence, and economic stability.

The collaborations in the database represent a striking change in the relationship between medicine and public health. Although the two sectors have a history of having worked together in the past, for most of this century they have interacted very little, evolving along separate, and virtually independent, tracks. Their distant relationship has not been due to a dearth of opportunities for improving individual and community health through cross-sectoral collaboration. If anything, opportunities to work together expanded with the emergence of bacteriology and, later, the increasing prevalence of chronic diseases. Instead, it reflects the lack of compelling reasons to engage in collaborative activities. Working independently, the medical and public health sectors were able to make great strides in achieving their missions. Moreover, few, if any, financial and professional incentives encouraged them to interact. In this context, it is not surprising that neither sector invested the time or effort that collaboration requires, or made serious attempts to overcome cross-sectoral tensions or the growing "cultural divide."

Today, continuing on separate tracks is no longer in the interest of either medicine or public health. In the current environment, the two sectors are becoming increasingly dependent on one another—in achieving their missions, in addressing challenging health problems, and in responding to economic and performance pressures. At the same time, new incentives and organizational structures are making cross-sectoral interactions more rewarding and more feasible than they have been in the past. As the 414 cases in the database demonstrate, the need for the two sectors to work together, and the support they can provide each other, are more than hypothetical. Current circumstances are persuading quite a few health professionals and organizations to work more closely with colleagues in the other sector—and often with partners in the broader community as well. Although many of the partners in these collaborations initially were unfamiliar with each other, and were separated by deep cultural differences, the cases demonstrate that it is possible for them to engage in common endeavors.

By combining their resources and skills in various ways, professionals and organizations in the two sectors are able to achieve benefits that none of them can accomplish alone. These benefits often are different for different partners, addressing important problems that each partner faces.

Often, professionals and organizations in medicine and public health get involved in collaborative activities to strengthen their capacity to carry out their missions—in practice, education, and research. Collaboration enhances the quality of medical care and patient satisfaction with care in a number of ways: by providing clinicians with up-to-date information relevant to their practices; by overcoming logistical and financial barriers that some patients face in obtaining access to care; by improving the ability of medical practitioners to modify risk behaviors and to address underlying causes of illness and disability; by providing organizations delivering care with methodologic tools to support quality improvement; and by developing better quality assurance standards and performance measures. Collaboration also provides health departments and community-based organizations with valuable support in carrying out population-based strategies that are essential to improving the health status of the community at large, such as surveillance, health assessment, public education, the adoption of health-protecting laws and regulations, health promotion campaigns, and the assurance of medical care. Collaboration furthers the teaching and research missions of academic institutions by providing additional sources of support for faculty salaries, meaningful training experiences for students and residents, and new opportunities for investigation and consultation.

Another benefit of collaboration is the enhancement of each health sector's stature and sphere of influence. For public health, interacting with the medical sector and other partners in the community increases the extent to which medical professionals, the public, and policymakers understand and value what the public health sector does. This understanding can help build a stronger constituency to support public health funding and activities—especially for community-wide public health services about which many people are unaware. Working more closely with the medical sector also facilitates the translation of public health knowledge into mainstream clinical practice, providing effective preventive care and treatment to a much broader population. For the medical sector, collaborative strategies make it possible for clinicians to have more far-reaching effects than they can by caring for patients on an individual basis. Working with the public health sector and other community partners gives clinicians the power to address health problems—such as HIV/AIDS, sexually transmitted diseases, cardiovascular disease, domestic violence, and substance abuse—that depend on more than what they can accomplish one-to-one in practice. Collaboration also enables medical practitioners to apply what they learn in their encounters with individual patients to broader populations. Both sectors find their policy voice strengthened through collaboration, giving them more control over health problems, their working environment, and the future direction of the health system.

A final benefit of collaboration—critical in today's environment—is its capacity to help professionals and organizations in both health sectors deal with economic and performance pressures. As the personal health care system becomes more competitive, the success of medical professionals and institutions is becoming increasingly dependent on their ability to form networks, to manage financial risk, and to achieve performance goals. For the public health sector, market forces and the devolution and downsizing of government are making it advantageous to work with and through the medical sector to achieve many of the most important health objectives, and to protect and effectively leverage limited budgets. Collaborative strategies enable the two health sectors to meet these pressures in several important ways: by linking them up with partners who can support their activities; by establishing organizational ties that decrease financial risk while enhancing negotiating leverage and efficiency; by providing them with needed data and analytic tools; and by increasing their sources of revenue.

Clearly, cross-sectoral collaboration offers American health professionals powerful strategies for dealing with current challenges. Recent papers addressing the relationship between medicine and public health, and the need for intersectoral action in Europe, suggest that these strategies may be applicable to other countries as well.[16,77] In spite of the value of collaboration in today's environment, however, the cases in the database are far from the norm. Moreover, few, if any, of the participants in the focus groups we conducted recognized the value of collaborative strategies in dealing with their current predicament.

The Committee on Medicine and Public Health as well as the partners involved in this project—the American Medical Association (AMA), the American Public Health Association (APHA), The New York Academy of Medicine (NYAM), and The Robert Wood Johnson Foundation (RWJF)—believe that vigorous efforts should be made to promote understanding about cross-sectoral collaboration among health professionals around the country, and to encourage its further development. To begin that process, two further issues need to be addressed:

- What is the collaborative paradigm? How does it affect the identity of the two health sectors and the way they think and work?

- What plans are underway to make more people aware of medicine and public health collaboration, and to provide professionals and organizations engaged in these activities with technical and policy support?

The Collaborative Paradigm

Bridging the cultures of medical care and public health is not choosing one or the other, nor is it creating an artificial culture which denies their diversity. Rather, it requires grasping and making real a whole which encompasses both, and which requires the contributions of both to achieve the goals of either.

— Kristine M. Gebbie, 1992[66]

Health professionals and organizations considering engaging in collaborative endeavors are concerned about how these activities will change them—not only in terms of the investments and benefits involved, but also in terms of what they are expected to know, to do, to value, and to be responsible for. These factors, which describe the paradigm in which health professionals work, also are of importance to educators who are charged with training future generations of health professionals.

Although none of the cases in the database explicitly describe the conceptual framework in which the partners function, the "collaborative paradigm" suggested by these cases represents a significant shift from both health sectors' status quo. The key change required by collaboration is that professionals and organizations in medicine and public health no longer consider themselves in isolation, but rather as partners in a larger, common health system. Working in a comprehensive framework, professionals in the two health sectors can appreciate each others' perspectives, and combine their resources and skills, without altering their mission or identity.

A METAPHOR FOR THE PARADIGM SHIFT

The paradigm that has characterized the relationship between medicine and public health for most health professionals working today might be visualized as two people standing back-to-back, looking in opposite directions, unaware of each other's existence. One of these people, the medical sector, is using a microscope to examine the nearby landscape, consisting of diagnosis, treatment, and biological mechanisms of disease. The other, public health, is using a telescope to view a completely different, nonoverlapping landscape encompassing health protection, health promotion, and the behavioral, socioeconomic, and environmental determinants of health. Living in their own worlds, the two health sectors interact very little with one another, attempting to address the problems they encounter independently.

The paradigm suggested by the cases in the database turns the two health sectors around so that they are now side-by-side, aware of each other's existence, looking at a common scene that encompasses both points of view. Instead of a microscope and a telescope, each sector now has a zoom lens. In this way the medical sector can start from the perspective of the individual, bringing in the broader context in which illness occurs to make clinical practice more effective. The public health sector can start with the big picture, zooming in to appreciate the role that biological factors and clinical care can play in improving the health of the community. From their new positions, functioning as part of a common universe, the two health sectors are not only able to relate their perspectives to each other, but also to reinforce each others' goals and activities.

KEY ELEMENTS OF THE COLLABORATIVE PARADIGM

Health professionals are legitimately concerned about paradigm shifts that challenge their sectoral identity. Indeed, some of the previous attempts to bridge the gap between medicine and public health—discussed earlier in the text—could be interpreted as expanding the paradigm of the medical sector to encompass (and perhaps take over) much of the mission, knowledge base, and responsibilities of public health. The same could be said about changes in the scope of public health.

Such transformations are not involved in the cases we discussed. These collaborations do not involve merging the two health sectors, turning one into another, or choosing one over the other. Quite the contrary, they reveal the benefits of having a health system with two distinct perspectives: one looking out for the health needs of the individual patient, the other committed to improving the health of the entire population. The power of collaboration derives from having each partner contribute what it does best or more efficiently. Consequently, the collaborative paradigm gives the highest return to the unique perspectives and skills that each sector brings to the table. Working in the context of this paradigm, each health sector maintains its own identity. There is no need for professionals or organizations in medicine or public health to change their mission. Moreover, they do not need to develop expertise in the other sector's knowledge base and skills, or take on responsibilities of the other sector, which could compete with their own mission.

Although collaboration does not involve a transformation of the two health sectors, it does require them to understand each others' perspectives and to appreciate how their expertise and activities relate to, and can reinforce, each other. In addition, it entails a willingness to work with other partners whose contributions complement their own. Thinking and working in this way represents a striking change in outlook for the medical and public health sectors. On the one hand, it means seeing themselves not as two separate enterprises but as parts of a larger, common health system. On the other hand, it means that professionals and organizations in the two sectors need to relinquish their "do-it-all-yourself" mentality and become more open to the notion of support.

The collaborative paradigm recognizes the value of differentiation in the health system, since there is only so much that any one person or organization can do. At the same time, however, it acknowledges that the health needs and health problems of individuals and populations are not discontinuous and cannot be neatly categorized or addressed according to the domains of particular specialties, programs, sectors, or institutional settings. In order to integrate the activities of the many specialized components of this health system—as described in the six synergies—the health sectors need a structured, comprehensive framework that allows them to appreciate the diverse resources inherent in the larger health system, as well as the relevance of different aspects of that system to their own mission and activities. This type of framework was shared by leaders in medicine and public health in the 19th century when they worked together around health boards and sanitary reforms. Today, it would include the following:

- a goal that both health sectors can share, such as maximizing health and minimizing disease, disability, and suffering

- the full range of biological, behavioral, socioeconomic, and environmental determinants of health and disease

- the broad spectrum of people and organizations—in the medical and public health sectors as well as the broader community—that can make an impact on these determinants

- the diverse resources and skills that partners in the health system can contribute

- the types of strategic interventions—health protection, health promotion, treatment, and rehabilitation—that can be mounted

Using such a framework enhances the ability of partners to achieve the powerful synergies of cross-sectoral collaboration. It provides a solid basis for identifying the types of problems that can be addressed through collaborative strategies, the different partners that can be included in a collaboration, and the ways that these partners' resources and skills can be combined (see Figure II-2). Because the framework explicitly includes a broad spectrum of people and organizations as potential partners, it helps professionals in the two health sectors relate not only to each other but also to the broader community.

In addition to thinking about themselves as part of a larger health system, professionals and organizations engaging in collaborative enterprises need to be willing to involve other partners in many of their activities. The cases in the database demonstrate that the medical and public health sectors have the capacity to reinforce each other in virtually everything they do—in medical and public health practice, policy, education, and research; and in activities focused on individuals, subpopulations, and entire communities. In these interactions, the health sector with primary responsibility and authority for a particular function allows other partners to play supportive roles. In many of the cases in

Synergies I and II, centering around the delivery of medical care, the public health sector supports the activities of the medical sector. In Synergies V and VI-A, by contrast, the medical sector enhances the ability of the public health sector to protect and promote the health of the entire community. Although functional support is primarily one way in these cases, both sectors derive meaningful benefits from the interaction. Collaborations also can be mutually supportive, of course. In Synergies III and IV, which focus on individuals as well as populations, each sector supports the functions of the other. In the process, they become considerably more responsive to the mission, constraints, and sources of professional satisfaction of the other health sector.

While the collaborative paradigm respects the identity, authority, and responsibility of each health sector, it does not impose on them fixed or pre-scribed roles. Because each health sector can reinforce so much of what the other sector does, a Venn diagram attempting to delineate roles for medicine and public health in the context of collaborative endeavors would show extensive overlap. This overlap is compounded by substantial local variation in roles—depending on such factors as available expertise and sources of funding—and by changes in roles that occur in the course of some collabora-tions. By providing valuable supports, collaboration makes it possible for each health sector to take on new roles or to give up other roles. It also provides health professionals trained in one sector with opportunities to work in orga-nizations run by the other sector.

ILLUSTRA-TIONS OF "COLLABO-RATIVE PARADIGM" THINKING

The collaborative paradigm influences the way health professionals think and work. The comprehensive framework helps them understand the perspective of their colleagues in the other sector. That framework, and a willingness to allow other partners to provide support, facilitates better integration of the two sectors' resources and skills. Because of these characteristics, the collaborative paradigm can be very useful in helping the medical and public health sectors deal with challenging health problems. Below, we illustrate the value of that paradigm in dealing with issues related to asthma, HIV/AIDS, and emerging technologies.

Consider first a physician caring for a young boy with asthma. Trained in the biomedical paradigm, this physician has previously focused her attention on biological mechanisms undergirding asthma and on prescribing an appro-priate therapeutic regimen for her patient. With a comprehensive framework that encompasses the full range of determinants of health, however, she is in a better position to appreciate that control of her patient's condition depends not only on her interpersonal skills and how "up-to-date" she is with the literature, but also on her patient's ability to get to her office, his access to supplies and drugs, the appropriateness of his family's health-seeking behavior, his com-pliance with his medical regimen, and the presence of cockroaches, mites, or other precipitants in his home. Working in the collaborative paradigm, this physician continues to do what she does best: care for her individual patient. Now, however, she can harness the resources and skills of a broad range of partners to help her address the nonbiological determinants of health that influence the success of her treatment.

The problem of asthma is equally revealing if viewed from the perspective of a public health officer responsible for developing programs to address the rising epidemic of this disease among inner-city children. Previously, his local health department had mounted asthma programs primarily on its own. But with a comprehensive framework, the health officer now can strategize how to work with and through the medical sector—as well as other groups in the community—to achieve his goals. By linking its individual-level services and population-based strategies to the activities of other partners, the health department can extend its sphere of influence and achieve a greater impact with its limited funds. Synergy I and II collaborations provide the health officer with a mechanism for assuring that children with asthma get access to medical care and are referred to programs that can eradicate precipitants in their homes. Synergy III-A collaborations can help keep clinicians in practice up-to-date about the most effective approaches to asthma therapy. Synergy III-B collaborations can link children identified as having asthma in school screening programs with medical practitioners who provide appropriate asthma treatment. Through Synergy IV-A collaborations, the health department can develop and implement a more effective surveillance system for asthma. And through Synergy V collaborations, it can obtain valuable support for its public education campaigns and environmental policies.

Another benefit of the collaborative paradigm is that it allows health professionals to understand and relate their different approaches for dealing with health problems. Without a comprehensive framework—and without the dialogue it allows—it has been difficult in the past to sustain preventive measures against a disease when drug treatment becomes available. The response to tuberculosis is a good example of this problem, and has lead to serious consequences—the failure to maintain an adequate focus on prevention contributed to the epidemic of multidrug-resistant tuberculosis in this country.[26,120] Now, with the recent introduction of expensive protease inhibitors to treat HIV/AIDS, there is increasing pressure to shift limited funds targeted to community-wide prevention of HIV/AIDS to the treatment of infected patients. The collaborative paradigm provides the medical and public health sectors with a framework for considering the prevention and treatment of HIV/AIDS together and for developing policies that maximize the benefits of these complementary strategies. If they do so, they may be able to avert the development of yet another drug-resistant epidemic.

As new technologies become available, the collaborative paradigm is likely to become even more important—not only to reconcile prevention and treatment, but also to integrate new biomedical approaches, such as molecular genetics, into the health system's prevention armamentarium. Consider as an example the recent research demonstrating the genetic effects of a component of tobacco smoke.[46] This research identified the specific molecule in cigarette smoke that interacts with the genetic receptor responsible for lung cancer. While the findings of this study could be used to support aggressive public policies aimed at discouraging the use of tobacco, they also could lead to a screening test that enables individuals to determine whether or not they are susceptible to lung cancer from cigarette smoke and to modify their behavior accordingly. The development of such a test could lead to the relaxation of anti-tobacco policies. If this were to happen, some people resistant to developing lung cancer might increase their use of cigarettes, putting others who are not resistant more at risk through second-hand smoke. Moreover, since the smokers would not necessarily be resistant to other effects of tobacco, this scenario could lead to a resurgence in non-malignant tobacco-related diseases, such as coronary artery disease, stroke, obstructive lung disease, and macular degeneration. The comprehensive framework we have been discussing provides a mechanism for integrating what we learn about molecular causation with environmental, social, and behavioral factors that are equally important determinants of health outcomes. Working through the collaborative paradigm, the two health sectors can use this information to jointly develop more effective health policies.

Moving Forward with Medicine and Public Health Collaboration

As we noted earlier, a striking dichotomy exists between the partners identified in the database collaborations and the participants in the focus groups that we conducted around the country. The former are pioneers in the development of a collaborative paradigm that can change the nature of the American health system, making it more responsive to the needs of individuals, communities, and health professionals. The latter are health professionals, in practice and in training, who are overwhelmed with the changes that are occurring in the health system, and are unaware of the relevance of medicine and public health collaboration to the pressures they face. Taking these two groups into account, the further development of cross-sectoral collaboration requires at least four types of actions:

- increasing awareness and understanding of these strategies among medical and public health professionals

- legitimizing this approach among health professionals in both sectors

- providing people in the field with useful tools to help them initiate and sustain collaborative relationships

- identifying and addressing barriers to cross-sectoral collaboration in the policy environment

It is hoped that this monograph will contribute to accomplishing these objectives. By providing compelling reasons for professionals in the two health sectors to reevaluate their relationship, as well as concrete descriptions of how cross-sectoral collaboration actually works and what it can achieve, we hope to stimulate readers' interest in collaboration and to give them a practical framework for thinking about and engaging in these types of activities. In April 1997, 350 health professionals reviewed the preliminary findings of the Committee on Medicine and Public Health at a symposium at NYAM. Through the leadership of APHA, AMA, and RWJF, copies of the completed monograph are being distributed to 200,000 health professionals around the country. It is also available on the World Wide Web (http://www.nyam.org/pubhlth).

AMA and APHA are engaged in other initiatives to promote collaborative interactions among medical and public health professionals—some of which predated this monograph. In March 1994, the two associations took steps to establish the Medicine/Public Health Initiative,[138,139] whose National Committee now consists of over 50 leaders in the two health sectors, representing the perspectives of a large (and expanding) group of organizations. In March 1996, the Initiative convened a National Congress in Chicago, IL. Engaging 400 medicine and public health delegates in dialogue about collaboration, the Congress was designed to encourage participants to work together on their home ground. Subsequently, the Initiative has administered a small-grant program, which is supporting research collaborations as well as meetings and medicine and public health congresses in various states. The University of Texas-Houston Health Science Center (U-T Houston) serves as the national coordinating office for the Initiative, maintaining an active web site (http://www.sph.uth.tmc.edu/mph). Funding for the Initiative's activities has come from the Agency for Health Care Policy and Research, the Centers for Disease Control and Prevention, The Josiah Macy, Jr. Foundation, RWJF, and The W. K. Kellogg Foundation (WKKF).

Additional projects are underway to provide professionals in the field with tools that can help them initiate or sustain cross-sectoral partnerships. RWJF and WKKF have funded NYAM to produce a *Pocket Guide to Medicine and Public Health Collaborations*—in print and electronic form—which will provide readers with a multi-indexed compilation of the cases on which this monograph is based. Closely correlated with the framework of the monograph, the *Pocket Guide* will categorize cases according to their location, the types of partners that are involved, the way they combine resources and skills (the synergies), and the structural foundation(s) they employ. By using this resource, readers will be able to identify the types of collaborations that are most relevant to their particular circumstances and needs, individuals directly involved in these collaborations whom they can contact for further information, and organizations in their region that are currently involved in various kinds of collaborative activities. The Internet version of the *Pocket Guide* will permit users to search the database through multiple index terms simultaneously, and will support two-way networking. New cases will be added to the electronic database as they are identified.

The next phase of the Medicine/Public Health Initiative has just been funded by a new grant from RWJF. Led by the Initiative's convening members—AMA and APHA—and assisted by U-T Houston and NYAM, this grant will facilitate a major extension of the Initiative's outreach to regional, state, and local areas. The grant's activities will be coordinated with two other programs supporting partnerships between medicine and public health. Turning Point, funded jointly by RWJF and WKKF, is a program to transform and strengthen the public health infrastructure in the United States so that states, local communities, and their public health agencies can respond to the challenge to protect and improve the public's health in the 21st century.[181] As part of the strategic plans that will be developed through this initiative, states and localities will redefine the relationship between the clinical health care and public health systems, and will strengthen partnerships between the two sectors to improve the public's health. The Community Care Network (CCN) Demonstration Partnerships, funded by WKKF and being evaluated with support from RWJF, aspire to improve the health status of communities by focusing on community health, establishing a seamless continuum of care among health care providers, managing within fixed resources, and promoting community accountability.[39-41] Those CCN demonstrations that involve partners from both the medical and public health sectors are included in the database of cases that informed this monograph.

A final—and critical—action that is needed to support cross-sectoral collaboration relates to the establishment of a conducive policy environment. Although relatively few cases in the database provided explicit information about policy barriers, analysis of the case material suggests that three types of obstacles inhibit participants from moving forward with their projects. One impediment relates to requirements of health programs, and "strings" attached to funding streams, which prevent some health professionals and organizations from working with other partners or from taking broader action to achieve health goals. In some cases, participants have had to negotiate more flexible funding or obtain waivers from program requirements in order to carry out their collaborative enterprise. The second policy issue concerns incentives for health professions training. There is little doubt that the further development of cross-sectoral collaboration will require changes in both medical and public health training. Few incentives exist, however, to encourage the broad range of schools that educate medical and public health professionals to develop collaborative approaches to training or to prepare their students to work within the collaborative paradigm. The third, and most basic, policy issue revolves around public goods. The market forces that are threatening funding for research, health professions training, population-based public health programs, and care for the un- and underinsured are also threatening the existence of key partners in some collaborative enterprises.

Clearly, more work needs to be done to identify the policy barriers that partners in cross-sectoral collaborations face. In addition, options need to be developed and advocated that can address these barriers. Until recently, it would have been difficult to think of a group to take on such responsibilities. Two of the initiatives mentioned above, however, can play important roles. Turning Point will provide a mechanism for bringing policies that inhibit cross-sectoral collaboration to the attention of state and local governments. The National Committee of the Medicine/Public Health Initiative can function as a powerful cross-sectoral coalition to identify problems in the field and to advocate policy changes at the national level. With these supports, and *your* active involvement—in the field and at policy levels—the strategies exemplified in the database collaborations may some day become the norm.

References

1. Alpha Center. 1996. Public health and managed care organizations—a new era of collaboration? *State Initiatives* (May/June 1996):2–4, 10.

2. Alter, C., and Hage, J. 1993. *Organizations working together.* Newbury Park, CA: Sage Publications, Inc.

3. Altman, D. 1995. The market and regulation: where community forces fit. *Frontiers of Health Services Management* 11 (4):49–50.

4. American Hospital Association. 1994. Healthy Communities in action. Chicago: Hospital Research and Educational Trust of the American Hospital Association.

5. Anderson, R. J., and Boumbulian, P. J. 1995. Comprehensive community health programs: a new look at an old approach. In *Academic health centers in the managed care environment,* edited by D. Korn, C. J. McLaughlin, and M. Osterweis: Association of Academic Health Centers.

6. Baker, E. L., Melton, R. J., Stange, P. V., Fields, M. L., et al. 1994. Health reform and the health of the public: forging community health partnerships. *Journal of the American Medical Association* 272 (16):1276–1282.

7. Barker, W., Bennett, N., Lewis, B., Bell, K., et al. 1993. Public health and private sector collaboration in Medicare influenza vaccination demonstration: the Monroe County experience. Paper read at 26th National Immunization Conference, at Atlanta, GA.

8. Barker, W. H., Menegus, M. A., Hall, C. B., Betts, R. E., et al. 1995. Communitywide laboratory-based influenza surveillance focused on older persons, 1989–1992. *American Journal of Preventive Medicine* 11 (3):149–155.

9. Bennett, N. M., Lewis, B., Doniger, A. S., Bell, K., et al. 1994. A coordinated communitywide program in Monroe County, New York, to increase influenza immunization rates in the elderly. *Archives of Internal Medicine* 154 (August 8, 1994):1741–1745.

10. Bennis, W., and Biederman, P. W. 1997. *Organizing genius: the secrets of creative collaboration.* Reading, MA: Addison-Wesley Publishing Company.

11. Berenson, R. A. 1996. New market relationships and their effects on patient care. Paper read at a Robert Wood Johnson Foundation Invitational Meeting—A Market in Turmoil: Evolving Relationships, September 11, at Washington, DC.

12. Bergman, A. B., Rivara, F. P., Richards, D. D., and Rogers, L. W. 1990. The Seattle's children's bicycle helmet campaign. *American Journal of Diseases in Children* 144 (June):727–731.

13. Berkman, L. F., and Breslow, L. 1983. *Health and ways of living: the Alameda County study.* New York: Oxford Press.

14. Bernier, R. H. 1994. Toward a more population—based approach to immunization: fostering private- and public-sector collaboration. *American Journal of Public Health* 84 (10):1567–1568.

15. Bernstein, E., and Bernstein, J. 1996. *Case studies in emergency medicine and the health of the public.* Sudbury, MA: Jones and Bartlett Publishers, Inc.

16. Bhopal, R. 1995. Public health medicine and primary health care: convergent, divergent, or parallel paths? *Journal of Epidemiology and Community Health* 49 (2):113–116.

17. Black, D. J., Smith, C., and Townsend, P. 1982. *Inequalities in health: the Black report.* New York: Penguin Books.

18. Blumenthal, D., and Thier, S. O. 1996. Managed care and medical education: the new fundamentals. *Journal of the American Medical Association* 276 (9):725–727.

19. Bodenheimer, T. S., and Grumbach, K. 1995. *Understanding health policy: a clinical approach.* Norwalk, CT: Appleton & Lange.

20. Bogue, R., and Hall Jr., C. H., eds. 1997. *Health networks innovations: how 20 communities are improving their system through collaboration.* Chicago: American Hospital Publishing, Inc.

21. Bondurant, S. 1995. Metamorphosis of health care: transcendent values. Paper read at National Area Health Education Centers Workshop, at Chicago, IL.

22. Boumbulian, P. J., and Anderson, R. J. 1994. Survival through community services: from sick care to health care. *Health Management Quarterly*:17–22.

23. Bowditch, H. 1874. Preventive medicine and the physician of the future. In *Fifth Annual Report of the State Board of Health of Massachusetts.* Boston: Wright and Potter (State Printers).

24. Braun, K. L., and Conybeare, C. R. 1995. HealthScope: a model for a low cost health education program using commercial television. *Public Health Reports* 110 (4):483–492.

25. Breslow, L. 1990. The future of public health: prospects in the United States for the 1990's. *Annual Review of Public Health* 11:1–28.

26. Brewer, T. F., Heymann, S. J., Colditz, G. A., Wilson, M. E., et al. 1996. Evaluations of tuberculosis control policies using computer simulation. *Journal of the American Medical Association* 276 (23):1898–1903.

27. Buffington, J., Bell, K., LaForce, M., and The Genessee Hospital Medical Staff. 1991. A target-based model for increasing influenza immunizations in private practice. *Journal of General Internal Medicine* 6 (May/June 1991):204–209.

28. Bulger, R. J. 1990. Reductionist biology and population medicine— strange bedfellows or a marriage made in heaven? *Journal of the American Medical Association* 264 (4):508–509.

29. Bulletin of the New York Academy of Medicine. 1988. Medicine and Public Health/Injury Issue. 64 (7):610–837 (entire).

30. Bullough, B., and Rosen, G. 1992. *Preventive medicine in the United States, 1900–1990: trends and interpretations.* Canton, MA: Science History Publications.

31. Bunker, J. P. 1995. Medicine matters after all. *Journal of the Royal College of Physicians of London* 29 (2):105–112.

32. Bureau of National Affairs. 1997. Surveys and studies. *BNA's Health Care Policy Report* 5 (2/17/97):288–292.

33. Carlson, R. J. 1975. *The end of medicine.* New York: John Wiley & Sons.

34. Center for Studying Health System Change. 1996. Tracking changes in the public health system: what researchers need to know to monitor and evaluate these changes. *Issue Brief* (No. 2):1–4.

35. Centers for Disease Control. 1995. Prevention and managed care: opportunities for managed care organizations, purchasers of health care, and public health agencies. *Morbidity and Mortality Weekly Review* 44 (No. RR-14).

36. Centers for Disease Control. 1997. Estimated expenditures for essential public health services-selected states, fiscal year 1995. *Morbidity and Mortality Weekly Report* 46 (7):150–152.

37. Cohen, J. J. 1995. Learning to care, for a healthier tomorrow. Paper read at Annual Meeting of the Association of American Medical Colleges, at Washington, DC.

38. Committee on the Costs of Medical Care. 1932. *Medical care for the American people.* Chicago: University of Chicago Press.

39. Community Care Network Demonstration Program. 1996. The demonstration & finalist partnerships. Chicago: Hospital Research and Educational Trust.

40. Community Care Network Demonstration Program. 1996. Examples of emerging rural community networks. Chicago: Hospital Research and Educational Trust.

41. Community Care Network Demonstration Program. 1997. The 25 Community Care Network Demonstration partnerships: profiles in progress. Chicago: Hospital Research and Educational Trust.

42. Community Choices 2010. 1996. Choosing to swim: Year-end report. Clark County, WA: Community Choices 2010.

43. Corrigan, A., and Pickens, S. 1997. Measuring health improvements in your community: evaluation measures must be included in strategic planning process. *Inside Preventive Care* 3 (3):6–8.

44. Council on Scientific Affairs. 1990. The IOM report and public health. *Journal of the American Medical Association* 264 (4):508–509.

45. Cunningham, R. 1996. Renegotiating the social contract in public health. *Medicine & Health Perspectives* (August 5, 1996):1–4.

46. Denissenko, M. F., Pao, A., Tang, M., and Pfeifer, G. P. 1996. Preferential formation of benzo[a]pyrene adducts at lung cancer mutational hotspots in P53. *Science* 274 (5286):430–432.

47. Dever, G. E. A. 1976. An epidemiological model for health policy analysis. *Social Indicators Research* 2:453–466.

48. DiGusseppi, C. G., Rivara, F. P., Koepsell, T. D., and Polissar, L. 1989. Bicycle helmet use by children: evaluation of a community-wide helmet campaign. *Journal of the American Medical Association* 262 (16):2256–2261.

49. Dismuke, S. E., Roberts, D., and Postic, S. 1993. Academia, public health and a private foundation join forces in Kansas. *The Link* 4 (Fall, 1993):1, 3–4.

50. Duffy, J. 1979. The American medical profession and public health: from support to ambivalence. *Bulletin of the History of Medicine* 53 (1):1–22.

51. Eggert, R. W., and Parkinson, M. D. 1994. Preventive medicine and health system reform. *Journal of the American Medical Association* 272 (9):688–693.

52. Estes, E. H. 1983. Educating primary care practitioners of the 1980s in preventive medicine and health promotion. In *Teaching preventive medicine in primary care*, edited by W. H. Barker. New York: Springer Publishing Company.

53. Evans, R. G., and Stoddart, G. L. 1990. Producing health, consuming health care. *Social Science and Medicine* 31 (12):1347–1363.

54. Evans, R. G., Barer, M. L., and Marmor, T. R. 1994. *Why are some people healthy and others not? The determinants of health of populations.* New York: Aldine De Gruyter.

55. Fee, E. 1991. Designing schools of public health for the United States. In *A history of education in public health: health that mocks the doctors' rules*, edited by E. Fee and R. M. Acheson. New York: Oxford University Press.

56. Fee, E., and Rosenkrantz, B. 1991. Professional education for public health in the United States. In *A history of education in public health: health that mocks the doctors' rules*, edited by E. Fee and R. M. Acheson. New York: Oxford University Press.

57. Fee, E. 1997. The origins and development of public health in the United States. In *Oxford Textbook of Public Health*, edited by R. Detels, W. W. Holland, J. McEwen, and G. S. Omenn. New York: Oxford University Press.

58. Flexner, A. 1910. Medical education in the United States and Canada, Bulletin no. 4. New York: Carnegie Foundation for the Advancement of Teaching.

59. Flynn, B. C. 1996. Healthy cities: toward worldwide health promotion. *Annual Review of Public Health* 17:299–309.

60. Foundation for Accountability. 1995. Guidebook for performance measurement: prototype. Portland, OR: Foundation for Accountability.

61. Friede, A., O'Carroll, P. W., Nicola, R. M., Oberle, M. W., et al. 1997. *CDC prevention guidelines: a guide to action*. Baltimore: Williams & Wilkins.

62. Frost, F. J., Cawthon, M.L., Tollestrup, K., Keny, F.W., et al. 1994. Smoking prevalence during pregnancy for women who are and women who are not Medicaid-funded. *American Journal of Preventive Medicine* 10 (2):91–96.

63. Fuchs, V. R. 1997. Managed care and merger mania. *Journal of the American Medical Association* 277 (11):920–921.

64. Galdston, I. 1949. *Social medicine: its derivations and objectives.* New York: The Commonwealth Fund.

65. Gardner, J. W. 1990. *On leadership.* New York: The Free Press.

66. Gebbie, K. 1992. Continental divide: blending the cultures of public health and medical care. Paper read at Sun Valley Forum—Rebalancing the Triad: Cure, Care, and Prevention, at Sun Valley, ID.

67. Glaser, B. G., and Strauss, A. L. 1967. *The discovery of grounded theory: strategies for qualitative research.* Chicago: Aldine Publishing.

68. Gordon, R. L., Baker, E. L., Roper, W. L., and Omenn, G. S. 1996. Prevention and the reforming U.S. health care system: changing roles and responsibilities for public health. *Annual Review of Public Health* 17:489–509.

69. Gore, A. 1995. Reinventing government: national performance review. Washington, DC: Office of the Vice President of the United States.

70. Gray, B. 1989. *Collaborating: finding common ground for multiparty problems.* San Francisco: Jossey-Bass.

71. Gray, B. H. 1992. World blindness and the medical profession: conflicting medical cultures and the ethical dilemmas of helping. *Milbank Quarterly* 70 (3):535–556.

72. Grayson, C. G., Kirkpatrick , D. J., Wilber , J., Melton, D. M., et al. *1992. A clinician's guide to AIDS and HIV infection in Georgia.* Atlanta, GA: Public Health Committee of the Medical Association of Georgia and the Division of Public Health, Georgia Department of Human Resources.

73. Greenlick, M. R. 1995. Educating physicians for the twenty-first century. *Academic Medicine* 70 (3):179–185.

74. Hafferty, F., and Salloway, J. C. 1993. The evolution of medicine as a profession: a 75-year perspective. *Minnesota Medicine* 76 (January):26–35.

75. Halverson, P. K., Mays, G. P., Kaluzny, A. D., and Richards, T. B. 1997. Not-so-strange bedfellows: models of interaction between managed care plans and public health agencies. *Milbank Quarterly 75* (1):113–139.

76. Hancock, T. 1993. The evolution, impact and significance of the healthy cities/healthy communities movement. *Journal of Public Health Policy* 14:5–18.

77. Hellberg, H. 1987. Health for all and primary health care in Europe. *Public Health* 101 (3):151–157.

78. Hippocrates; Jones WHS. 1923. Airs, waters, places. In *Hippocrates.* Cambridge, MA: Harvard University Press.

79. Hogness, J. R., McLaughlin, C. J., and Osterweis, M., eds. 1995. *The university in the urban community: responsibilities for public health.* Washington, DC: Association of Academic Health Centers.

80. Hughart, N., Guyer, B., Stanton, B., Strobino, D., et al. 1994. Do provider practices conform to the new pediatric immunization standards? *Archives of Pediatric Adolescent Medicine* 148 (9):930–935.

81. Hughes, D. C., Runyan, S.J. 1995. Prenatal care and public policy: lessons for promoting women's health. *Journal of the American Medical Women's Association* 50 (5):156–159, 163.

82. Illich, I. 1982. *Medical nemesis: the exploration of health.* New York: Pantheon Books.

83. Imershein, A. W. 1982. Integration of health and human services in Florida. In *Health services integration: lessons for the 1980s.* Washington, DC: Institute of Medicine.

84. Institute of Medicine. 1982. *Health services integration: lessons for the 1980s.* Washington, DC: National Academy Press.

85. Institute of Medicine. 1984. *Community-oriented primary care: a practical assessment: summary.* Washington, DC: National Academy Press.

86. Institute of Medicine. 1988. *The future of public health.* Washington, DC: National Academy Press.

87. Institute of Medicine. 1994. *Overcoming barriers to immunization: a workshop summary.* Edited by J. S. Durch. Washington, DC: National Academy Press.

88. Institute of Medicine. 1996. *The hidden epidemic: confronting sexually transmitted diseases.* Washington, DC: National Academy Press.

89. Institute of Medicine. 1996. *Healthy communities: new partnerships for the future of public health.* Edited by M. A. Stoto, C. Abel, and A. Dievler, *A report of the first year of the committee on public health.* Washington, DC: National Academy Press.

90. Institute of Medicine. 1997. *Improving health in the community: a role for performance monitoring.* Edited by J. Durch, L. A. Bailey, and M. A. Stoto. Washington, DC: National Academy Press.

91. Ireys, H. T., Anderson, G. F., Shaffer, T. J., Neff, J. M. 1997. Expenditures for care of children with chronic illnesses enrolled in the Washington State Medicaid program, fiscal year 1993. *Pediatrics* 100 (2 Pt 1):197–204.

92. Joint Commission on Accreditation of Healthcare Organizations. 1996. *Joint commission standards:* URL http://www.jcaho.org.

93. Joint Commission on Accreditation of Healthcare Organizations. 1996. Joint commission to create National Library of Healthcare Indicators. *Joint Commission Perspectives* 16 (2):1, 4.

94. Kaluzny, A. D., Zuckerman, H. S., and Ricketts III, T. C. 1995. *Partners for the dance: forming strategic alliances in health care.* Ann Arbor, MI: Health Administration Press.

95. Kanter, R. M. 1994. Collaborative advantage: the art of alliances. *Harvard Review* 72:96–108.

96. Keener, S. R., Baker, J. W., and Mays, G. P. 1997. Providing public health services through an integrated delivery system. *Quality Management in Health Care* 5 (2):27–34.

97. Kennedy Kreiger Institute. 1997. Lead poisoning prevention and treatment center. Baltimore: Kennedy Kreiger Institute.

98. Kirkpatrick, D. J., Taylor, C. G., Klein, E. R., Nesheim, S. R., et al., eds. 1996. *A pediatric clinician's guide to AIDS and HIV infection in Georgia.* Atlanta, GA: Public Health Committee of the Medical Association of Georgia and the Division of Public Health, Georgia Department of Human Resources.

99. Kitzman, H., Olds, D.L., Henderson Jr., C.R., Hanks, C., et al. 1997. Effect of prenatal and infancy home visitation by nurses on pregnancy outcomes, childhood injuries, and repeated childbearing. A randomized control trial. *Journal of the American Medical Association* 278 (8):644–652.

100. Kletke, P. R., Emmons, D. W., and Gillis, K. D. 1996. Current trends in physicians' practice arrangements. *Journal of the American Medical Association* 276 (7):555–560.

101. LaLonde, M. 1974. *A new perspective on the health of Canadians: a working document.* Ottawa: Canadian Department of National Health and Welfare.

102. Lambrew, J. M., Ricketts III, T. C., and Morrissey, J. P. 1993. Case study of the integration of a local health department and a community health center. *Public Health Reports* 108 (1):19–29.

103. Lasker, R. D., Humphreys, B. L., and Braithwaite, W. R. 1995. Making a powerful connection: the health of the public and the national information infrastructure. Washington, DC: U.S. Public Health Service Public Health Data Policy Coordinating Committee.

104. Leavitt, J. W. 1980. Public health and preventive medicine. In *The education of American physicians: historical essays*, edited by R. L. Numbers. Berkeley, CA: University of California Press.

105. Lee, P. R., Benjamin, A. E., and Weber, M. A. 1997. Policies and strategies for health in the United States. In *Oxford Textbook of Public Health*, edited by R. Detels, W. W. Holland, J. McEwen, and G. S. Omenn. New York: Oxford University Press.

106. Lipton, F., Hannigan, T., Siegel, C., Samuels, J., et al. 1996. New York-New York Housing study. Paper read at the American Public Health Association Annual Meeting, at New York, NY.

107. Litman, T. J. 1984. Appendix: chronology and capsule highlights of the major historical and political milestones in the evolutionary involvement of government in health and health care in the United States. In *Health politics and policy*, edited by T. J. Litman and L. S. Robins. New York: John Wiley & Sons.

108. Lorber, B. 1996. Are all diseases infectious? *Annals of Internal Medicine* 125 (10):844–851.

109. Ludmerer, K. M. 1985. *Learning to heal: the development of American medical education.* New York: Basic Books, Inc.

110. Madison, D. L. 1996. Preserving individualism in the organizational society: "cooperation" and American medical practice, 1900–1920. *Bulletin of the History of Medicine* 70:442–483.

111. Mann, J. M. 1997. Medicine and public health, ethics and human rights. *Hastings Center Report* 27 (May–June):6–13.

112. Margolis, P. A., Lannon, C. M., Stevens, R., Harlan, C., et al. 1996. Linking clinical and public health approaches to improve access to health care for socially disadvantaged mothers and children: a feasibility study. *Archives of Pediatric Adolescent Medicine* 150 (8):815–821.

113. Martin, P. Y., and Turner, B. A. 1986. Grounded theory and organizational research. *Journal of Applied Behavioral Science* 22 (2):141–157.

114. McCarton, C. M., Brooks-Gunn, J., Wallace, I. F., Bauer, C. R., et al. 1997. Results at age 8 years of early intervention for low-birth-weight premature infants. The infant health and development program. *Journal of the American Medical Association* 277 (2):126–132.

115. McDermott, W. 1978. Medicine: the public good and one's own. *Perspectives in Biology and Medicine* 21 (2):167–187.

116. McGinnis, J. M., and Foege, W. H. 1993. Actual causes of death in the United States. *Journal of the American Medical Association* 270 (18):2207–2212.

117. McGinnis, J. M. 1997. What do we pay for good health? *Journal of Public Health Management and Practice* 3 (3):vii–ix.

118. McKeown, T. 1979. *Role of medicine: dream, mirage or nemesis.* Princeton, NJ: Princeton University Press.

119. Miller, C. A., Moore, K. S., Richards, T. B., Kotelchuck, M., et al. 1993. Longitudinal observations on a select group of local health departments: a preliminary report. *Journal of Public Health Policy* Spring:34–50.

120. Miller, B., and Castro, K. G. 1996. Sharpen available tools for tuberculosis control, but new tools needed for elimination. *Journal of the American Medical Association* 276 (23):1916–1917.

121. Millis, J. S. 1996. Report of the citizens commission on graduate medical education. Chicago: American Medical Association.

122. Mittelmark, M. B., Luepker, R. V., Jacobs, D. R., Bracht, N. F., et al. 1986. Community-wide prevention of cardiovascular disease: education strategies of the Minnesota Heart Health Program. *Preventive Medicine* 15:1–17.

123. Nadler, D. A., Gerstein, M. S., and Shaw, R. B. 1992. *Organizational architecture: designing for changing organizations, The Jossey-Bass Management Series.* San Francisco: Jossey-Bass.

124. National Association of County and City Health Officials. 1990. Report on the nature and level of linkages between local health departments and community migrant health centers.

125. National Association of County and City Health Officials. 1991. *APEXPH: Assessment protocol for excellence in public health.* Washington, DC: National Association of County & City Health Officials.

126. National Committee for Quality Assurance. 1997. *Health plan employer data and information set, version 3.0 (HEDIS 3.0)*. Washington, DC: National Committee for Quality Assurance.

127. National Health Policy Forum. 1996. Trends in health network development: community and provider initiatives in a managed care environment. *Issue Brief* 690:1–12.

128. National Research Council. 1997. *Assessment of performance measures for public health, substance abuse, and mental health*. Washington, DC: National Academy Press.

129. New York Academy of Medicine Standing Committee on Public Health and Legal Medicine. 1852. Medical aid to the indigent-sanitary police. New York: The New York Academy of Medicine.

130. Olds, D. L., Eckenrode, J., Henderson Jr., C.R., Kitzman, H., et al. 1997. Long-term effects of home visitation on maternal life course and child abuse and neglect. Fifteen-year follow-up of a randomized trial. *Journal of the American Medical Association* 278 (8):637–643.

131. Osborne, D. E., and Gaebler, T. 1992. *Reinventing government: how the entrepreneural spirit is transforming the public sector.* Reading, MA: Addison-Wesley Publishing Company.

132. Osterweis, M., McLaughlin, C. J., and Manasse, J., Henri R., eds. 1996. *The U.S. health workforce: power, politics, and policy.* Washington, DC: Association of Academic Health Centers.

133. Parran, T., and Ferrand, L. 1939. Report to the Rockefeller Foundation on the education of public health personnel. New York: Rockefeller Foundation.

134. Pearson, T. A., Spencer, M., and Jenkins, P. 1995. Who will provide preventive services? The changing relationships between medical care systems and public health agencies in health care reform. *Journal of Public Health Management and Practice* 1 (1):16–27.

135. Pew Health Professionals Commission. 1995. *Critical challenges: revitalizing the health professions for the twenty-first century.* San Francisco: University of California at San Francisco Center for the Health Professionals.

136. Pickens, S., Boumbulian, P., and Tietz, M. 1995. Community assessment: strengths, assets and management. *Inside Preventive Care* 1 (6):3–7.

137. Public Health/Managed Care Advisory Panel to the Pew Charitable Trusts. 1996. Academic public health and managed care: strategies for collaboration. New York: Columbia School of Public Health.

138. Reiser, S. J. 1996. Medicine and public health: pursuing a common destiny. *Journal of the American Medical Association* 276 (16):1429–1430.

139. Reiser, S. J. 1997. Topics for our times: the medicine/public health initiative. *American Journal of Public Health* 87 (7):1098–1099.

140. Rivara, F. P., Thompson, D. C., Thompson, R. S., Rogers, L. W., et al. 1994. The Seattle children's bicycle helmet campaign: changes in helmet use and head injury admissions. *Pediatrics* 93:567–569.

141. Robert Wood Johnson Foundation. 1996. Annual Report. Princeton, NJ: The Robert Wood Johnson Foundation.

142. Robinson, J. C., and Casalino, L. P. 1995. The growth of medical groups paid through capitation in California. *New England Journal of Medicine* 333 (25):1684–1687.

143. Rosen, G. 1947. What is social medicine? A genetic analysis of the concept. *Bulletin of the History of Medicine* 21:674–733.

144. Rosen, G. 1971. The first neighborhood health center movement—its rise and fall. *American Journal of Public Health* 61 (8):1620–1637.

145. Rosenbaum, S., and Richards, T. B. 1996. Medicaid managed care and public health policy. *Journal of Public Health Management and Practice* 2 (3):76–82.

146. Rosenkrantz, B. G. 1974. Cart before horse: theory, practice and professional image in American public health, 1870–1920. *Journal of the History of Medicine* (January 1974):55–73.

147. Rundall, T. G. 1994. The integration of public health and medicine. *Frontiers of Health Services Management* 10 (4):3–24.

148. Ryle, J. A. 1949. Social medicine: its derivations and objectives. In *Social Medicine: its derivations and objectives,* edited by I. Galdston. New York: The Commonwealth Fund.

149. Schauffler, H. H., Hennessey, M., and Neiger, B. 1997. Health promotion and managed care: an assessment of collaboration by state directors of health promotion. Berkeley, CA: Association of State and Territorial Directors of Health Promotion and Public Education.

150. Schroeder, S. A., Zones, J. S., and Showstack, J. A. 1989. Academic medicine as a public trust. *Journal of the American Medical Association* 262 (6):803–812.

151. Scutchfield, F. D., and Keck, C. W. 1997. *Principles of public health practice.* Albany, NY: Delmar Publishers.

152. Senge, P. M. 1990. *The fifth discipline: the art and practice of the learning organization.* New York: Doubleday/Currency.

153. Shonick, W. 1995. *Government and health services: government's role in the development of U.S. health services, 1930–1980.* New York: Oxford University Press.

154. Showstack, J., Fein, O., Ford, D., Kaufman, A., et al. 1992. Health of the public: the academic response. *Journal of the American Medical Association* 267 (18):2497–2502.

155. Showstack, J., Lurie, N., Leatherman, S., Fisher, E., et al. 1996. Health of the public: the private sector challenge. *Journal of the American Medical Association* 276 (13):1071–1074.

156. Smith, D. R., and Anderson, R. J. 1990. Community-responsive medicine: a call for a new academic discipline. *Journal of Healthcare for the Poor and Underserved* 1 (2):219–228.

157. Smith, D. R., Anderson, R. J., and Boumbulian, P. J. 1991. Community responsive medicine: defining an academic discipline. *American Journal of Medical Sciences* 302 (5):313–318.

158. Sommer, A., Tielsch, J. M., Katz, J., Quigley, H. A., et al. 1991. Racial differences in the cause-specific prevalence of blindness in East Baltimore. *The New England Journal of Medicine* 325 (20):1412–1417.

159. Starfield, B. 1996. Public health and primary care: a framework for proposed linkages. *American Journal of Public Health* 86 (10):1365–1369.

160. Starr, P. 1982. *The social transformation of medicine.* New York: Basic Books.

161. Stevens, R. 1971. *American medicine and the public interest.* New Haven, CT: Yale University Press.

162. Stevens, R. 1989. *In sickness and in wealth: American hospitals in the twentieth century.* New York: Basic Books.

163. Stieglitz, E. J. 1949. The integration of clinical and social medicine. In *Social medicine: its derivations and objectives*, edited by I. Galdston. New York: The Commonwealth Fund.

164. Stone, E. J., Citters, R.L., Pearson, T.A. 1990. Perspectives in physician education. *American Journal of Preventive Medicine* 6 (Suppl 1).

165. Susser, M., and Susser, E. 1996. Choosing a future for epidemiology. *American Journal of Public Health* 86 (5):668–677.

166. Tengs, T. O., Adams, M. E., Pliskin, J. S., Safran, D. G., et al. 1995. Five-hundred life-saving interventions and their cost-effectiveness. *Risk Analysis* 15 (3):369–390.

167. Thompson, R. S., Rivara, F. P., and Thompson, D. C. 1989. A case-control study of the effectiveness of bicycle safety helmets. *New England Journal of Medicine* 320 (21):1361–1367.

168. Thompson, R. S., Thompson, D. C., Rivara, F. P., and Salazar, A. A. 1993. Cost-effectiveness analysis of bicycle helmet subsidies in a defended population. *Pediatrics* 91:902–907.

169. Thompson, R. S., Taplin, S. H., McAfee, T. A., Andelson, M. T., et al. 1995. Primary and secondary prevention services in clinical practice: twenty years' experience in development, implementation, and evaluation. *Journal of the American Medical Association* 273 (14):1130–1135.

170. Thompson, R. S. 1996. What have HMO's learned about clinical services? An examination of the experience at Group Health Cooperative of Puget Sound. *Milbank Quarterly* 74 (4):469–509.

171. Tocqueville, A. de. 1996. *Democracy in America.* New York: Harper & Row.

172. True, S. J. 1995. Community-based breast health partnerships. *Journal of Public Health Management and Practice* 1 (3):67–72.

173. U.S. Department of Health and Human Services. 1980. Ten leading causes of death in the United States, 1977. Atlanta, GA: Center for Disease Control, Bureau of State Services.

174. U.S. Department of Health and Human Services. 1991. *HHS Secretary's Report to Congress on the Status of Health Personnel in the United States.* Washington, DC.

175. U.S. Department of Health and Human Services. 1994. Ten leading causes of death in the United States, 1990. Atlanta, GA: Center for Disease Control, Bureau of State Services.

176. U.S. Department of Health and Human Services. 1996. *Health United States 1995.* Hyattsville, MD: DHHS Pub. No. (PHS) 96-1232.

177. U.S. Department of Health and Human Services. 1996. *Healthy People 2000 review 1995–96.* Washington, DC: DHHS Pub. No. (PHS) 96-1256.

178. U.S. Department of Health and Human Services—Public Health Service. 1980. *Promoting health/preventing disease: objectives for the nation.* Atlanta, GA.

179. U.S. Department of Health and Human Services—Public Health Service. 1991. *Healthy People 2000: national health promotion and disease prevention objectives.* Washington, DC: DHHS Pub. No. (PHS) 91-50212.

180. U.S. Preventive Services Task Force. 1996. *Guide to clinical preventive services: report of the U.S. Preventive Services Task Force, 2nd edition.* Washington, DC: Williams & Wilkins.

181. W. K. Kellogg Foundation, and The Robert Wood Johnson Foundation. 1997. Turning Point: collaborating for a new century in public health. National Program Offices: National Association of County and City Health Officials (NACCHO) in Washington, DC, and the University of Washington School of Public Health and Community Medicine in Seattle, WA.

182. Welch, S. W. 1924. Cooperative relations between official and unofficial health agencies. *Public Health Report* 39:3243–3251.

183. Welton, W. E., Kantner, T. A., and Katz, S. M. 1997. Developing tomorrow's integrated community health systems: a leadership challenge for public health and primary care. *Milbank Quarterly* 75 (2):261–289.

184. Wendy Knight & Associates. 1996. Improving the public's health: collaborations between public health departments and managed care organizations. Vergennes, VT: Joint Council of Governmental Public Health Agencies.

185. Wennberg, J., and Gittelsohn, A. 1982. Variations in medical care among small areas. *Scientific American* 246 (4):120–134.

186. Weschler, H., Levine, S., Idelson, R. K., Schor, E. L., et al. 1996. The physician's role in health promotion revisited—a survey of primary care practitioners. *The New England Journal of Medicine* 334 (15):996–998.

187. White, K. 1991. *Healing the schism: epidemiology, medicine, and the public's health*. New York: Springer Verlag.

188. White, K., and Connelly, J. 1992. *The medical school's mission and the population's health*. New York: Springer Verlag.

189. Willard, W. R. 1966. Report of the ad hoc committee on education for family practice. Chicago: American Medical Association.

190. Wisniewski, J. J., and Childress, L. 1994. Managed care college: a continuing education program for primary care physicians. *Medical Interface*, 7 (10):56–67.

191. Wood, D. J., and Gray, B. 1991. Toward a comprehensive theory of collaboration. *Journal of Applied Behavioral Science* 27 (2):139–162.

192. Yin, R. K. 1984. *Case study research: design and methods*. Thousand Oaks, CA: Sage Publications.